D1202727

human deviance,
social problems,
and social control

Prentice-Hall, Inc., Englewood Cliffs, New Jersey

Edwin M. Lemert

SECOND EDITION

human deviance,

social problems,

and social control

PRENTICE-HALL SOCIOLOGY SERIES
Neil J. Smelser, editor

Library of Congress Catalog Number: 71-166980

ISBN: 0-13-444885-5

10   9   8   7   6   5   4

Printed in the United States of America

Prentice-Hall International, Inc., London
Prentice-Hall of Australia, Pty. Ltd., Sydney
Prentice-Hall of Canada, Ltd., Toronto
Prentice-Hall of India Private Limited, New Delhi
Prentice-Hall of Japan, Inc., Tokyo

Contents

I

deviation
as a process

II
deviation and social control

III
some forms of deviance

Preface

I prefer to think that the papers in this volume have been selected, rather than collected, with a view to their maximum consistency and continuity. They reflect research interests which are in some instances remote from the familiar subject grounds of sociology if, indeed, not exotic. In part this is explained by my early joint training in anthropology and sociology and a yen for rustic islands; in larger part it is a consequence of my preoccupation with sociopsychological problems logically subservient to cross-cultural exploration and study.

Despite the seeming diversity of the pieces, they have rendezvous points in theoretical issues crucial or central to sociology. Their common concern is with social control and its consequences for deviance. This is a large turn away from older sociology that tended to rest heavily upon the idea that deviance leads to social control. I have come to believe that the reverse idea, (i.e., social control leads to deviance) is equally tenable and the potentially richer premise for studying deviance in modern society.

The concept of secondary deviance is a logical extension of the formulation of deviance as problems of social control. It proposes that changes in psychic structure accompany transitions to degraded status, during which the meaning of deviance changes qualitatively, as well as in its outward expressions. Deviance is established in social roles and is perpetuated by the very forces directed to its elimination or control. This, of course, has to be understood as a process of meaningful social interaction.

My allegiance to symbolic interaction as a perspective is qualified. I take care to add that I regard myself neither as an "interactionalist" nor as a phenomenological sociologist. As several of the papers show, there is a limiting or cost aspect of meanings and values, based upon physiological, ecological, and technological facts. Furthermore, the rise of new moral categories is related to changes in such facts, although the precise nature of these relationships is often elusive.

All save two of the articles have been published previously. "Role Enactment, Self, and Identity in the Systematic Check Forger" was first read at meetings of the California Psychological Association in 1962, and later revised. The discussion of secondary deviance was specially written for the first edition to give the concept some historical depth and to consider more fully some of the theoretical issues it raises. Two pieces have been replaced in this revision. One of the new papers, "Sociocultural Research on Alcohol," provides some theoretical and methodological perspectives on alcohol studies that were absent in the earlier papers on this topic. The other, "Social Problems and the Sociology of Deviance," is an extension of an article which appeared in the *New International Encyclopedia of the Social Sciences*. It seeks to update my ideas on deviance by considering criticisms that have arisen around theories of societal reaction and labeling. It is hoped that including such historical materials on social problems will enhance teaching uses of the papers.

E.M.L.

I

deviation as a process

1 SOCIAL PROBLEMS
AND THE SOCIOLOGY OF DEVIANCE

Social problems are best described simply as perplexing questions about human societies proposed for solution. The distinctiveness of such questions as a separate object of sociological study rests upon their topicality, currency, and pragmatic derivation. Social problems are part of the climate of opinion in a society which centers around expressed needs for public policies and anticipated requirements for social control. Social problems study or research consists of the ordering of perspectives and social facts in relation to the ends and means of collective action.

Proceeding beyond this general statement to a more precise definition of social problems poses a complicated task of sorting out the wide diversity of views held by sociologists as to the nature of the subject matter and perspectives from which it should be studied.[1] These conflicting viewpoints, as well as salient misgivings shared by many as to whether social problems is a "field," or can validly be included with

This paper was originally published as "Social Problems." Reprinted with permission of the Publishers from The International Encyclopedia of the Social Sciences, David L. Sills, Editor, Volume 14, pp. 452–58. Copyright © 1968 by Crowell Collier and Macmillan, Inc.

[1] Francis E. Merrill, "The Study of Social Problems," *American Sociological Review* 13 (1948): 251–59. For divergent views see the accompanying "Discussions" by Ernest R. Mower and Stuart A. Queen, pp. 260–62.

sociology, are in part understandable in the context of the origins and history of sociology itself.

HISTORY OF SOCIAL PROBLEMS APPROACH

Concern with social problems has been singularly American or Anglo-Saxon. Antecedents can be found in the literature of socioeconomic criticism and reform which was directed at many of the consequences of commerce, industrialism, and urban growth in western Europe, particularly eighteenth-century and nineteenth-century England. The more immediate forerunners of what came to be the social problems approach emerged from writings, reports, essays, and surveys by Protestant clergymen, philanthropists, and middle-class humanitarians in the United States as well as England who were dedicated to a variety of social reform activities. These included prison reform, settlement work, child rescue, promotion of temperance, housing betterment, elimination of poverty, and improvement of conditions of employment of women and children; by the middle of the nineteenth century many of these had crystallized into organized actions or associations.

The roots of the intellectual orientation toward social problems as an academic subject are more precisely located in the broadly based American reform movement from which, in 1865, there issued the American Social Science Association. This represented a merger of a variety of local and regional associations, whose constituted objectives were clearly meliorative.[2] In large part it was responsible for the introduction of social science courses in American colleges and universities, beginning in 1865 and reaching a peak between 1885 and 1895. Many, if not most, of these courses, however titled, dealt with topics subsequently recognized as the substance of social problems courses in sociology—with possibly somewhat greater attention paid to education and law.

The development of such courses reflected motivations of persons both within and outside the universities who were seeking to arouse and prepare students for careers of legislative reform. The courses attained quick popularity with students, many of whom were repelled by limitations of the classical or science curricula and who were fired by the social ferments of the post-Civil War period. Toward the end of the nineteenth century, when sociology began to receive formal departmental recognition in colleges and universities, many of those recruited to teach it came from backgrounds of the ministry and charity work. The lineal ties of their

---

[2] Luther L. Bernard and Jessie Bernard, *Origins of American Sociology: The Social Science Movement in the United States* (New York: Crowell, 1943); see especially pp. 554 ff.

versions of sociology with the older social science movement are attested by the substantial numbers of those early sociologists who were members of the National Conference of Charities and Corrections and of the American Prison Congress.[3]

The scientific rationale.

Such facts strongly tempt one to the conclusion that American sociology was fathered by the study of social problems. However, this is opposed by another theme, reflecting continuity with the thought of Auguste Comte and Herbert Spencer, holding to a scientific purpose in the study of society, which was present almost from the first in the social science movement. To the scientific emphasis in pioneer American sociology was added an antireform bias, stemming from the laissez-faire philosophy of Spencer and sounded in W. G. Sumner's strident disdain for social welfare activities. The conflict of purposes among early sociologists is epitomized by the lengths to which Sumner himself went in devising titles which would sharply distinguish his courses from the reformistic ones taught by his colleagues at Yale Divinity School.

It is generally accepted that Lester F. Ward's teleological philosophy outweighed the influences of Spencer and Sumner in the formative years of American sociology and that the notion of an "applied sociology" became or remained dominant. Yet the applied sociology of Ward [4] was little more than an idea which took its concrete meaning from classroom teaching, student field trips to charitable institutions, and the writing of textbooks, a number of which appeared in the first decade of the twentieth century. These, as well as the ones which followed, drew heavily on factual data from a variety of sciences construed to have a bearing on the problems under discussion, roughly ordered into "causes," "effects," and "solutions." This was consistent with Spencer's conception of sociology as a synthetic, "capstone" science, but this scientific rationale probably made a virtue of necessity. The amount of "pure" sociology available for application to social problems was severely limited; early sociologists, like Yankee inventors, made do with materials at hand.

Changing perspectives.

The passing of time saw the social problems approach in sociology lose ground as the socioeconomic characteristics of recruits to the field

---

[3] Edwin H. Sutherland, "Social Pathology," *American Journal of Sociology* 50 (1945): 429–35.

[4] Lester F. Ward, *Applied Sociology: A Treatise on the Conscious Improvement of Society by Society* (Boston and New York: Ginn, 1906).

changed and as the need to validate sociology's status as a distinctive science was increasingly accepted. In the middle decades of the twentieth century sociologists turned more and more to self-conscious discussion of methodology, research design, and theory, with a growing attention to the European sociology of Max Weber and Émile Durkheim. A kind of ideological commitment to social neutrality and nonevaluative research took hold of the discipline. The gulf between social theory and the study of concrete social problems grew wide, intellectually stranding many sociologists with continuing interest in the latter.[5] Their discontent culminated in the establishment in 1952 of the Society for the Study of Social Problems, which, while affiliated with the American Sociological Association, nevertheless has held to its separate identity.

Despite the shift in perspective regarding the fundamental tasks in sociology, the flow of textbooks on social problems continued unabated, and courses so titled continue to be taught—albeit more restively by a younger generation of sociologists trained to demand theoretical meaning in materials with which they deal. The attenuated identification of sociologists with social problems courses is perpetuated by the relatively large number of students attracted to their offerings who nevertheless do not plan to follow sociology as a course of study. Instruction in social problems courses in otherwise scientifically oriented sociology departments is given various rationales—general education, a "service function," or a means of recruitment of students to the field.

Other pressures also have made it difficult for sociologists to disengage themselves from the old ties to social problems. Government recognition of military uses of sociology during World War II, plus research support from industry, government, and private foundations after the war, drew the interest of sociologists toward applied research on problems posed by persons or agencies outside the field. The massive surge of the American Negro after 1954 toward greater equality of opportunity multiplied the contingents of sociologists at work on applied research. The looming threat of thermonuclear war motivates others toward immediately useful, rather than abeyant, "scientistic" sociology. A number of highly articulate critics both within and outside sociology have inveighed against the sterility or inapplicability of much contemporary theory, directly challenging the claim that sociology can or should aspire to ethical neutrality. Efforts to make the study of social problems more policy directed and subservient to social action have been conspicuous among younger sociologists who were sensitized by the ghetto riots and student revolts of the 1960s, and prolongation of the Vietnam war.

[5] Arthur K. Davis, "Social Theory and Social Problems: Fragments for a Philosophy of Social Science," *Philosophy and Phenomenological Research* 18 (1957): 190–208.

THEORETICAL ISSUES

The most sweeping indictment of social problems writings appeared in an article by C. Wright Mills [6] in 1943 entitled "The Professional Ideology of Social Pathologists." With slashing phrases he more or less condemned an entire generation of social pathologists for the low conceptual level of their textbooks, the discrete and unrelated nature of their treatments of various social problems, and insertions of rural-biased value judgments in the guise of objective terminology. These observations, while undeniably cogent and pointed, were overdrawn and given selective emphasis to support Mills's own brief for structural analysis of social problems data.

Closer study and more sanguine assessment of the field in the past make it less atheoretical than it would seem, especially if the textbooks are disregarded in favor of provocative articles by Frank, Waller, Fuller, and Fuller and Myers.[7] These writers, especially Fuller, both saw and sought to analyze social problems in a general setting of values and value conflict. Fuller's distinction between ameliorative problems and moral problems, the implications of which he developed in a paper on morals and the criminal law,[8] bears insightfully on structural questions concerning the relationship of values to norms and the contingency of legal action on variations in this relationship.

Both Frank and Fuller stressed a holistic view which is axiomatic among contemporary sociologists, i.e., that situations or behavior considered to be problems, on finer analysis may prove to be expressions of cherished values or institutionalized norms crucial to the operation of society. From this came Fuller's conclusion—dismal to some—that solutions to social problems may be impossible. This, when fitted with his later effort to demonstrate a natural history of social problems,[9] closely

[6] C. Wright Mills, "The Professional Ideology of Social Pathologists," *American Journal of Sociology* 49 (1943): 165–80.

[7] L. K. Frank, "Social Problems," *American Journal of Sociology* 30 (1925): 462–73; Willard W. Waller, "Social Problems and the Mores," *American Sociological Review* 1 (1936): 922–33; Richard C. Fuller, "Sociological Theory and Social Problems," *Social Forces* 15 (1937): 496–502; Richard C. Fuller, "Problem of Teaching Social Problems," *American Journal of Sociology* 44 (1938): 415–25, 433–35; Richard C. Fuller and Richard R. Myers, "Some Aspects of a Theory of Social Problems," *American Sociological Review* 6 (1941): 24–32.

[8] Richard C. Fuller, "Morals and the Criminal Law," *Journal of Criminal Law and Criminology* 32 (1942): 624–30.

[9] Richard C. Fuller and Richard R. Myers, "The Natural History of a Social Problem," *American Sociological Review* 6 (1941): 320–28; Edwin M. Lemert, "Is There a Natural History of Social Problems?" *American Sociological Review* 16 (1951): 217–23.

allies his thinking with the laissez-faire philosophy of Sumner, but it is also akin to the political conservatism many sociologists believe to inhere in "system" theories of society. In sum, these critics seem to say that putting social problems into a structural context destroys both ideological rationale and the individual motivation for reform, by showing the problems to be "necessary" consequences of a given type of value system or by making clear that deeply held values will have to be sacrificed and institutions disrupted if the problems are to be eliminated.

DEFINITION AS AN ISSUE

The early authors of books, tracts, and essays of social criticism in the Anglo-Saxon tradition bothered little about definitions of social problems. They drew uncritically on inner convictions about those aspects of society or of the human condition that needed correction or reform. In many instances they relied on a sense of propriety as "natural" or as the product of natural law. Jeremy Bentham was among the first to attack laws, law making, and judicial procedure based on this kind of morality, which he saw as expressions of irrational sympathies and antipathies. He and his followers urged the substitution of the criteria of utility as a rational basis for morality and legislation. However, pragmatism or experience, rather than logically derived principles of utility, became the underlying guide for American writers seeking to define social problems.

Among the first attempts at definition were those of Ellwood, Howerth, Kelsey, and Hart.[10] The prevailing definition, however, came from Clarence Case, who was attracted to ideas of W. I. Thomas dealing with generic elements in the process of cultural origins. Predominant among these was an element of *attention*, defined as the subjective or reciprocal aspect of social control, which is activated by crisis.[11] These ideas led Case to propose that social problems are situations impressing a large number of competent observers as needing remedy by collective action. They became for him and many others after him sociopsycho-

[10] Charles A. Ellwood, *The Social Problem: A Reconstructive Analysis,* rev. ed. (New York: Macmillan, 1915); Ira W. Howerth, *Work and Life: A Study of the Social Problems of To-day* (New York: Sturgis and Walton, 1913), especially see chapter 1, "The Social Problem To-day"; Carl Kelsey, "How Progress Causes Social Problems," *University Lectures Delivered by Members of the Faculty in the Free Public Lecture Course* (University of Pennsylvania, 1914–1915), 9–16; Hornell N. Hart, "What is a Social Problem?" *American Journal of Sociology* 29 (1923): 345–52.

[11] Clarence M. Case, "What is a Social Problem?" *Journal of Applied Sociology* 8 (1924): 268–73; W. I. Thomas, *Social Behavior and Personality: Contributions of W. I. Thomas to Theory and Social Research,* ed. Edmund H. Volkart (New York: Social Science Research Council, [1917–1937] 1951).

logical phenomena; social problems, stated most simply, are whatever a goodly number of informed members of society say they are.

This definition more or less identifies sociologists with the lay populace and makes public opinion sociological opinion, with implied faith in a democratic process. Its difficulties accrue from recognition of the irrational or spurious qualities in public expressions or collective behavior, which counsels considerable discounting of public reactions or moral indignation as guides for sociological criticism of society or its institutions. Moreover, questions must be faced as to how many or what persons qualify as an acceptable panel for making judgments as to what are social problems. Many issues in modern society are articulated almost exclusively within coteries of specialists in health, medicine, welfare, correction, and education. They reflect technical interests, often couched in esoteric language, which are projected into the arena of public opinion only ephemerally or adventitiously.

Superficially, Fuller's distinction between moral and ameliorative problems seems to reconcile the older conception of social problems with these facts of technical specialization. However, the division between moral and technical problems often becomes vague or disappears, for means may become ends or ends means, depending upon the vantage point of the beholder. The idea that social problems could be defined by a consensus of professional and welfare experts made little headway with sociologists, largely because judgments of specialists outside their own or adjacent areas of interest can claim no greater validity than those of educated lay persons. Representative specialists often are spokesmen for organized groups, necessarily supporting vested agency values as well as conveying judgments derived from technical knowledge. Finally, it must be noted that the ordering of social problems with respect to their priority or importance cannot be determined by consulting specialists who define them distributively.

SOCIAL PATHOLOGY

The subjectivism inherent in the "popular" definition of social problems runs athwart the conception of sociology as a body of knowledge which rises above common sense and is accumulated through application of special methods by observers or researchers at least relatively detached from the social facts under scrutiny. If social problems are defined in terms of such a body of knowledge, they become objective rather than subjective facts, "discoverable" from laws or generalizations about necessary conditions of social life. Despite its well-documented shortcomings, the bare idea of social pathology is more congenial to such a formulation of sociology than is that of social problems.

Social pathology was an effort to apply a biological or medical model to the analysis of problematical phenomena of society. It rests on the idea that societies or their constituent parts may develop abnormally or anomalously and that they can be described or "diagnosed" in the light of some pristine or universal criterion of normality or health. The orientation of social pathology was, however, toward man rather than society, being heavily pervaded with the nineteenth-century concern about the relevance of institutions to the perfectibility of human nature. The notion of individual maladjustment figured large in discussions of social pathology, revolving about the consequences of physical illness, mental deficiency, mental disorders, alcoholism, lack of education, or incomplete socialization for the realization of life goals regarded as normal for most people. The fact that many of these conditions are indeed associated with organic pathologies or were assumed to have a hereditary foundation lent strength to the idea that social problems were external, or objective, facts. Sociological residues of this idea persist today among those who believe alcoholism and mental disorder to be diseases. In the perspective of time it may be said that so long as American society was dominated by middle-class values, laissez-faire individualism, localism, and southern regionalism, the more absolutistic conception of social problems as social pathology remained tenable.

SOCIAL PROBLEMS AND SOCIAL DISORGANIZATION

The growth of cultural relativity in sociology, infiltrating from the critical–historical themes of American anthropology, together with the general questioning of paramount American values that was generated by the great depression of the 1930s, foreign revolutions, and totalitarian war put an end to social pathology as a viable perspective on social problems. The need for concepts to organize thought about societies in wholesale flux and crisis was conjoined with the need to place discussion of social problems in a more comprehensive intellectual scheme that would be in keeping with the methodological aspirations of sociologists. The needs in part seemed met by restatement of conceptions of social disorganization originally set down by Thomas and Znaniecki [12] and Charles H. Cooley.[13] Many of the phenomena that had long been the subject matter of social problems or social pathology now were postulated as symptoms

[12] W. I. Thomas and Florian Znaniecki, *The Polish Peasant in Europe and America*, 2nd. ed., 2 vols. (New York: Dover, [1918–1920] 1958). An unabridged edition of the original five-volume work.

[13] Charles H. Cooley, *Social Process* (New York: Scribner, 1918). See especially pages 153–68, "An Organic View of Degeneration."

or products of such processes as uneven cultural development, cultural lag, conflict, dissensus, and dialectical change. Taken together, these processes meant social disorganization. A pivotal distinction was set up between social disorganization and personal disorganization, with the latter assumed to be functionally associated with the former. On this point most textbook writers followed the organic analogy of Cooley rather than the ideas of Thomas and Znaniecki, who saw no necessary relationship between the two. /

While some sociologists have decried texts on social disorganization as being little different from those on social problems, apart from their introductory chapters, this ignores the lively development of ecological studies by sociologists at the University of Chicago and elsewhere, whose findings appeared to give statistical support for the notion that social problems are expressions of a common underlying social process. For a while, at least, the idea of "disorganized areas" in urban communities became established sociology and a welcome new way of ordering the data in textbooks. Vice, crime, poverty, divorce, and mental disorder all became part of a zonal or area parcel explainable in terms of generic ecological growth, change, and deterioration.

Social disorganization as a subject has the look of an impressive theoretical façade which on closer analysis is disillusioning. The concept of process on which it relies is vague at best, and the distinction between social and personal disorganization is difficult to maintain. Serious doubt has been cast on the method of ecological correlation, undermining the neat idea of disorganized areas. Careful ethnographic studies of the slum, such as W. F. Whyte's *Street Corner Society*,[14] made it undeniably clear that such areas can be or are relatively well organized.

The idea of social disorganization still has its theoretical partisans and, defined simply as human activities or failures to act which impede or block other activities, is indeed demonstrable and of heuristic value. Thus, if artillerymen fire shells that, by reason of faulty communication or poor manufacture, fall on their own troops, the result is fittingly enough described as social disorganization. But if questions are asked whether the attack was part of integral tactics, or whether the associated campaign advanced overall strategy, or whether the war should have been fought in the first place, theoretical analysis quickly moves into speculation where fact and value blur. In any but a specifiable, closed social system or subsystem with consensual goals, the formulation of social disorganization reduces to value choices of its author.

[14] William Foote Whyte, *Street Corner Society: The Social Structure of an Italian Slum*, 2nd. ed., enl. (Chicago: University of Chicago Press [1943] 1961); Gerald D. Suttles, *The Social Order of the Slum* (Chicago: University of Chicago Press, 1968).

SOCIAL PROBLEMS AS DYSFUNCTIONS

Forms of thought from the traditions of European sociology and English anthropology offer the theoretical alternative of subsuming the data of social problems under the category of social dysfunctions. This descriptive and analytic device proceeds from assumptions that there are functional prerequisites of social life around which institutional structures operate, mutually supporting each other, meeting psychobiological needs of individuals, and contributing to an over-all integration of society. Practices or activities which run counter to functional prerequisites, which disrupt the institutional nexus, or which frustrate individual needs are defined as social dysfunctions.

The difficulties of functional analysis are well known. Determining what is indispensable to maintain a specific complex of behavior and what is adventitious is made difficult by the fact that the range of cases or time series in human societies from which to generalize often is small and some kinds of events have only a few instances. Culture comes to each generation in unsorted bales or packets, and historical, comparative, or cross-cultural studies are limited in their potential for sorting out that which is functional or dysfunctional. When cultures change or undergo disruption, that which may have seemed to participants or observers to be a causal or functional association may turn out to be dispensable. The social problems of yesteryear often live only as the quaint reminiscences of today.

The persistence of ancient social problems or dysfunctional activities in such forms as crime, political corruption, gambling, or prostitution in the face of collective efforts to eradicate them is not readily explained by functional analysis. An explanation for such seeming paradoxes was proposed by Robert K. Merton [15] in the form of a distinction between "manifest" and "latent" functions; R. M. Williams [16] also dealt with this matter in his discussion of "patterned evasions of institutional norms." However, these explanations seem secondary or residual at best. They call attention to the fact that actions may have functions as well as dysfunctions. In another light, they are implicit concessions that determination of functions in a culturally diverse society depends in large degree on the particular needs, perspectives, or values adopted by the observer.

A more crucial but closely related issue in functional analysis is whether it can reveal those activities which can be established in objective

[15] Robert K. Merton, *Social Theory and Social Structure*, rev. and enl. ed. (Glencoe, Ill.: Free Press [1949] 1957), chapter 1.

[16] Robin M. Williams, Jr., *American Society: A Sociological Interpretation*, 2d. ed. (New York: Knopf, [1951] 1960). See especially chapter 10, "Institutional Variation and the Evasion of Normative Patterns."

terms as social problems, even though they are not necessarily subjects of popular awareness or collective action. In a general way Case [17] heeded this question when, in defining social problems primarily as aspects of the collective mind, he nevertheless recognized that statisticians and others could describe *adverse conditions* of society; furthermore, the inclusion of a "situation" in definitions by a number of other sociologists was recognition that objective factors were a necessary part of social problems.[18] Ogburn,[19] more clearly of functionalist persuasion and impressed by the discrepancies between dynamic technology and institutional adaptation, sought a totally objective definition of social problems as consequences or expressions of "cultural lag." Subsequent critics showed that this conception was not, as hoped, free from value judgments and strongly argued against its underlying dichotomy of material and nonmaterial culture.

The causal relationships between technology, culture, and moral ideas and the sequence in which they change continue to be among the great moot questions of sociology. They have grown more prominent as ruling groups in some societies, seeking to assist others to industrialize or raise agricultural productivity. The discovery that introduced technology in many instances does not always lead to the expected consequences has compelled students of socioeconomic development to conclude that their judgment of what is functional and dysfunctional for others is not easily imposed for the purpose of directing change.

SOCIAL PROBLEMS AS DEVIANCE

Since 1940 a sizable portion of the traditional subject matter of social problems, such as crime, delinquency, prostitution, drug addiction, and physical handicaps, has been categorized as deviance, deviation, or deviant behavior. The amoral, statistical, or descriptive implications of the terms carry a strong appeal, although they tend to acquire morally invidious connotations. Generally, deviance is defined as violations of norms, or departures from social expectancies, but beyond this minimal agreement the ideas projected for its analysis differ considerably.

One group of sociologists, following Durkeim, Parsons, and Merton, has been primarily concerned with the etiology of deviance and its different rates of occurence between or within societies. They have sought

---

[17] Clarence M. Case, "What is a Social Problem?"

[18] Thomas Lynn Smith, et al., *Social Problems* (New York: Crowell, 1955). See especially chapter 1.

[19] William F. Ogburn, *Social Change: With Respect to Culture and Original Nature*, new ed., with supplementary chapter (New York: Viking, [1922] 1950).

to locate the sources of deviation in discontinuities, anomie, or strain within the structure of a society that is assumed to be more or less an integrated system. The analysis of deviation in this theoretical context is voluntaristic, in contrast with deterministic or strictly causal versions of functionalism.* Deviation originates from permutations of choice by individuals motivated by culturally given ends and confronted with means of varying accessibility.*The most cogent statement or theoretical design derived from these ideas appeared in Merton's widely influential article "Social Structure and Anomie." [20]

Critical assessment of the structural or "anomie" interpretations of deviation was slow to crystallize but was finally made by a symposium of sociologists qualified by extensive research in areas of deviation. In this volume, *Anomie and Deviant Behavior*, edited by Marshall B. Clinard,[21] they raised serious doubts as to whether Merton's effort to design an embracing theory of deviation was sufficient for the complexities of the data. The ends–means distinction is not an easy one to maintain with concrete data, and the individual motivational base of structural sociology is barren ground for the production of a theory of group-related deviation in any but reactional terms. The heavy accent on conditions of social order in works of Parsons [22] reduces social control to a negative mechanism for repressing deviation; the recognition of deviation as a creative necessity for social change is absent from structural theories or appears only in revised afterthoughts.

THE NEW DEVIANCE SOCIOLOGY

The past two decades have seen the emergence and growth of a new deviance sociology, which stands at considerable distance from theories concerned with structural sources of deviance.\Those identified with the new point of view on deviance are distinguished by the importance they assign to symbolic interaction and social control in the understanding and analysis of deviance. An article I wrote on a general theory of socio-

[20] Robert K. Merton, "Social Structure and Anomie," *American Sociological Review* 3 (1938): 672–82. A revision of this article appears on pages 161–94 in the 1957 edition of Merton's *Social Theory and Social Structure* as "Continuities in the Theory of Social Structure and Anomie."

[21] Marshall B. Clinard, ed., *Anomie and Deviant Behavior: A Discussion and Critique* (New York: Free Press, 1964). Includes "An Inventory of Empirical and Theoretical Studies of Anomie," by Stephen Cole and Harriet Zuckerman.

[22] Talcott Parsons, *The Social System* (Glencoe, Ill.: Free Press, 1951). See especially chapter 7, "Deviant Behavior and Mechanisms of Social Control."

pathic behavior in 1948, and my book *Social Pathology* in 1951,[23] were the first attempts at a systematic statement of the emerging point of view, although some brief interpretive ideas similar in nature were presented by Tannenbaum in his book *Crime and the Community*, published in 1938.[24] A paper by Kitsuse on the societal reaction to deviant behavior read in 1960,[25] Goffman's book *Asylums* in 1961,[26] an article by Erikson entitled *Notes on the Sociology of Deviance* which appeared in 1962,[27] plus the publication of Becker's book *Outsiders* in 1962,[28] more or less set the prevailing themes and mood of what is loosely known as a school. This has been dubbed variously the Neo-Chicagoans, the West Coast School or the Pacific Seminar—designations serving to contrast it with deviance studies by sociologists of the eastern establishment primarily concerned with etiology. /

The western-looking deviance sociologists have focused their work on the consequences of the moral order and social control, seeking to show how categories of deviance are invoked and applied to individuals and groups. They have given currency to such concepts as societal reaction, stigma, degradation, mortification of self, police discretion, and typification, ideas which are especially suited to showing how agencies and institutions ostensibly organized for welfare, reform, rehabilitation, and treatment give form and meaning to deviance and stabilize it as secondary deviation. While research on the process by which individuals become deviant has tended to be subordinated to the suffusing concern with legally instituted agencies of deviance control, nevertheless it has been illumined by the concepts of moral careers, deviant careers, contingency, drift, sense of injustice, encapsulation, turning points, identity crises, and secondary deviance.

[23] Edwin M. Lemert, "Some Aspects of a General Theory of Sociopathic Behavior," *Research Studies, State College of Washington*, 16 (1948), 23–29; *Social Pathology* (New York: McGraw-Hill, 1951).

[24] Frank Tannenbaum, *Crime and the Community* (New York: McGraw-Hill, 1938).

[25] John Kitsuse, "Societal Reaction to Deviant Behavior: Problems of Theory and Method," paper read at meetings of the American Sociological Association in 1960. Published in *The Other Side: Perspectives on Deviance*, ed. Howard Becker (New York: The Free Press, 1964), 87–102.

[26] Erving Goffman, *Asylums* (New York: Anchor, 1961).

[27] Kai Erikson, "Notes on the Sociology of Deviance," *Social Problems* 9 (1962): 307–14.

[28] Howard Becker, *Outsiders* (New York: The Free Press, 1963). The work of Thomas Scheff also belongs with the western school; see his "The Role of the Mentally Ill and the Dynamics of Mental Disorder: a Research Framework," *Sociometry* 26 (1963): 436–53.

LABELING THEORY

What began as some tentative and loosely linked ideas about deviance and societal reaction in my writings subsequently were replaced by the theoretical statement of Becker that social groups create deviance and that deviant behavior is that which is so labeled.[29] This position got further elucidation in Erikson's functionalist derived assertion that the social audience is the critical factor in deviance study.[30] In retrospect these must be regarded as conceptual extrusions largely responsible for the indiscriminate application of "labeling theory" to a diversity of research and writing on deviance. Unfortunately the impression of crude sociologistic determinism left by the Becker and Erikson statements has been amplified by the tendency for many deviance studies to be preoccupied with the work of official agencies of social control, accenting the arbitrariness of official action, stereotyped decision-making in bureaucratic contexts, bias in the administration of law, and the general preemptive nature of society's controls over deviants.

The mood or tone of much deviance research and writing has been that of ironic commentary or indictment of institutional controls; the perspective often has been that of the exploited, degraded, or victimized deviant, more or less caught and shaped by fateful circumstances over which he has little or no control. This perspective has been defended on grounds that conventional sociology narrowly reflects the viewpoints of established authority and power groups. It also has been asserted that perspectives have an inherent polarity and that it is impossible to take over the viewpoints of controllers and those controlled at the same time.[31] These "background assumptions" of deviance sociology owe a good deal to the historical context out of which it has developed.

The rise of the new deviance sociology beginning in the 1950s roughly corresponds to the postwar acceleration of social change and vast alterations in the form of society in the United States, most conspicuous being the preeminence and intrusion of large-scale, bureaucratized organizations in the lives of individuals. The resultant pattern of social structure has been described variously as the "welfare state," the "administrative state," the "garrison state," and the "military industrial combine," terms which caption the powerlessness of individuals necessarily dependent on specialized group organization to satisfy their needs. The kinds of problems generated and perceived in this societal context have revolved around fundamental issues of human dignity and distributive

[29] Howard Becker, *Outsiders*, p. 9.
[30] Kai Erikson, "Notes," p. 11.
[31] Howard Becker, *Outsiders*, pp. 170–76.

justice. In this climate of the times the emergence of labeling theory has the air of historical necessity. In any event a good deal of the style, themes, and findings of deviance research has made its way into the literature and expressions of civil libertarians, activists, and pariah groups seeking to advance their causes or convert their interests into legal rights.

Appreciation of the vulgarization of labeling theory and its assimilation to popular causes undoubtedly has accelerated the growth of criticisms. While these to a degree have been pointed and relevant they also betray a malaise over the discontinuity between labeling theory and much of the rest of sociology. The most serious charge is that labeling theory depicts social control as arbitrary, and more or less washes out any causative significance substantive actions may have for persons who become deviants, as well as denying their objective harm or social damage. Pushed to the extreme, the theory makes deviance a kind of artifact or spurious imputation of social control.[32]

While this difficulty theoretically can be resolved by fully exploiting the conception of symbolic interaction, the adoption of a subordinate, "underdog" perspective makes this difficult. Even when more completely utilized, however, symbolic interaction in the Meadian sense leaves important aspects of deviance unexplained.

SYMBOLIC INTERACTION AND DEVIANCE

A good deal of the interaction described in the writings of labeling theorists is unilinear and unidirectional. "Others" vis à vis the deviant initiate interaction: for the most part they are instigators who intentionally or inadvertently degrade, discredit, or invade the privacy and territories of deviants. When "others" are agents of groups their decisions and actions are reduced to "routine practices," "common typifications" and

[32] Critical articles: David Bordua, "Recent Trends: Deviant Behavior and Social Control," *Annals of the American Academy of Political and Social Sciences* 57 (1967): 149–63; Jack Gibbs, "Conceptions of Deviant Behavior: The Old and the New," *Pacific Sociological Review* 9 (1969): 9–14; Roland Akers, "Problems in the Sociology of Deviance: Social Definitions and Behavior," *Social Forces* 46 (1968): 455–65; Clarice Stoll, "Images of Man and Social Control," *Social Forces* 47 (1968): 119–27; John De La Mater, "On the Nature of Deviance," *Social Forces* 46 (1958): 445–55; Edwin Schur, "Reactions to Deviance," *American Journal of Sociology* 75 (1969): 309–22; Lawrence D. Haber and Richard T. Smith, "Disability and Deviance: Normative Adaptations of Role Behavior," *American Sociological Review* 36 (1971): 87–97; Prudence Rains and John Kitsuse, "Comments on the Labeling Approach to Deviance," unpublished paper; Nanette J. Davis, "Labeling Theory in Deviance Research: A Critique and Reconsideration," *Sociology Quarterly*, 13 (Fall 1972) 447-474.

"proverbial characterizations" or racial-class bias, all strongly reminiscent of Durkheim's collective representations. Reification of power, insistence on group-sustaining functions of deviance, and uncritical acceptance of the notion that treatment and rehabilitation institutions are "total" give a further cast of Durkheimian solidarity to groups against which deviants stand as "outsiders."

In more extreme labeling theory the process of becoming deviant appears ineluctable; deviants lose individuality and become like "empty organisms" who are "successfully" labeled by others.[33] A qualifying theme admitting of variations in response by the individual deviant is that of the countervailing self, who is resigned to deviant status ascription but seeks to nullify or mitigate its impact through information control and reduction of the visibility of deviance.[34] The resultant interaction takes on qualities of a contest or game.

DEVIANCE AS THE DRAMATIZATION OF EVIL

A dramatistic or dramaturgic model is both explicit and implicit in the approach of labeling theorists to deviance, owing much to Mead's conception of symbolic interaction as analogous to dramatic play and participation in the game. Such interaction by definition requires striking conjunction of action, outward expression of inner conceptions, and denouement to an unequivocal end. The dramatic model of deviance interaction makes "others" solidary groups, actors with a scenario, or agents with common goals, seeking to set and keep the deviant apart from society. Goodness and badness are irreconcilable opposites incorporated into all facets of society. Mead termed the process "modern organization of the taboo"; Tannenbaum made it the equivalent of early Hebraic scapegoating; and Garfinkel described it as ceremonial degradation based on "suprapersonal values of the tribe." The primitive outgrouping in these metaphors is further reflected in Becker's choice of clan reactions to incest in far-off Melanesian islands to epitomize the dynamics of the labeling process.[35]

The extent to which dramatistic analysis suffices for the study of deviance in modern society is a question labeling theorists neither raise nor

[33] David Bordua, "Recent Trends."

[34] See Erving Goffman, Stigma (Englewood Cliffs, N. J.: Prentice-Hall, 1963).

[35] See G. J. Mead, "The Psychology of Punitive Justice," American Sociological Review 23 (1928), 577–602; Frank Tannenbaum, Crime and the Community, chapter 1; Harold Garfinkel, "Conditions of Successful Degradation Ceremonies," American Journal of Sociology 61 (1956): 420–24; Howard Becker, Outsiders, pp. 10, 11; the same primitive analogy is found in Shlomo Shoham, The Mark of Cain: the Stigma Theory of Crime and Deviation (Jerusalem: Israel University Press, 1970), chapters I, V.

answer. Obviously it does not comprehend a great deal of relevant inter-action which is prosaic, mundane, or a process of drift in which perceptions of self and other change with no great demonstration. Indeed, for some forms of deviance the more subtle, vague, and unstated implications of interaction become its essence. Moreover, it must be recognized that indi-viduals define themselves as deviant on their own terms and independent of specific societal reactions. Finally, the interaction process seen in full organic reciprocity allows that individuals court, risk, even create condi-tions of their own deviance.

THE SOCIETAL REACTION AND DEVIANCE

Despite the considerable attention given to agencies of social control, deviance research has not greatly clarified the complexities of societial re-actions. The dramatistic model, noted previously, is not sufficient to the task; and Mead's unformed ideas of society, largely a description of one generalized other, are poor sources for a modern theory of the societal reaction.[36] Yet a sociopsychological model which reduces the complexities of the societal reaction to interpersonal interaction is pervasive, both in speculation about the emergence of new legal and moral categories and in explanations of how extant deviance designations are applied.

One kind of theory proposes that the rise of new moral and penal definitions is the work of "moral entrepreneurs," or "moral crusaders" im-bued with a sense of mission to impose their own morality on others in order to preserve a threatened way of life. Such people are unconcerned with means to ends and often become professional reformers.[37] This in brief is a type of *reductio ad personam* theory, illustrations of which may be found—more in the past than the present—narrowly centering on issues like alcohol and drug use, gambling and sex, which are characterized by ambivalence, value conflict, and absence of victimization. In decided contrast, the law of theft, while at times affected by public opinion, scarcely can be said to have resulted from moral crusades. Similar cases are many of the fiduciary laws, and regulatory and licensing law, important to the definition of deviance.[38]

A number of researches attest to the influence of vested interests and

[36] Bernard N. Meltzer, "Mead's Social Psychology," in *Symbolic Inter-action*, eds. Jerome G. Morris and Bernard N. Meltzer (Boston: Allyn and Bacon, 1967), p. 21.

[37] Howard Becker, *Outsiders*, chapter 8; Joseph Gusfield, *Moral Crusade* (Urbana: University of Illinois Press, 1963).

[38] Jerome Hall, *Theft, Law, and Society* (Indianapolis, Ind.: Bobbs-Merrill, 1935); William J. Chambliss, "A Sociological Analysis of the Law of Vagrancy," *Social Problems* 12 (1964): 67–77.

specialized associations in shaping criminal and regulatory legislation. Acquaintance with the workings of legislatures reveals the multi-faceted interaction they have with such groups, as well as the intricacies of their own internal interaction through committees, majorities, and minorities. Judges, courts, administrators, and police interact further to qualify new substantive law by jurisdictional and procedural adaptations. To understand the interplay of so many groups in the development of new categories of legal and moral control requires a model of group interaction rather than interpersonal interaction.[39]

When a chain of interaction mediated by groups precedes decisions and actions, what is an end value for one person may be no more than an expendible means to another; hence predicting the societal reaction by taking the role of the other and intuiting what is in the mind of the civic reformer, legislator, judge, policeman, psychiatrist, or correctional officer fails. Accordingly a model of group interaction shifts from persons as such to interests, values, or claims of others, and to the order in which they are likely to be sacrificed or satisfied in the light of group commitments, the availability of means, and the costs of the means. Laws and rules produced in group interaction often reflect the values or norms of no group or persons but rather their dilemmas, compromises, expeditious adherence to procedures, and strictures of time and budgets.

Much of the work on variations in police processing of deviants seems to justify reductionist interpretations based on role conceptions, occupational culture, prejudice, and the interpersonal dynamics of encounters. But as more macrocosmic studies are made it will be apparent that police action differs greatly by jurisdiction, and that technology of dispatching, electronic data processing, departmental organization, accommodative patterns, external claims on police resources, and the nature of complaint situations greatly affect police decisions to process deviants and their purposes in so doing. Often the concomitant interaction is confusion, uncertainty, and inconsistency instead of the unanimity and consensus implied in "successful labeling." Total rejection and relegation as an "outsider" does not well describe the handling of the deviant in modern society, for often he or she is subjected alternately to penalty and aid, assistance then rejection. For some types of deviance, notably alcoholism, stuttering, and shoplifting, ambivalence, duality, and intermittency seem to be the most significant aspects of the societal reaction.[40]

[39] For an older view of the temperance movement differing from Gusfield's "moral crusade" interpretation, see Alfred McClung Lee, "Techniques of Social Reform: An Analysis of the New Prohibition Drive," *American Sociological Review* 9 (1944): 65–77; on law, see Edwin M. Lemert, *Social Action and Legal Change* (Chicago: Aldine, 1970).

[40] See, for example, Raymond Nimmer, "St. Louis Diagnostic and Detoxification Center: An Experiment in Non Criminal Processing of Public Intoxicants," *Washington University Law Quarterly* (Winter 1970), pp. 1–27.

No one theory or model will suffice to study the societal reaction; models must be appropriate to the area under study, to the values, norms, and structures indentifiable in the area, as well as the special qualities of the persons and their acts subject to definition as deviant. The fact that analysis begins with the societal reaction does not deny the significance of these last, the objects of the societal reaction.

OBJECTIVE ASPECTS OF DEVIANCE

Discussion of the objective aspects of deviance is complicated by the fact that in some cases, such as stuttering and other childhood and adolescent "behavior disorders," research can demonstrate no objective differences between children who do and who do not become deviants. Studies of "hidden delinquency" and "untreated mental disorders" also emphasize similarities in the behavior of those who get formally defined as deviant and those who don't. White collar crime is sometimes cited as evidence that the societal reaction alone accounts for differential criminality between social classes. Seeking to fix this idea, Becker refers to the open recognition of incest among the Trobriand islanders as a highly variable contingency of clan conflict.[41]

\ Striving to validate a conception of deviance as primarily a definitional phenomenon overlooks the way in which the societal reaction varies with objective differences in behavior, its situational context, and its consequences. An important reason why white collar crime is seldom punished is that it is not the same kind of behavior as other crime and there are different attitudes towards it. The same point has been made about traffic offenses.[42] Malinowski's instance of incest, which impressed Becker, actually was between cousins, quite different from incest within the nuclear family, almost invariably punished in primitive societies. /

In rapidly changing societies and in relatively unstructured situations emphasis is properly placed on the societal reaction in deviance study. In societies and situations with stable, patterned values and norms having sacred connotations it may be more profitable to place the emphasis on attributes of persons and their actions. Still it has to be heeded continually that deviance outcomes flow from interaction between the two sets of factors, to which their identifiable attributes contribute at all times. Interaction clarifies the changing weight of the two. Thus while idiosyncratic parental disapproval of a child's normal speech hesitations may

[41] Howard Becker, "*Outsiders*," pp. 10, 11.

[42] Sheldon Messinger, "The View" (unpublished paper, Center for the Study of Law and Society, University of California at Berkeley, 1964), p. 3; H. Lawrence Ross, "Traffic Law Violation: A Folk Crime," *Social Problems* 8 (1960–61): 231–41.

"cause" stuttering, later the speech may become sufficiently nonfluent to "cause" rejecting reactions from others outside the family group. Likewise for adolescent "incorrigibility," which, while often subjective in origin, becomes objective in effects.

\ The extreme relativism in some statements of labeling theory leaves the unfortunate impression that almost any meaning can be assigned to human attributes and actions. To the contrary, human interaction always occurs within limits: biological, psychological, ecological, technological, and organizational. These explain why certain general kinds of behavior are more likely to be deemed undesirable than others. Practically all societies in varying degrees and ways disapprove of incest, adultery, promiscuity, cruelty to children, laziness, disrespect for parents and elders, murder, rape, theft, lying, and cheating.[43] Perhaps the point to make is that certain kinds of actions are likely to be judged deleterious in any context: wilfully causing the death of others, consuming large amounts of alcohol for long periods of time, spreading infectious disease, or losing one's eyesight. It is not so much that these violate rules as it is that they destroy, downgrade, or jeopardize values universal in nature. /

Negative valuations, derived either from symbolic learning or from direct experience, in a sense inhere in many human anomalies, conditions, and actions and furthermore are necessary factors in explaining the societal reaction, although obviously not sufficient in themselves to account for the variable relationships between the two. The more complete account of the interplay between objective and subjective aspects of deviance must be sought by considering how it becomes a social problem.

DEVIANCE AS A SOCIAL PROBLEM

Although social disorganization and social pathology are now outmoded concepts, that of social problems still serves the study of deviance if attention is given to the ways in which problems are perceived and to the kinds of adaptations made to them. If we accept the proposition that life is adaptive, then many or most difficulties arising from variations in human actions, temperament, and appearances are seen as transitory problems, those of everyday living, calling for little beyond forebearance, patience, or average ingenuity for their solution. The process of adaptation is one of normalization, which may range from completely ignoring the difficulty, through a kind of mindless acceptance, to invention of plausible

[43] Ralph Linton, "Universal Ethical Principles: an Anthropological View," in *Moral Principles of Action*, ed. Ruth N. Anshen (New York: Harper & Row, 1952), pp. 645–60.

excuses and explanations, all without raising issues about compliance with rules. /

Persistent actions or their consequences which confront others, discomfit them, or complicate their lives are less easily normalized because they are likely to intrude on awareness and because they challenge the easy assumption that time will solve the problem. They pose questions of valuation, reciprocity, and consequences or cumulative costs of the actions to others, so that special adaptation is called for. The actions, conditions, or situations are apt to be singled out by others as deviant or the result of deviance, i.e., contrary to values and norms, but not necessarily defined as such or made the object of social control. Instead accommodations are made, in which the behavior is in some way contained, its consequences minimized, or its costs made bearable—in some cases by passing them on to others. A secretary "covers" for her drunken employer, the husband hires a servant to take over duties of a schizophrenic wife, or a department store manages shoplifting primarily as a problem of "inventory shrinkage" whose costs are added to sales. Large-scale accommodations between law enforcement people and racketeers may become patterned, particularly in connection with "crimes without victims," such as gambling and prostitution.

The most important fact about such accommodations in modern society is their instability. They may break down due to changing values, resources, and status of those in positions to assume or activate control, or due to changes in the form of the actions to which they have accommodated. That which has been treated as a difference increases in frequency or in its costs to others—individuals or the community at large. Increased costs may mean that resources are insufficient to maintain dominant conventional values in the face of the problem, or that hitherto protected values are brought under direct attack. Most likely this occurs when the behavior in question becomes highly visible, openly and flagrantly flaunting the values of those in positions of dominance. The problem becomes one of social control, one solution of which is to define a person or persons categorically as deviant. /

Whether or not a social problem is defined as one of deviance and what kind of deviance it designates at all times needs to be conceived in terms of social dynamics. This may require a synchronic analysis of deviance as the outcome of an administrative process, or a diachronic analysis in which new categories of deviance and deviants emerge from a process of sociocultural change. A number of classifications have been devised to help clarify the kinds of problems of social control represented by deviance and deviants: criminal deviants, transgressors, renegades, educands, sick deviants, repentant deviants, cynical deviants, enemy deviants, and innovators, all of which indicate something more and something less than the crude designation of deviants as "outsiders." [44] These are useful to the degree that they are not reified or mistaken for roles or personality types; they shed light primarily on deviants as they are perceived and evaluated by persons who hold to certain values and regard related norms as binding. At the same time they are not entirely dissociated from objective difference in the form and context of deviance.

CONCLUSION

Deviance sociology is an understandable outgrowth of dissatisfaction with older conceptions of social problems, social pathology, social disorganization, and anomie, which on closer examination failed to yield testable hypotheses or predictions of human events, and which in use were not independent of values they presumed to study objectively. On the surface deviance sociology seems to offer a relatively detached or scientific way of studying certain types of social problems. Yet its mood and tone and choice of research subjects discloses a strong fixed critical stance towards the ideology, values, and methods of state-dominated agencies of social control. In extreme statements deviance is portrayed as little more than the result of arbitrary, fortuitous, or biased decision-making, to be understood as a sociopsychological process by which groups seek to create conditions for perpetuating established values and ways of behaving or enhancing the power of special groups. One impression left is that agencies of social control are described and analyzed to expose their failures in what they try to do and their incidental encroachments on "inalienable rights" and "freedom." Thus seen, deviance sociology is more social criticism than science. It offers little to facilitate and foster the kinds of decisions and controls actually necessary to maintain the unique quality of our society— the freedom to choose.

Although sociological theory has failed to yield answers to the "functional question," i.e., what is necessary to maintain our social system, the need for objective measures independent of the sociopsychological process of evaluation is more critical today than in the past, given the avalanche of population growth and the swift decline of our natural resources. Measures are needed not only of the amount and kinds of damage done by deviants to our society but also of the costs of various modes and means of defining and dealing with them. Undoubtedly some forms of behavior have been

---

[44] Florian Znaniecki, *Cultural Sciences: Their Origin and Development* (Urbana: University of Illinois Press, 1963), pp. 344–52; Vilhelm Aubert and Sheldon Messinger, "The Criminal and the Sick," *Inquiry* 1 (1958): 137–60; Joseph Gusfield, "Moral Passage: the Symbolic Process in Public Designations of Deviance," *Social Problems* 15 (1967): 175–88.

unnecessarily defined as deviant, and the amount of their damage to society has been exaggerated. The costs of maintaining controls over these are considerable. However, the consequences of other forms of behavior treated as deviant are unclear and they need to be discovered by research. Those who would settle such problems by appeals to "freedom" and sacred "rights" of individuals often fail to appreciate that removal of one set of controls may initiate another whose consequences may be not only less desirable for the deviants but more costly to society.

The sociology of deviance must be a science of deviance and must be made an integral part of a science of social control broadly conceived to discover things necessary to do as well as those not to do.

2

SOCIAL STRUCTURE,
SOCIAL CONTROL,
AND DEVIATION

Deviation, deviancy, or deviant behavior now seem to be legitimized concepts in sociology, demarcating more sharply a modern field of study formerly laid out by the rough "metes and bounds" concepts of social problems, social pathology, and social disorganization. The statistical implications of the idea of deviation, its amoral connotation, and its ready adaptation to the analysis of social systems have made it congenial to modern sociologists for purposes of both general theoretical interpretation and empirical research. Increasingly, it has become a part of textual sociology.

However, there is reason to believe that all is not well with deviation as currently conceived and that its adoption into the official lexicon of our discipline may be premature. Caution is prescribed by continuing controversies over the definition and etiology of delinquency and crime, and to a lesser extent by the uncertainty and disagreement over definitions of such phenomena as mental disorder and alcoholism. Looming in the background of these particular controversies are larger debates, sometimes polemics, over the theoretical sufficiency of "functionalism" and "social-system" analysis.

Further reasons for guarding against unqualified commitment to the deviation concept come from recognizing the weakness of relevant socio-logical theory and limitations of empirical knowledge about social norms, which in many ways have built little beyond Sumner's older natural law concepts of the folkways and mores. It is also apparent that many pre-vailing usages of deviation place strictures upon the concept of social control which are unacceptable to those who see control in relation to the dynamics of power. Finally, as yet, no suitable way of integrating the notion of deviation into a theory of social change has been devised, which is of no small embarrassment to those who would heed the strident voices of the policy scientists and others who write to the urgencies of the times.[1]

The weight of these considerations suggests that in the present state of our thinking, deviation is better regarded as a conception than as a concept. Large questions are still very much in order as to the sufficiency of theoretical formulations of deviation, which, we make so bold as to suggest, are trending in at least two directions. Their emergent forms, while revealing areas of overlap and continuity, may or may not be reconcilable. One conception of deviation can be called structural, perhaps "substantive," the other, one of social control or "process."[2] The struc-tural conception has been most symmetrically stated by Merton in his discussion of social structure and anomie; an equally express formulary of the alternative, "control" conception awaits development. This critical examination of the structural analysis of deviation may, we hope, dialec-tically lead to further clarification of the social-control conception of deviation. /

THE STRUCTURAL VERSION OF DEVIATION

Merton's perspective of society, like that of Parsons and of Durkheim before him, gives central importance to the concept of structure. This Merton sees as a variable source of "pressures" or "strain" whose conse-quences can be calculated or described as differential rates and forms of deviation between and within societies. According to Merton, societies have a cultural structure separate and distinguishable from a social struc-ture, the former consisting of "an organized set of normative values," the

[1] Arthur K. Davis, "Social Theory and Social Problems," *Philosophy and Phenomenological Research* 18 (1957): 190–208.

[2] Edwin M. Lemert, "Deviation: Substance or Process" (Unpublished manuscript, 1963), pp. 1–12.

latter of "an organized set of social relationships." Anomie arises from or describes a disjunctive relationship between the two. The seeming paradox by which an anomic society generates both conformity and deviation is explained by reference to a rigid or dilapidated social structure, which restricts opportunity for some categories of the population. Put in barest form: The social structure allows some people to compete for universally inculcated goals, and other persons it does not. The former follow the institutionally prescribed norms; the latter do not. The "modes of adaptation" the latter make to their anomalous position in the social structure are forms of deviation.[3]

It is important to note that the term cultural structure as employed by Merton makes it explicit that goals are "more or less integrated" and "roughly ordered in some hierarchy of value." In other words, culture, presumably through socialization, supplies individuals with a standardized order of values. At the same time we note his contention that "the cultural structure defines, regulates, and controls the acceptable modes of reaching out for these goals." This is further emphasized by the statement that regulatory norms are "rooted in the mores of institutions." To the norms are imputed substantive attributes of prescription, preference, permissiveness, and proscription.[4]

Although Merton is careful to qualify his statement and to acknowledge, if somewhat obliquely, some of their less defensible implications, it is doubtful that he escapes the difficulties which inhered in Durkheim's assignment of qualities of "externality and constraint" to collective representations. Thus, for example, while he recognizes the statement that "controls are in the mores" as elliptical, he presumes that this embarrassment is evaded by grading the norms according to the above indicated attributes of varying compulsiveness.[5]

Close examination of literature on the subject compels us to admit that the term culture has never been satisfactorily or fully defined, and it is highly doubtful that a theoretical line between culture and social structure can be maintained in data analysis, save in the most general way.[6] This is not to deny the usefulness of the term culture as a conceptual orientation

[3] Robert Merton, *Social Theory and Social Structure,* rev. ed. (New York: Free Press, 1957), chapter IV.

[4] Ibid., pp. 132–35.

[5] Ibid., p. 133.

[6] See Evon S. Vogt, "On the Concepts of Structure and Process in Cultural Anthropology," *American Anthropologist* 62 (1960): 18–33; A. L. Kroeber and Talcott Parsons, "The Concepts of Culture and of Social System," *American Sociological Review* 23 (1958): 582–83; Claude Lévi-Strauss, "Social Structure," in *Anthropology Today,* ed. A. L. Kroeber (Chicago: University of Chicago Press, 1953), pp. 524–53.

to certain kinds of data. The difficulties begin to plague us when, as Barnett says, "unsupportable demands (are) made upon it and . . . undemonstrable claims made for it as an explanatory device." [7] The common tendency is to reify what can be no more than a mental construct and to give it properties appropriate to an order of phenomena, different from that which it describes, i.e., in Merton's usage, culture "defines, regulates, and controls." Inescapable circularity lies in the use of culture as a summary to describe modal tendencies in the behavior of human beings and, at the same time, as a term of designating the causes of the modal tendencies.

/ The empirically more tenable alternative is that only human beings define, regulate, and control behavior of other human beings. Beyond this it is dubious that clear and exclusive referents can be found either for a "cultural system" or a "cultural hierarchy of values." This is not to deny the existence of hierarchies of values, but merely to insist that only individuals have hierarchies of values, which by minimal agreement specify affective as well as cognitive responses. To claim otherwise forces the animistic admission that cultures *feel* for and against things, or that they feel more strongly about some things than others. /

Groups, which are empirically demonstrable phenomena, do not have value hierarchies identical to those of feeling, cognating human beings. It is, however, possible to show that groups, through social interaction and control, can determine that certain values will necessarily be satisfied by members before others, or that certain values will be maintained in a dominant position in group interaction. Furthermore, it is possible to show with factual data a series of interlocking or intermeshing groups, which, due to their positions in relation to accessible means of power and social control, can determine that certain values will be dominant, i.e., satisfied first by various persons in the constituent groups. Again, it must be cautioned that such associational values orders are not the same as individual hierarchies.

The more associational networks there are in a society, and the more rapidly they change, the more important it becomes to adopt this limited set of postulates about the relationship of values, groups, and individuals. One consequence of doing so is that conformity, which Merton makes no attempt to explain, becomes problematical as well as deviation. The persistence of patterned behavior and the extent to which it is a relevant factor in individual and collective behavior, conforming and deviating, must be explained rather than assumed. In doing so, particular care must be taken to avoid identifying conforming behavior with patterned behavior.

---

[7] H. G. Barnett, "Comment on Acculturation: An Exploratory Formulation," *American Anthropologist* 56 (1954): 1001.

THE ENDS-MEANS SCHEMA

It is plain that Merton's conception of deviation can gain acceptance as a theory and become empirically useful in proportion to the validity of the ends-means schema upon which it rests. Some sociologists object to the concept of value as vague and shy away from its use. Others argue more strongly that it adds nothing to the explanation of behavior.[8] Yet, despite such dissident notes, both sociologists and anthropologists are being pushed towards some such concept by the nature of the problems with which they must deal.[9] A more pertinent criticism, less easily set aside, is the assertion that the distinction between values and means cannot be maintained; Turner raises this issue in a commentary on the anomie formulation.

> This scheme is difficult to apply, however, since the distinctions between means and ends are not easily made in practice. Values become ends or means only in the context of a particular act in progress, and there are no values which constitute ends all of the time or means all of the time. To apply the scheme requires that the investigator determine what are really ends—a highly dubious process. Thus in American society the pursuit of money (an end) without respect to the approved means can be called an excessive emphasis on goals. But it is equally logical to insist that money be regarded as a means toward more ultimate goals such as happiness, and that the excessive pursuit of money is a concentration on means at the expense of ends.[10]

Part of the problem, then, in the analysis of deviation, is that the nature of a social value has not been sufficiently clarified, which necessarily compromises any theory resting upon it. However, the confusion between values and means is less a conceptual weakness in deviation theory than the failure to recognize and make a place for it. Instead of making the confusion a reason for rejecting the value-means distinction, sociologists should turn it to use for interpretation and research. The empirical facts behind the confusion may well be the most important ones with which we have to deal in the study of deviation in modern society.

[8] Franz Adler, "The Value Concept in Sociology," *American Journal of Sociology* 62 (1956): 272–79.

[9] Don Martindale, "Social Disorganization: The Conflict of Normative and Empirical Approaches," in *Modern Sociological Theory*, ed. H. Becker and A. Boskoff (New York: Holt, Rinehart & Winston, 1957), p. 348.

[10] Ralph Turner, "Value-conflict in Social Disorganization," *Sociology and Social Research* 38 (1954): 305.

VALUES AND VALUATION

For our purposes here, values are defined as factors that, within physical and biological limits, affect choice.[11] As such, they are abstractions inferred from acts. However, in making such inferences it is mandatory to distinguish between the act of valuation by an individual and the observable pattern of action which demonstrates the position of a value in a hierarchy or order. The act of valuation is a sorting out and ordering process which occurs when events are mediated by the cognitive processes of the cerebral cortex, which results in preferences for various courses of action.

Valuation immediately precedes action to a greater or lesser degree in all societies because individual members seldom are supplied with means for satisfying their values at costs which correspond to their wishes. The concept of costs here is taken to mean those other values which must be sacrificed in order to satisfy any given value. It is assumed that costs can be at least roughly gauged by the amount of time, energy, and psychic stress required to reach a chosen goal. Costs are important variables in analysis because changes in the costs of means can modify the order of choice, even though the "ideal" values order of the individual remains constant.

The order of value satisfaction in groups must be understood as the product of the interaction of many individuals, each pursuing his hierarchy, sacrificing something of lesser value for something of greater. In so doing, the individual frequently sees the group as a means to ends; he is adjusting to the fact that services of others, whose value hierarchies differ from his own, become means whereby he can achieve his own ends. For this reason the pattern of his choices in a group setting may not correspond to his subjective hierarchy, a fact which cannot be overemphasized in trying to understand the sociopsychological contexts of conformity and deviation.

｜ One of the salient difficulties in most discussions of values and one apparent in Merton's or any purely structural analysis of deviation is the failure to separate out (1) acts of individuals which embody values learned symbolically and transmitted as part of culture during childhood, largely through primary groups; and (2) acts which, as explained above, are products of contingent valuation. In the first instance, actions of individuals are unreflective, and carried out without calculation of consequences or consideration of alternatives. Conformity of this kind can be, in Merton's sense, a consequence of structured or patterned relationships between values and norms. In the second instance the prelude to action is

---

[11] I have closely followed the ideas of W. Fred Cottrell in discussing valuation. See his "Men Cry Peace," in *Research for Peace* ed. Quincy Wright, W. F. Cottrell, and C. H. Boasson (Oslo: Institute for Social Research, 1954), pp. 112–25.

a conscious selective process in which the costs of means, rather than a sacred or internalized "emphasis," play upon a range of alternatives. Two resultant actions of conformity or deviation may be overtly similar but subjectively quite different.

PATTERNED VALUES AND SOCIAL STRUCTURES

It is theoretically conceivable that there are or have been societies in which values learned in childhood, taught as a pattern, and reinforced by structured controls, serve to predict the bulk of the everyday behavior of members and to account for prevailing conformity to norms. However, it is easier to describe the model than it is to discover societies which make a good fit with the model. Durkheim apparently drew upon descriptions of primitive Australian societies in arriving at his ideal of an integrated society.[12] Yet these descriptions were highly selective and undoubtedly biased by a concern with an exceptional, totemic marriage and clan system. Students of American Indian societies, among them Opler, have been at least as impressed by the normal occurrence or high incidence of fragmentation, autonomy, and competition of cultural elements as by their unity or consistency.[13] Divisive elements in Moslem societies are well known, and pluralism is conspicuous in societies of southeast Asia and the Caribbean area.[14] It is safe to say that separatism, federation, tenuous accommodation, and perhaps open structuring are at least as characteristic of known societies of the world as the unified kind of ideal social structure based on value consensus which impressed Durkheim,[15] Parsons, and Merton.

ETHNIC, PLURALISM, ACCOMMODATION, AND DEVIATION

One form of value pluralism arises when dominant values of a culturally distinct group are extended to become a basis for normative regula-

[12] Howard Becker, "Anthropology and Sociology," in *For a Science of Social Man*, ed. John Gillin (New York: Macmillan, 1954), p. 107.

[13] Morris E. Opler, "Themes as Dynamic Forces in Culture," *American Journal of Sociology* 51 (1945): 192–206.

[14] See papers on "Social and Cultural Pluralism in the Caribbean," *Annals of New York Academy of Sciences* 83 (1960): 761–916; review of same by R. T. Smith in *American Anthropologist* 63 (1961): 155–56.

[15] It should be noted that Durkheim recognized a kind of negative solidarity based upon abstention from interference with rights of others rather than upon ends. See Emile Durkheim, *The Division of Labor*, trans. George Simpson (New York: Free Press, 1947), pp. 115–22.

tion of ethnic or religious populations having divergent values. The resultant social integrations follow from conquest, territorial expansion, or migration and are largely accommodative in nature. By definition or fiat, certain cultural practices of the minority cultural groups become crimes, subject to sanctions and penalties imposed by the dominant group or elite. Sellin called attention to the implications of such facts, years ago, in his discussion of culture conflict and crime.[16] Examples abound in the extension of Soviet law into Siberia, imposition of French law in Algeria, and the establishment of English, French, German, and American legal institutions in Pacific Island dependencies. Closer to home can be seen the continuing subjection of American Indians and Mexicans to Anglo-Saxon law, and the consequence of the migration of rural Negroes into northern, urban jurisdictions.

\ The important conclusion from examination of such pluralistic value situations is that criminal deviation in the ethnic minorities can be explained in the same way as conformity among members of the dominant population segment, i.e., by reference to traditionally patterned values and norms where there is no socially structured restriction of means. Numerous examples of such deviant behavior in our society, without disjunctive ends-means concomitants, can be cited: violations of fish and game laws by Indians; common law marriage, statutory rape, marihuana use, and carrying concealed weapons by Mexican migrants; common law marriage, "totin' " (petty theft) and assault by rural Negro migrants; gambling and opium use by Chinese; informal sororal polygyny, gambling, and statutory rape ("sex sixteen" cases) among Hawaiians; drunkenness among older Japanese in Hawaii; and cockfighting among Filipinos.

This kind of unreflective, subcultural behavior is seen most clearly among newly migrant peoples, whose offenses sometimes seem naïve and childlike in the eyes of law enforcement agents. However, if the law is persistently enforced, its effects will be to create new costs for the traditional means of the minority group, leading to a gradual growth in awareness among the minority peoples of the legal implications of their behavior and introducing valuational phenomena into their behavior. Much, of course, depends upon the way in which the laws are enforced and the subgroups or elites to whom control is delegated. /

Conformity of ethnic groups in a pluralistic society, or in situations where intercultural values and norms compete, frequently has to be comprehended as a function of a variety of accommodative relationships which require that subgroup values be satisfied through the instrumental use of associations in the larger, culturally differentiated society. Thus,

[16] Thorsten Sellin, "Culture, Conflict, and Crime," *Social Science Research Council Bulletin* 41 (1938).

when native peoples or migrants become involved in a money economy, technological arrangements, and government health and welfare projects, conformities are produced, not through acceptance of dominant values but rather through treating the values and norms of the dominant group as alternative means to their own unchanged ends. Nowhere is this more clearly exemplified than in the sporadic or cyclical patterns of participation of native peoples in the work-money complexes which have been superimposed on their societies by colonizing elites of western nations. Similarly revealing are the uses they make of the money earned by their labors.[17]

NEO-TECHNIC PLURALISM AND SOCIAL STRUCTURE

It may be protested that the kinds of deviation and conformity we have just discussed are special problems or are tangential to the main concern of Merton's theory, which deals with populations presumed to have been socialized within a common cultural tradition. However, when attention is shifted to a contemporary, urban, secular, technologically based society such as our own, the notion that such a society has a common value hierarchy, either culturally transmitted or structurally induced, strains credulity. Thomas and Znaniecki quite early recognized and stated the fact that the association has become the structural unit of American society and that there is no one association which seeks to or can impose an over-all system of values:

> With the growing social differentiation and increasing wealth and rationality of social values, the complex of traditional schemes constituting the civilization of a group becomes subdivided into several more or less independent complexes. The individual can no longer be expected to make all these complexes his own; he must specialize. There also arises between the more or less specialized groups representing . . . systematic complexes of schemes a conscious or half conscious struggle for supremacy. . . . It is clear . . . that no special social complex, however wide, rich and consistent, can regulate all the activities which are going on in the group. Moreover the broad complexes which we designate by the terms "religion," "state," "nationality," "industry," "science," "art," split into smaller ones and specialization and struggle continue between these. The prevalent condition of our civilization . . . can thus be characterized as that of a plurality of rival complexes of schemes each regulating in a definite traditional way certain activities and each contending with others for supremacy within a given group. The antago-

---

[17] Edwin M. Lemert, "Alcohol Use in Polynesia," *Tropical and Geographic Medicine* 14 (1962): 183–91.

nisms between social stability and individual efficiency is further complicated by conflicting demands put on the individual by these different complexes, each of which tends to organize personal life exclusively in view of its own purposes.[18]

The current relevance of these propositions about modern society has been echoed in Cottrell's observations on the special relationship of associations to values held by individual members.

> Associations and institutions such as the national state and "functional groups," by which we mean groups devoted to a limited number of fairly closely defined objectives, such as trade unions, merchant associations, insurance companies, or corporations, constitute value-creating, value-mediating structures, which differ in very significant ways from the family or local community. The number of such differences is large and has received considerable attention. Of great import here is the fact that such groups attempt to impose no complete pattern of values as the "primary groups" do. That is to say, they disregard many of the values of the individuals who make up the group.[19]

In life-history retrospect, when the individual leaves the arena of primary groups and enters into numerous associations and unstructured situations with individual members representing disparate values, the patterned values acquired in primary groups are overlaid with social interactions which change the meaning of his early experiences. For those who follow patterned values and get the consequences they were taught to expect, the pattern is reinforced in overt behavior and presumably in psychic structure. For those who follow the pristine pattern and meet with other than anticipated consequences there is a modification of either overt behavior or psychic structure, or both.

Because of the disparity in individual members of associations the values which emerge as dominant therein may vary greatly from those of individuals considered distributively. When the association becomes part of an alignment with other associations, the values made dominant in society through the activities of such alignments are even further removed from those of individuals in the various constituent associations. By the same token, the norms set up or legislated to insure the dominance of these

[18] W. I. Thomas and F. T. Znaniecki, *The Polish Peasant in Europe and America* (New York: Dover, 1958), part III, pp. 1894–96.

[19] Cottrell, "Men Cry Peace," *op. cit.*, p. 116. See also David Aberle, "Shared Values in Complex Societies," *American Sociological Review* 15 (1950): 495–502; Frank E. Hartung, "Common and Discrete Values," *Journal of Social Psychology* 38 (1953): 3–22.

remote values may be greatly discrepant or in direct conflict with those held to be appropriate by individuals. It thus becomes doubtful whether study of ideal or presumably indoctrinated values and norms of individuals will generally predict conformity in modern society. Individuals, because they necessarily utilize groups as means to ends, continuously and characteristically conform to norms they have not been taught or to norms whose moral concomitants have been highly attenuated in the course of time. Conformity in groups represents some kind of aggregation of values of individuals, but the form or process of aggregation cannot be presumed from the mere overt facts of conformity. If we are correct that conformity and deviation are complementary aspects of the same phenomena, then much the same generalizations apply to deviation.

INDIVIDUAL CHOICE IN PLURAL SOCIETY

One objection to Merton's view of choice and action by individuals in our society is that it simplifies something enormously complex. Instead of seeing the individual as a relatively free agent making adaptations pointed toward a consistent value order, it is far more realistic to visualize him as "captured," to a greater or lesser degree, by the claims of various groups to which he has given his allegiance. It is in the fact that these claims are continually being preemptively asserted through group action at the expense of other claims, frequently in direct conflict, that we find the main source of "pressures" on individuals in modern society, rather than in "cultural emphasis on goals." Overt behavior, whether it be conforming or deviant, frequently reflects contingent ordering of values and compromised positioning, and their unresolved dilemmas. The likelihood that these will be similar in any two individuals is small.

The captured position of individuals in modern, pluralistic society sheds light on the choice of means to ends. One general consequence of this position is the increase of calculational behavior and a heightened awareness of alternatives, a necessary willingness to consider a wide variety of values and norms as functional alternatives to ends.[20] In a different type of society, this would not be possible. The pressures for individuals to do this have been parallelled by freedom to do so through the widespread secularization of values, largely a product of science and technology.

[20] A related point of view is held by Goode, who states that "accepting dissensus [sic], nonconformity, and conflicts among norms and roles . . . develops the idea that the total role system of the individual is unique and overdemanding." William J. Goode, "A Theory of Role Strain," *American Sociological Review* 25 (1960): 495.

Now a very great number of changes in the modern world have altered the traditional means of obtaining man's values. Some of the "sacred" values of another time have by the development of science become secularized, that is, they are considered as alternatives to other values, and also the means to their achievement can be rationally considered in terms of functionality to achieve them rather than as ends in themselves.[21]

Understanding the way in which illegitimate means are used to satisfy values is complicated by the fact that associations in many areas of choice strive to have, and in many cases succeed in having, their special values advanced, protected, or entrenched through enactment of legal norms. Thus, in addition to an older traditional body of criminal laws revolving around sacred values of life, person, and property, there is a vast proliferation of criminal statutes having to do with health, welfare, public safety and order, conservation, taxes, banking, fiduciary operations, insurance, and transportation, largely representing the specialized values of associations. In many instances the legal norms represent no values of individuals or groups, but rather are the results of compromises reached through group interaction in legislatures.[22]

Our argument here is that criminal laws of the first class can still be regarded as "sacred," but that those of the latter generally fall into a category of secularized, functional alternatives to ends, irrespective of the fact that they have been given political sanction or public, ethical connotation. It is further contended that it is impossible to speak of a cultural or broadly indoctrinated "emphasis" on such norms and equally unrealistic to try to classify them in terms of the degree of their compulsiveness, as proposed by Merton. Objective emphasis on such norms is shifting or ephemeral, to a large extent unsteadily resting on associational alignments having access to political power or on illusory ideologies. Subjectively, the emphasis which individuals place upon such norms depends upon the relationship of the individual to the groups whose values the norms have been designed to give dominance. Seen somewhat differently, the emphasis placed on normative means is determined by their cost, that is, by the particular values that must be sacrificed in order to adopt means.

The kind of orientation towards norms emerging in modern society is epitomized in attitudes of the traffic offender toward his punishments.

---

[21] Cottrell, "Men Cry Peace," op. cit., p. 118.

[22] R. C. Fuller, "Morals and the Criminal Law," *Journal of Criminal Law and Criminology* 32 (1941–42): 624–30; Albert Morris, "Changing Concepts of Crime," in *Encyclopedia of Crime*, V. C. Branham and S. B. Kutash, eds. (New York: Philosophical Library, 1949), pp. 47–55; John J. Honigmann, "Value Conflict and Legislation," *Social Problems* 7 (1959): 34–40.

According to one study, he characteristically regards fines either as "a cost of doing business" or "an unjust penalty for something he could not have avoided." [23] Data of my own indicate that fines for violations of weight regulation for trucks in areas of northern California are accepted by companies, as well as by individual truck drivers, as a necessary cost of doing business. Compliance or noncompliance becomes purely a matter of dollars and cents; thus the cost of two trips to move freight from one terminal to another may be higher than the cost of one trip plus fines assessed at so much per pound. Evidence that the illegal alternative is conceived in purely functional terms exists in the formalized arrangements whereby issuance of a certain type of "trip ticket" insures that the driver's fines will be paid by the company. The reciprocal functionality of attitudes of state officials likewise is revealed by the practice of sending monthly statements to the trucking companies of total fines due.[24]

While it is difficult to determine the extent to which costs become the basis for choosing illegal alternatives to ends in various areas of our society, there seems to be evidence of a growth of "practical morality," under the influence of the dominant world of business, industry, and the large association.[25] Research is confused by the tendency of persons to continue to pay lip service to older, patterned moral concepts. Some indication of the "real" situation is gained from one study of chiseling on unemployment compensation, which disclosed that the "nearness" of persons to the actual conflict situation and the particular issue (sickness) was an important factor in their willingness to regard non-compliance as an acceptable alternative.[26]

RISK TAKING AND DEVIANT BEHAVIOR

At this juncture it is possible to bring several of the ideas so far developed into a somewhat different, perhaps novel, concept of deviant behavior. This concept refers to situations in which persons who are caught in a network of conflicting claims or values choose not deviant alternatives but rather behavioral solutions which carry risks of deviation. Deviation

[23] H. Lawrence Ross, "Traffic Law Violation: A Folk Crime," *Social Problems* 8 (1960–61): 231–40. Clinard gives data to show that blackmarket violators looked upon fines in much the same way. Marshall Clinard, "Criminological Theories of Violations of Wartime Regulations," *American Sociological Review* 11 (1946): 264.

[24] Lemert, "Deviation: Substance or Process."

[25] Solomon Rettig and Benjamin Pasamanick, "Changes in Moral Values as a Function of Adult Socialization," *Social Problems* 7 (1959): 117–25.

[26] Erwin O. Smigel, "Public Attitudes Toward Chiseling," *American Sociological Review* 18 (1953): 59–67.

then becomes merely one possible outcome of their actions, but it is not inevitable. It hinges rather on the turn of circumstances or convergence of external factors. Such an explanation has been proposed by Firth to explain suicide—a subject on which Merton is strangely silent.

Taking issue with Durkheim's analysis of suicide, Firth has shown how suicide among people in the island setting of Tikopia cannot be related to rigidities of social structure nor to any consistent psychic states, largely because the persons attempting suicide were responding to a variety of competing values and because the nature of the act of suicide has culturally variable meanings of goodness and badness, depending upon the specific form of the act and the groups viewing it. Furthermore, it is important that the acts differed in their lethal probabilities; only in certain cases could it be ascertained that the person had definitely chosen to end his or her life. In a large range of cases the most that could be said was that death was one possibility, other possibilities being that the act could eventuate as a daring exploit or lead to a reintegration of the individual into the island social life. A not unimportant factor in the outcome was the efficiency and dispatch with which the rescue fleets were organized and put to sea to locate the lone swimmer or canoe voyager—whose behaviors were among the most common forms of suicide-possible acts.[27]

This analysis of suicide suggests the more general possibility that there are many instances in which people do not elect deviant solutions to problems but instead initiate lines of behavior which, according to how circumstances unfold, may or may not become deviant. In other words, risk-taking, rather than deviation, is perceived by the conflicting person as a "way out." In effect the decision becomes "let chance decide," which indicates that *several* ends-means possibilities inhere in the behavior. While it would be presumptuous in the absence of supporting research to push this interpretation as a general theory of deviant behavior, nevertheless its pertinence to the facts of suicide in our society seem as great as for suicide among the Polynesians of Tikopia. Evidence that risk-taking may be a predominant theme in other forms of deviant behavior comes from the writer's own research on check forgery, in which a substantial number of cases revealed persons who were not motivated to pass bad checks but who simply took chances that under certain circumstances their checks might not be honored. Examples are building contractors who, in anticipation that construction loan payments would be released on schedule, issued checks to laborers and to others for services and materials in such a way

[27] Raymond Firth, "Suicide and Risk-Taking in Tikopia Society," *Psychiatry* 24 (1961): 2–17; James M. A. Weiss, "The Gamble with Death in Attempted Suicide," *Psychiatry* 20 (1957): 17–25. Explanations in terms of anomie have been found not generally applicable to African data on suicide and homicide. Paul Bohannan, ed., *African Homicide and Suicide* (Princeton, N. J.: Princeton University Press, 1960), chap. 9.

that liabilities were created. When the expected payments were not deposited in the bank, their checks became (in California) insufficient funds felony offenses. Although sociology has yet to explore the possibility, it is fair to assume that a considerable amount of risk-taking is built into our business culture—particularly in some areas such as contracting, brokerage and commission selling, and salvage and distress merchandising.[28]

INTERVENING VARIABLES IN DEVIATION

If Merton has excessively simplified the complexities of ends and means and their interrelationships in modern society, much the same charge can be made in regard to his treatment of social structure. His theoretical leap from a single, abstracted element of social structure—class-limited access to means—to deviation in its several typologized forms is a broad one, to say the least. However commendable such parsimony may be in the interests of codifying research, it requires at least prima facie evidence that the assumed differential rates of deviation between upper and lower social strata do exist. Furthermore, some logical exercise or empirical argument seems a preliminary necessity to justify the view, certainly tangential to sociology, that deviation is the result of *individual adaptations.*

A general purview of extant research leaves serious doubts that deviant behavior is proportionately more common at lower than at other class levels of our society. The doubts increase as one proceeds away from crime rates, which are the starting point for Merton's formulation. Crime rates are shaky grounds for any theory, largely because of the widely recognized unreliability of crime statistics. Even if it is granted that crime is relatively more frequent for lower class populations, there are outstanding exceptions when certain types of crimes are noted, such as check forgery, embezzlement, automobile theft, and possibly sex offenses.[29] Further difficulties

---

[28] A good deal of deviant sex behavior can be looked upon as an outcome of risk-taking. The deviant status (for it can scarcely be called behavior) of the unmarried mother is a case in point. A whole range of ends may be present in decisions of single girls to engage in non-marital sexual intercourse. It seldom is the case that a girl chooses to become pregnant and have an illegitimate child. For a study of the characteristic conflicts and dilemmas in this "deviation" see Vincent Clark, *Unmarried Mothers* (New York: Free Press, 1961).

[29] See Edwin M. Lemert, "The Behavior of the Systematic Check Forger," *Social Problems* 6 (1958): 141–49; A. C. Krusiz, et al., *Sexual Behavior in the Human Male* (Philadelphia, Pa.: W. B. Saunders, 1948), pp. 327–93; William Wattenberg and James Balistrieri, "Automobile Theft: A 'Favored Group' Delinquency," *American Journal of Sociology* 57 (1952): 575–79.

with the assumed priority of class handicaps in the explanation of illegal behavior are met in the equal or greater variations in crime rates when they are computed by age, sex, locality, and ethnic identity.

When attention is drawn to such forms of deviation as alcoholism, suicide, and drug addiction, there are no consistent data to show that these are more common adaptations of members of lower class society.[30] Some studies agree with the idea that psychosis rates are inversely related to class or occupational status, but when rates for psychoneuroses are considered, the relationship becomes positive.[31] The contention that radicalism or rebellion are lower class adaptations is perhaps the most difficult of all to fit the facts. Proclivities of middle-class persons for radical protest and action have long been known to writers on the subject.[32] Cottrell's case study of the death of a railroad town due to dieselization portrays dramatically how technologically induced crisis may evoke a shift towards radicalism or ideological rebellion in the settled, "moral," propertied class, rather than in the lower class, which in this instance had the low cost alternative of migrating from the town. Geographic location, age, and seniority as expressions of technological structure largely determined which persons experienced pressures to deviate.[33]

The degree and rapidity with which technology differentiates social organization in modern society and the difficulty of discovering measures of social status generally applicable to a variety of populations and areas speak of the necessity to use a more discriminating concept or concepts than social class in seeking to explain how social structure influences deviation. It is possible to share with Merton a modest assumption that position

[30] On alcoholism see W. M. Wellman, M. A. Maxwell, and P. O'Hollaren, "Private Hospital Alcoholic Patients and the Changing Conception of the Typical Alcoholic," *Quarterly Journal of Studies on Alcohol* 18 (1957): 388–404; Edwin M. Lemert, "The Educational Characteristics of Alcoholics," *Quarterly Journal of Studies on Alcohol* 12 (1951): 475–88. On suicide see J. P. Gibbs, "Suicide," in *Contemporary Social Problems*, eds. Robert K. Merton and Robert A. Nisket (New York: Harcourt Brace Jovanovich, 1961), pp. 244 ff. The data on drug addiction are inconclusive in regard to the original occupational status of addicts to the United States; however, in England addicts apparently are drawn largely from the middle and upper classes. Physicians appear to have the highest rates of drug addiction of any occupational groups in the United States, England, and Germany. Charles Winick, "Physician Narcotic Addicts," *Social Problems* 9 (1961): 174–86; Edwin M. Schur, "Drug Addiction Under British Policy," ibid., pp. 156–66.

[31] August B. Hollingshead and Frederick C. Redlich, *Social Class and Mental Illness* (New York: John Wiley, 1958), chapter 8.

[32] Edwin M. Lemert, *Social Pathology* (New York: McGraw-Hill, 1951), pp. 184–86.

[33] W. F. Cottrell, "Death by Dieselization," *American Sociological Review* 16 (1951): 358–65.

in social structure is important in determining what means become available to reach ends, but other factors are equally important. Among these are groups, technology, psychic processes, and sociobiological handicaps.

COLLECTIVE ADAPTATIONS

Nothing seems more obtrusive in modern society than the dependence of individuals upon groups as means of reaching their ends and the collective context in which ends and means assume importance. For this reason we may wonder why Merton made no allusions to groups as dynamic variables in deviant behavior, in his original and revised essays. It was only subsequently, and then in a very limited way, that he recognized the need to link theoretically some aspects of deviation to groups. Thus, in order to account for forms of deviation that do not arise from private "autistic" adaptations, he advocates the concept of nonconformity as "a basis for consolidating the theory of deviation and reference group behavior." Following Cooley, Merton defines this as a kind of conformity in reverse, that is, conformity to values and normative standards of reference groups representing "an earlier condition of society or that of future society."

Reference group is a term with several meanings in sociology, but it is employed by Merton to account for the individual's perceptions which are at variance from those expected from an inventory of values of the group or social category of which he is currently a member. The problem in its use is that it easily becomes reductionistic,[34] and insofar as the group becomes an inert repository of values assumed to determine the behavior of the individual for whom it is a referent, the criticism is justifiable. Actually, the "group" is an illusory variable in Merton's suggested analysis of nonconformist behavior, for it corresponds to no extant or identifiable body of persons. The discrete individual remains for Merton the unit of analysis; the group as an arena of interaction, variably influencing conformity and deviation, nowhere comes to the fore in his treatment.[35]

It seems almost gratuitous to insist that many forms of deviation, professional crime, prostitution, "vagrancy," skid-row drinking, use of opiates and marihuana smoking, even bureaucratic "ritualism," are collective acts in which group derived and group maintained values, as well as

[34] Marie Jahoda, "Conformity and Independence," *Human Relations* 12 (1959): 101.

[35] This seems to be what Dubin says of Merton's and his own formulations of deviant behavior. Robert Dubin, "Deviant Behavior and Social Structure: Continuities in Social Theory," *American Sociological Review* 24 (1959): 163.

private values, are served. It is equally necessary to see that conformity, as numerous psychological studies and knowledge of monolithic, political-party behavior make plain, is a collective as well as an individual pheno-menon.[36]

In struggling with the perplexing problem of the relation of the indi-vidual to the group it is wise to note an emphasis in Cooley's figurative prose, other than that singled out by Merton, to wit, the nonconformity "results from an unusual way of *selecting* and *combining* accessible social influences . . ." and that the individual "*tries* to conform to the group standards to which he gives his allegiance." [37] Seen in this light the issue becomes one of whether the individual conforms or deviates because he shares both values and norms of a deviant subgroup or because he elects to participate in a group whose specialized ends coincide at certain points with his order of values.

A great deal of the confusion and disagreement as to whether juvenile gangs have substantive sub-cultures classifiable as delinquent comes from a failure to take into account the interaction through which certain values become dominant in a group. It is significant that only a small percentage of such gangs engages in delinquencies, and only a small part of the behavior of so-called delinquent gangs is delinquent. Close analysis discloses that gang members react to many value claims besides those of the gang and that group interaction is highly important in determining the incidence, form, and direction of, say, assault or violence.[38]

The need for a theory of associational groups as agencies which fix and alter the order of value satisfaction, as well as shape means to ends, has long been apparent in the study of what has been loosely designated white collar crime. I once asked E. H. Sutherland whether he meant by this term a type of crime or crime committed by a special class of people.

---

[36] For a review of pertinent literature on conformity see Richard H. Willis, "Social Influence and Conformity—Some Research Perspectives," *Acta Sociologica* 5 (1960): 100–114.

[37] Charles H. Cooley, *Human Nature and The Social Order* (New York: Free Press of Glencoe, Inc., 1956), p. 301.

[38] See Walter B. Miller et al., "Aggression in a Boys' Street Corner Group," *Psychiatry* 24 (1961): 283–98. Sykes and Matza describe some of the same value claims as does Miller, but from the vantage of the individual. Both papers appear to be a good start at analyzing the processes by which values are aggregated in deviant behavior. Gresham Sykes and David Matza, "Techniques of Neutralization: A Theory of Delinquency," *American Socio-logical Review* 22 (1957): 664–70. See also Lewis Yablonsky, "The Delinquent Gang as a Near Group," *Social Problems* 7 (1957): 108–17; Harold Pfautz, "Near-Group Theory and Collective Behavior: A Critical Reformulation," *Social Problems* 9 (1961): 167–74.

He replied that he was not sure, thus admitting to an ambiguity which, in our estimation, he never resolved. He was not alone, however, for the courts handle antitrust violations in two ways, fining the corporations and also punishing their individual officers. A vast amount of case evidence shows that illegal price-fixing, misrepresentation, adulteration, collusive bidding, abetting extortion by labor racketeers, tax evasion, restrictive covenants, as well as a modicum of more traditional crimes, including even behavior chargeable as treason, follow from informal, clandestine, policy decisions of associations.[39] Such decisions, reached through group interaction, reflect an order of values and choice or means not necessarily representative of decision-makers considered distributively, and increasingly less representative of persons and groups organizationally removed from the point of policy interaction. The same conclusion is applicable to corruption, crime, and radicalism within labor unions, where we have fuller documentation of the control systems and group interaction that create and preserve organizational values inconsistent with member values.[40] Insofar as workers narrowly look on the labor union as an effective means to higher wages and better working conditions, they will tolerate, and under certain circumstances will support or even share, criminal practices or communism among their leaders.

The behavior and verbal rationales of corporation executives which so incensed Sutherland—such as their willingness to put profits above patriotism—from our point of view can only be understood in the context of technological and cost imperatives that confront whole associations. Their consequences at the level of individual behavior is illustrated by differences in compliance with axle-load regulations on the part of private and armed forces trucking operations in the northern California area. Generally, private firms seem to disregard the required distibution of weight on axles of trucks, even though this practice shortens the life of trucks and raises maintenance costs. In contrast, truckers working for naval supply in the San Francisco area after the war apparently observed the regulations. The difference in behavior was largely due to the fact that

[39] For an exemplary case study see Richard A. Smith, "The Incredible Electrical Conspiracy," *Fortune* (April 1961): 132–80; (May 1961): 161–224. Although Sutherland points to individuals as white collar criminals, he states unequivocally that "crimes of business are organized crimes." E. H. Sutherland, *White Collar Crime* (New York: Holt, Rinehart & Winston, 1961), p. 255. Clinard cites cases to show that gasoline companies urged dealers to get into the black market. Marshall Clinard, *The Black Market* (New York: Holt, Rinehart & Winston, 1952), pp. 168 ff.

[40] David J. Saposs, "Labor Racketeering: Evolution and Solutions," *Social Research* 31 (1958): pp. 253–70; John Hutchinson, *Corruption in American Trade Unions*, Reprint 91 (Berkeley: University of California Institute of Industrial Relations, 1957), esp. p. 14.

while private firms quickly charged off their depreciated equipment, the Navy pool could not do this, and moreover, it had a relatively low budget for maintenance.

The interplay of technological factors and deviation also appears in problems of determining weight differences in truck loads where moisture content of such materials as sand and gravel cannot be gauged. Trucks loaded in the fields with agricultural produce also make compliance problematical, and it is undoubtedly correct to say that many truck drivers do not know and cannot know whether their equipment is overloaded. Technological factors and costs likewise have a direct influence on disregard for speed limits set for trucks and buses in California. The meeting of schedules for time-conscious customers and passengers can be compromised only at the risk of serious loss of patronage and profits.[41]

The relation of technology to conformity and deviation is unexplored territory so far as sociology is concerned, and our attempts to document its importance can only be faltering. Yet it seems clear from the trend of our analysis that there are numerous aspects of conformity and deviation in which it must be reckoned with as both a limiting and imperative factor.

PSYCHIC PROCESSES AND DEVIATION

Although Merton looks upon deviation primarily as the result of individual adaptations, nowhere in his essays does he make allowance for psychic processes as variables that can significantly affect the form of the adaptations. There is but one incidental reference to the possible relevance of such phenomena to deviation, in a comment that "truly private" nonconformity is a form of "autism." However, there is no effort to elaborate this concept or to place it in the larger context of his paradigm.

While culture-personality theory and speculation have yet to prove their worth to sociology, we need not reject the postulate that psychic processes vary with positions occupied by individuals in social structures, particularly when the processes are carefully defined in terms of commitment, involvement, and participation. Exclusion from groups and social isolation may be important variables in accounting for the development of certain forms of deviation. Cressey has stressed isolation as one of the variables necessary to explain embezzlement.[42] The present writer has offered what he calls an "isolation and closure" theory of certain kinds of

[41] Lemert, "Technology and Deviation," *op. cit.*

[42] Donald Cressey, *Other People's Money* (New York: Free Press, 1953), esp. chapter 2.

check forgery, as well as an explanation of paranoia as an interactional product of exclusion.[43] Meier and Bell have suggested, from their research, a more general conclusion that anomie may be a cause rather than an effect of circumscribed life chances.[44] Social isolation from others, arising in a variety of ways, can alter significantly, if only ephemerally, the emphasis placed upon certain values and the perception of means in terms of both their availability and moral acceptability.

The consequence of Merton's omission of any discussion of the psychic process is an unavoidable superficiality in his conception of the deviations that he subsumes as "retreatist." We find a certain tour de force quality in lumping together activities of such vaguely defined people as "vagabonds," "pariahs," "vagrants," and "autists" with chronic drunkards and drug addicts and, without specifying what the "activities" are, attributing to them a common "escapist" motivation which eventuates in "asocialized" individuals. Serious difficulties are met in any effort to reduce alcoholism and drug addiction to the simple kind of ends-means relationship which Merton makes a key to understanding deviant behavior. Alcohol and narcotics have manifest physiological and sociopsychological effects which, in ways as yet not well understood, alter the value orders of individuals. With persistent use they frequently become associated with organic and status changes (in our society) which radically modify the perception of the costs of means of reaching ends. Drugs and alcohol at certain stages of use become ends rather than means, a transformation of meaning which must be heeded in explaining how or why drug addicts and alcoholics engage in other forms of deviant behavior, such as petty theft or passing bad checks.

SOCIOBIOLOGICAL LIMITS

It would seem that any theory beginning with the idea that limited access to means of adaptation is a source of deviant behavior would turn thought to the limiting effects of biological handicaps and anomalies, if for no other reason than to justify their exclusion. It can, of course, be argued that to bring these into such theory introduces a synthetic element inconsistent with a disciplinary commitment to study only the "sociological" factors at work in deviation. More careful analysis and a modicum of familiarity with the data indicate that the central subject matter in question is at least as sociological, or sociopsychological, as it is biological

[43] Edwin M. Lemert, "An Isolation and Closure Theory of Naïve Check Forgery," *Journal of Criminal Law and Criminology* 44 (1953): 296–307; and "Paranoia and the Dynamics of Exclusion," *Sociometry*, 25 (1962): 2–20.

[44] Dorothy Meier and Wendell Bell, "Anomie and Achievement of Life Goals," *American Sociological Review* 24 (1959): 201.

—perhaps more so. 'Although physical handicaps partially restrict opportunities for achievement, the more critically operating limits come from an overlay of interpersonal and formal social barriers founded on cultural stereotypes about physical defects. As many physically disadvantaged people say, the problem is less the handicap than it is people.[45] /

The case is most clear with cosmetic defects, for here there are no biological limitations on behavior or choice in a strict sense. Yet the social exclusion encountered by persons so differentiated and their own withdrawal reactions are no less impressive than those seen in other kinds of physical disabilities. Much the same is true for one of the commonest forms of speech disorder, stuttering, which is almost entirely functional, appearing in otherwise normal children and adults. Equally significant is the fact that there is no necessary relationship between the extent and nature of physical disabilities and the variety of adaptations made to them. Individual responses range from withdrawal, through rebellion, to cynical or "professional" manipulation of cultural stereotypes and the rehabilitative arrangements organized by society to cope with the "problems" of the handicapped. Indications are strong that the special status given to the physically handicapped, as well as to many other deviants, differentiates the "psychic environment" within which they must live. A large part of this consists of imputation of special character qualities to deviant and defective persons, which become an objective framework for the development of subjective limits on meaning and choice.

⸗ There is a processual aspect to deviation, whose acknowledgement is forced on us by the fact that with repetitive, persistent deviation or invidious differentiation, something happens "inside the skin" of the deviating person. Something gets built into the psyche or nervous system as a result of social penalties, or degradation ceremonies,[46] or as a consequence of having been made the subject of "treatment" or "rehabilitation." The individual's perception of values, means, and estimates of their costs undergoes revision in such ways that symbols which serve to limit the choices of most people produce little or no response in him, or else engender responses contrary to those sought by others. /

PRIMARY AND SECONDARY DEVIATION

Considerations of this sort led the present writer, in an earlier paper, to pose a theoretical distinction between primary and secondary deviation.

[45] Joseph Himes, "Some Concepts of Blindness in American Culture," *Social Casework* 31 (1950): 21–28.

[46] Harold Garfinkel, "Conditions of Successful Degradation Ceremonies," *American Journal of Sociology* 61 (1956): 420–24.

This was devised to bring attention to two different kinds of research problems, the second of which is untouched in Merton's discussions of deviation: (1) *how deviant behavior originates;* (2) *how deviant acts are symbolically attached to persons and the effective consequences of such attachment for subsequent deviation on the part of the person.* Primary deviation is assumed to arise in a wide variety of social, cultural, and psychological contexts, and at best has only marginal implications for the psychic structure of the individual; it does not lead to symbolic reorganization at the level of self-regarding attitudes and social roles. Secondary deviation is deviant behavior, or social roles based upon it, which becomes means of defense, attack, or adaptation to the overt and covert problems created by the societal reaction to primary deviation. In effect, the original "causes" of the deviation recede and give way to the central importance of the disapproving, degradational, and isolating reactions of society.[47] The distinction between primary and secondary deviation is deemed indispensable to a complete understanding of deviation in modern, pluralistic society. Furthermore, it is held that the second research problem is pragmatically more pertinent for sociology than the first:

> In modern society it is difficult or impossible to derive theoretically a set of specific behavioral prescriptions which will in fact be normatively supported, uniformly practiced, and socially enforced by more than a segment of the total population. Under such conditions it is not the fact that individuals engage in behavior which diverge from some theoretically posited "institutional expectations," or even that such behaviors are defined as deviant by the conventional and conforming members of society. A sociological theory of deviance must focus specifically on the interactions which not only define the behavior as deviant but also organize and activate the application of sanctions by individuals, groups and agencies. For in modern society the socially significant differentiation of deviants from non-deviants is increasingly contingent upon circumstances of situation, place, social and personal biography, and bureaucratically organized agencies of social control.[48]

SOCIAL CONTROL AND DEVIATION

We can move now from a kind of revisionist critique of Merton's paradigm to the major theoretical issue between a purely structural conception

[47] Edwin M. Lemert, "Some Aspects of a General Theory of Sociopathic Behavior," *Proceedings of Pacific Sociological Society* 16 (1948): 23–29.

[48] John I. Kitsuse, "Societal Reaction to Deviant Behavior: Problems of Theory and Method," *Social Problems* 9 (1962): 256; see also Edwin M. Lemert, *Social Pathology* (New York: McGraw-Hill, 1951), chapter 3.

of deviation and the view of deviation as a consequence of the extent and form of social control. The latter rests upon the assumption that social control must be taken as an independent variable rather than as a constant, or merely reciprocal, societal reaction to deviation. Thus conceived, social control becomes a "cause" rather than an effect of the magnitude and variable forms of deviation.

Facts are readily marshaled to give body to this conception. Firth, in the previously cited study of suicide in Tikopia, brought out the importance of the organization and dispatch of rescue fleets among other factors determining the lethal probabilities in suicide behavior. In our own society differences in crime rates between communities can be related to variations in available means for policing, as measured, for example, by a ratio of police to population.[49] The differing efficacy of families as supervisory agencies similarly can be shown to have a notable effect on rate differences in juvenile delinquency.[50] Finally, the presence or absence of a "compliance section" in corporations undoubtedly has something to do with frequency with which antitrust laws are violated.

However, it is necessary to proceed beyond these obvious implications of social control for the incidence of deviation to those more closely connected with its operation in modern pluralistic society. In so doing we would like to note that new ways of thinking can be opened up by assuming that, in the absence of pressures to conform, people will deviate, or more precisely, express a variety of idiosyncratic impulses in overt behavior. When this assumption is joined with our earlier one, that our society increasingly shows fluid and open structuring of situations, categorically different ideas about deviation follow.

An equally flexible conception of norms is required to supplement these assumptions. So considered, norms become little more than a reference point for action, or, following Felix Cohen,[51] a set of probabilities that in some situations certain unpleasant things will happen to people either at the hands of associates or from actions of legal or other tribunals. When these probabilities are high we can assume that behavior of an individual and of those reacting to it express patterned values. When they are low we must make other assumptions about the outcome of the individual's actions and of the actions of those who react to him; we must, in so doing, adopt a social-interactional rather than a relationship perspective.

[49] W. F. Ogburn, "Factors in the Variation of Crime among Cities," *American Statistical Association Journal* 30 (1931): 12–34.

[50] Jackson Toby, "The Differential Impact of Family Disorganization," *American Sociological Review* 22 (1957): 505–11.

[51] Felix S. Cohen, *Ethical Systems and Legal Ideals* (Ithaca, N.Y.: Cornell University Press, 1959), p. 254.

CONSTITUTIVE NORMS

Garfinkel has originated an intriguing set of notions revolving around what he designates as "constitutive rules of social interaction," which appear to be promising concepts for research on behavior in unstructured situations. These are less specifications of substantive behavior than they are criteria of the possible locale, numbers of participants, and order of action an individual assumes must be chosen by himself and others in social interaction. These most nearly resemble ground rules or basic rules of a game. Thus, in a bridge game there are no rules requiring that a given card be played, only rules as to who should play it. Furthermore, players do not respond so much to the act as they do to its meaning in relation to the emerging strategy of the game. It is assumed that constitutive rules are discoverable as interactional guides in the course of daily events as well as in games.[52]

The germane conclusion is that in certain situations it is impossible to determine what is regarded as normal or deviant behavior merely by inspecting its external features. It must be known what rules are the basis of social interaction and at what point the participants are in an interactional sequence. In the course of such interaction, individuals may unilaterally change the rules or the rules may, by group interaction, be shifted to a new ground. In some cases this may take the form of a sliding scale of norms, as at a cocktail party where behavior which would not be allowable at the beginning may become so after "things get going." Courtship and sex behavior in general would seem to fall into the category of game-like interaction, in which rules are progressively changed by a variety of subtle cues, dress, or sententious silence. Often this applies not only to the courting pair but also to parents and the community.

When constitutive rules are breached, the situation becomes "confused," which may either lead to withdrawal of persons from interaction or to a redefinition of the unexpected behavior in terms of alternative meanings of what is constitutively "normal" or acceptable. The interim interaction which culminates in mutual acceptance of new constitutive rules is one of "normalization."\Normalization takes place between persons who "trust" one another, or who are bonded together by mutual claims, as in family, friendships, reciprocal business and professional relationships, or by informal ties which grow up within formal organizations. It also may occur in what Goffman calls "encounters," [53] when they are governed

[52] Harold Garfinkel, "Some Conceptions of and Experiments with 'Trust' as a Condition of Stable Concerted Actions" (Manuscript: Files of Center for Study of Law and Society, University of California, Berkeley); also his *Studies in Ethnomedology* (Englewood Cliffs, N.J.: Prentice-Hall, 1967).

[53] Erving Goffman, *Encounters* (New York: Bobbs-Merrill Co., Inc., 1961).

by some criteria of politeness or courtesy, or by humanitarian solicitude for physically handicapped persons.

From the point of view of valuational choice, normalization will persist so long as the value satisfactions contingent on the interactional bond are of a higher order than those sacrificed by continued normalization. In such a context anomie becomes the state of confusion during which social interactors are unable to discover alternately acceptable meanings for the departure from the rules. Deviant behavior and the possibility of control action arise from the assignment of unacceptable meanings to behavior in interaction which results in high costs or sacrifices of values to those associated with the bond of trust who have access to means of social control.

Normalization is readily perceived in family interaction where a wide variety of idiosyncratic behavior becomes acceptable by virtue of esoteric rules which evolve out of social interaction. A great deal of behavior which in another context would be defined as "delinquent" is normalized because the rules of interaction are different. Even more impressive is the normalization of behavior which, when projected against the diagnostic criteria of formal psychiatry, would be looked upon as "neurotic" or "psychotic." Equally revealing is the diversity of meaning of intoxication in courtship, marriage, and family settings, or even in occupational situations. One position established by research, as well as theory, in the field of speech disorders is that there is no such thing as abnormal speech among children, and that speech problems are a function of parental perception and evaluation.[54]

There are pressing reasons why primary groups go to what might be thought of as extreme lengths in normalizing the behavior of members. When confronted by a breach of constituted rules, voluntary withdrawal or "leaving the field" often is impossible for interacting members. Excluding the person who breaches the rules is a drastic step, for it betokens a betrayal of trust, which must be justified to group members as well as to others. The problem is even more critical if the group turns to formal or legal agencies of social control, or when the primary group is forced to interact with such formal agencies due to violation of formal rules by a member.[55]

[54] Wendell Johnson, "Perceptual and Evaluational Factors in Stuttering," in *Handbook of Speech Pathology*, ed. Lee H. Travis (New York: Appleton-Century-Crofts, 1957), chap. 28. For a discussion of normalization and exclusion in relation to physical handicaps, see Fred Davis, "Deviance Disavowal," *Social Problems* 9 (1961): 120–32.

[55] Normalization also can be related to positive functions of deviation for groups. See Robert A. Dentler and Kai T. Erikson, "The Functions of Deviance in Groups," *Social Problems* 7 (1959): 98–107. A related problem, no

While there is precious little information to draw from, it is likely that normalization increasingly characterizes internal interaction within large associations. The picture is muddied somewhat by the currency of the concept of the "organization man" and the assumed high standards of conformity set for him. However, there can be no doubt that accountable losses of time or unfavorable publicity, as well as the complexities of internal situations themselves, lead corporations, for example, often to consider acceptable employee behavior that in other contexts could be defined as deviant. Department stores seem to prefer, or are compelled, to define the unauthorized removal of merchandise by employees as part of losses covered under the accounting concept, "inventory shrinkage." [56] While the actions involved in some instances are clear violations of formal rules of the law of theft, in others, where the merchandise is damaged or remaindered, or is taking up space needed for other purposes, it is plausible that the situation is less clearly structured. Distinctions between "lost" and "stolen," and between accidental and deliberate breakage on docks and in warehouses, become unimportant to shippers who can adjust their costs or cover losses with insurance. Whether union rules or laws against discrimination in hiring and firing are "violated" on construction projects often depends on the kind of bargaining interaction which goes on between project supervisors and union representatives. Whether the divergent use of labor and materials authorized for construction projects, particularly public ones, is defined as illegal or contrary to rule often depends upon ephemeral or progressively modified agreements between contractors and supervisors. A revealing topic for examination would be the norms constituted for the use and disposition of military supplies and equipment which became "salvage" in South Pacific islands after World War II.

A recent interpretation by Janowitz of various data on military organization indicates that changing skill structures growing out of technology are revolutionizing military discipline, and that formal rules have less and less of a place in the work of a combat team, which is the prototype of the whole military organization.

The combat soldier, regardless of military arm, when committed to battle, is hardly the model of Max Weber's ideal bureaucrat following

---

less important, is the positive function that individuals' choice of deviant definitions or status may have as a means of preserving group ties. For an excellent study of how being hospitalized as insane or mentally ill may thus operate, see Sheldon L. Messinger, "The Mental Hospital and Marital Ties," *Social Problems* 9 (1961): 141–55.

[56] Herbert A. Bloch and Gilbert Geis, *Man, Crime, and Society* (New York: Random House, 1962), p. 207.

rules and regulations. In certain respects he is the antithesis. The combat fighter is not routinized and self-contained. Rather his role is one of constant improvisation, regardless of his service or weapon. Improvisation is the keynote of the individual fighter or combat group. . . . The military organization dedicated to victory is forced to alter its techniques of training and indoctrination. Rather than developing an automatic reaction to combat dangers, it requires training programs to teach men not only to count on instruction from their supervisors but also to exercise their own judgment about the best responses to make when confronted with given types of danger.[57]

It is desirable or even mandatory to ask whether associations in general have not become more or less dedicated to victory or, at least, to vigilant defense in our society. Insofar as this is true, and to the degree that goal consciousness pervades organizations, it can be anticipated that their operations will be less and less set by formal rules and that a form of social control appropriate to functionality and loose structuring will emerge.

ACTIVE SOCIAL CONTROL AND DEVIATION

Although the concept of social control has never been defined to the full satisfaction of sociologists, usages have pointed either in a kind of positivist, teleological direction, or towards the more conservative thought of W. G. Sumner. In an earlier effort to develop a modern idea of social control, the present author took issue with conceptions of social control fathered by the writings of Sumner, specifically with the notions that folkways, mores, and laws are predominant means of social control. Following older ideas of L. M. Bristol, I proposed that such control be termed "passive," in contrast to "active" social control.[58] The distinction, a pivotal one for our purposes, makes passive control an aspect of conformity to traditional norms; active social control, on the other hand, is a process for the implementation of goals and values. The former has to do with the maintenance of social order, the latter with emergent social integrations. More precisely stated, active social control is a con-

[57] Morris Janowitz, *Sociology and the Military Establishment* (New York: Russell Sage Foundation, 1959), pp. 37–38.

[58] L. M. Bristol, *Social Adaptation* (Cambridge, Mass.: Harvard University Press, 1915); Edwin M. Lemert, "The Folkways and Social Control," *American Sociological Review* 7 (1942): 394–99; and "The Grand Jury as an Agency of Social Control," *American Sociological Review* 10 (1945): 751–58. Janowitz proposes a distinction between domination and manipulation to explain the changing emphasis in military discipline toward goal achievement in *Sociology and the Military Establishment*, p. 38.

tinuous process by which values are consciously examined, decisions made as to those values which should be dominant, and collective action taken to that end. While it has individual aspects it is more typically a function of group interaction.

The saliency of active social control in modern society must be understood as an outcome of major changes in the nature of innovating processes. Directly contrary to Merton's view of innovation as a deviant or nonconformist response of structurally disadvantaged individuals, are the ubiquitous indications that innovation has become organized or institutionalized in our society.[59] This is reflected in the image and reality of corporations as research-oriented organizations; it can be demonstrated by data showing the changing ratio of patents granted individuals to those granted to corporations.[60] "Innovate or die" is no idle caveat for the association of today, be it a monster corporation, struggling parochial school system, or intrenched racial segregationists in Prince Edward County, Virginia.

Organized innovation has given us a dynamic technology which continuously differentiates, undercuts, and creates new values, or modifies their order of satisfaction by changing their costs. The dynamics of competition of subgroups within associations, of associations within coalitions, and of coalitions of associations within society to advance their values or maintain them in favored positions has no parallel in any society of the past. It demands that a radically different version of social control be brought into our horizons of thought: "instead of asking how society orders and controls the individual, students of social control might ask how society takes its organization and momentum from its behaving individuals." [61] We must also ask how society takes its organization and momentum from the interaction of groups. While the shadow of Thomas and Znaniecki's "creative man" has grown large, more often than not in society today the shadow cast is that of a creative group.

The implications of active social control for deviation are not easily stated in systematic form, but they can be made apparent by applying an ends-means schema, qualified by cost and other factors, to the agencies and agents of social control. Agencies of social control, not excluding those of law enforcement, when operating in areas of value conflict and in situations complicated by technological change, like other groups in

[59] Hedley Bull, "Systematic Innovation and Social Philosophy," *Inquiry* 3 (1960): 199–205.

[60] Jacob Schmookler, "Technological Progress and the Modern American Corporation," in Edward S. Mason, ed., *The Corporation in Modern Society* (Cambridge, Mass.: Harvard University Press, 1959), chap. 7.

[61] Roger Nett, "Conformity—Deviation and the Social Control Concept," *Ethics* 64 (1953–54): 43.

action select from and implement values in variable ways. The norms that individual agents of social control within organizations are called upon to enforce or follow frequently become functional alternatives to ends. Such individuals seek to gain conformity to norms they do not share, or ignore those they do share, depending upon the availability of means of control, the costs of action, and the competition of values within and outside the control agency. Unless such factors are known in particular situations, it is impossible to determine what norms will be invoked to define a given behavior, or a class of behavior, as deviant and to attach the behavior to persons.

Aubert convincingly states the case when he argues that rather than be concerned with the definition of white collar crime, sociologists should study the *controversy* over white collar crime. Speaking from his study of the regulation of business and of labor regulation in Norway, he says:

> It is frequently impossible to discover the socio-psychological origins and functions of criminal behavior without insights into the social processes behind the enactment of the criminal legislation. The social norms and mores that gave impetus to the enactment and the groups that uphold the norms are important to know for purposes also of tracing the criminal recruitment mechanisms. The nature of the norms thus legally sanctioned may for instance to some extent determine whether criminals tend to be rebels, psychopaths, or rational profit-seekers. . . . Unless we know the location and scope of the groups supporting the legislation, the function it serves in those groups, we shall not succeed in explaining and predicting offenses.[62]

Nowhere is the contingent nature of deviation made more apparent in our society than in the action of government regulatory agencies with adjudicative and punitive powers in situations where they are confronted by consequences of technological and organizational change. Large areas of action having to do with business, finance, health, labor, housing, utilities, safety, and welfare are subject to control through administrative rules discontinuous in origin and form from the culturally derived norms which impressed Merton and others seeming to favor a conception of passive social control. The real source of deviation in such areas is not necessarily change in the behavior of the subjects of regulation, but may be the imposition of new rules which define existing behavior, or behavior consistent with older norms, as now deviant. The object of so defining the behavior is to produce change, not to repress it.

Even when the scene changes from administrative agencies to tra-

[62] Vilhelm Aubert, "White Collar Crime and Social Structure," *American Journal of Sociology* 58 (1952–54): 263–71.

ditional courts, the nonsubstantive nature of legal norms remains clear. The vicissitudes in the interpretation of our antitrust laws are a record of shifting value dominance, in which court judgments have been taken, or frequently modified, by the perception of intolerable costs which literal enforcement of the laws would impose on socially important or strategic industries.[63] Furthermore, it has had to be recognized that literal application of the laws may have effects opposite to those intended by regulators, so that increasingly, policy or values guide court decisions rather than deviation per se. Unmistakable signs that this is true are seen in a recent antitrust decision.

> While it must be admitted that not all of these acts are prohibited, nevertheless we must view them in the broad panorama of other acts and their associations with each other to note, not only the effect, but to pierce the veil of intent . . . it is clear that the . . . result of the conspiracy was to restrict competitors, which is illegal.[64]

It is significant not only that courts are empirically moving toward an ends orientation, but that students of jurisprudence have consciously recognized this development, which places formalistic law in a broader setting of social control. Thus Pound speaks of the important, new directions of juristic thought:

> One is the insistence on function rather than on content; the tendency to ask how do precepts work, to ask whether they can be made to bring about just results rather than whether their abstract content is abstractly just. The moment we ask such questions, we are driven to inquire as to the end of law. For function means function toward some end. Thus for a generation philosophical discussion of the legal order has taken a continually larger place in jurisprudence.[65]

The growing preoccupation with ends in social control which is readily seen in administrative agencies and courts of law also gets expressed in policy awareness of agencies and agents charged with apprehension of law violators. This is most obvious in urban police departments, where the end becomes *regulation* of traffic rather than arrest of traffic law

[63] James E. Lemert, "The Licensing of Chemical Reprocessing Plants Under the Atomic Energy Act," *George Washington Law Review* 29 (1961): 750–52.

[64] "United States vs. Besser Manufacturing Company," in *Industrial Organization and Public Policy* (Homewood, Ill.: Richard D. Irwin, 1958), pp. 373 ff.

[65] Roscoe Pound, *Social Control Through Law* (New Haven, Conn.: Yale University Press, 1942), p. 123.

violators. Yet it can also be held that professionalized police today generally play regulatory roles which are more directly pointed to the end of maximum protection for the community than they are to enforcement of the criminal law. This is due in no small part to value dilemmas the policeman experiences, coupled with the limited time and energy he has available for his task.

> As the patrolman walks his beat his mind does not persistently dwell upon the code of criminal procedure or the latest report on juvenile delinquency. . . . He may observe a multitude of violations, some relating to laws and ordinances which were never intended by the enactors to be enforced, others involving minor regulations of public order, the conduct of trades and callings having some color of public interest or the use of private property. Their very number and variety are such that their requirements are largely unknown to the people to whom they apply. Hence violations are extremely common. The observing patrolman is thereby confronted with a dilemma. If warnings are issued to all such petty violators they will not prove effective unless those who persist in their infractions are arrested and summoned; and if such letter-of-the-law enforcement is attempted the patrolman will be so continuously engaged as a prosecuting witness before the courts that only a small proportion of his time will be devoted to patrolling his beat.
>
> The policeman's art, then, consists of applying and enforcing a multitude of laws and ordinances in such degree or proportion that the greatest degree of protection will be secured. The degree of enforcement and the method of application will vary with each neighborhood and community. There are no set rules, nor even general guides, to the policy to be applied. Each patrolman must, in a sense, determine the standard to be set in the area for which he is responsible. . . . Thus he is a policy-forming police administrator in miniature . . .[66]

The dilemma of the regulatory or enforcement agent and his need to make his own policy may also derive from the spurious qualities of the norm to which he must enforce compliance. This occurs when laws and rules represent no group's values nor values of any portion of a society. Instead they are artifacts of compromise between the values of mutually opposed, but very strongly organized, associations. Alcoholic beverage control furnishes many classic examples of the resultant vagaries of the process by which behavior can become deviant or conformist. Nowhere is this more dramatically illustrated than in the liquor laws of New Zealand, which a recent writer has dubbed the "patchwork monster." Speaking of the unrepresentativeness of the laws, he says:

[66] Bruce Smith, *Police Systems in the United States*, rev. ed. (New York: Harper & Row, 1960); pp. 18–19.

> Popular indignation . . . often ignores the dual nature of the forces behind the retention of the present law. "Both political parties," stated a night club manager recently, "are afraid to lose the votes of the breweries and the temperance people, and will not touch the laws." [67]

Such laws compel licensing agencies, which are creations of law and organs of government, to treat violations as normal conditions of administering the law. At the same time, they force regional variations in interpretation of the law and lead police to treat its enforcement as a functional alternative.

> The Report of the Royal Commission of Licensing in 1946 states that there is strong evidence that after-hours trading must be taken into account in fixing prices and rents of hotels, and that many licensees are under the economic necessity of supplying an after-hours trade. In country areas this merely means that the publicans could not make ends meet without evening and Sunday trade and that, being a necessary social amenity for the local inhabitants, it is catered for by the publicans in defiance of the law. Intelligent constables recognize this, and modify their enforcement of the licensing law accordingly. But in the cities the situation is different.[68]

The assignment of treatment functions to traditional law enforcement agencies, as with regulatory functions, has meant that the arrest and court processing of individuals as deviants must be studied in the light of the interplay of values within the agencies. In certain situations police, prosecutors, grand juries, judges, and probation and parole officers often are not enforcing norms so much as they are expressing conflicts and compromises between different sets of values.

The continuing debate over the nature and causes of juvenile delinquency derives in no small part from the confusion of passive and active social control in the juvenile court, where traditional values vie with scientific ones, where community protection values compete with those of child protection and treatment. Thus Tappan says of the juvenile court:

> There is a wide disparity of methods employed that reflects statutory variation somewhat, but more important, the relative strength of competing socio-legal values fostered by differing legal and administrative points of view in the particular jurisdiction.[69]

[67] Conrad Bollinger, *Grog's Own Country* (Wellington, New Zealand: Price, Milburn, 1959), p. 73.

[68] Ibid., p. 67.

[69] Paul Tappan, *Juvenile Delinquency* (New York: McGraw-Hill, 1949), p. 180; see also F. Killan, "The Juvenile Court as an Institution," *Annals of the American Academy of Political and Social Science* 201 (1949): 89–100.

Characteristically in the juvenile court and its related agencies, judges and workers (police to a lesser extent) respond to the style rather than the content of the behavior of youth who come under their influence and control. A conspicuous result of this is that frequently it is impossible to predict what kind of behavior will result in arrest and adjudication of a child as delinquent, unless it represents a highly visible threat to patterned values of property and person. It is significant in this connection that in California in 1960, 60 per cent of all juvenile arrests were not for delinquent behavior but for "delinquent tendencies." [70]

It seems pre-eminently clear that "delinquency" in our society has no substantive meaning in a sense of a form or essence of behavior which can be described independently of judgments and symbolically colored reactions of others to it. Whether given behavior of a youth is described as delinquent, leading to his adjudication, and the attachment of the label "delinquent" to his person depends upon the perception of arresting officers, availability of biographical data, estimates of the morality of his parents, monetary claims of victims, the biases in judges, and therapeutic ideologies of probation officers and social workers.[71]

The task of sociology is to study not the theoretically conceived "stuff" of delinquency but the process by which a variety of behaviors in contexts are given the unofficial and official meaning that is the basis for assigning a special status in society. That deviant status is assigned can scarcely be denied, despite efforts to define juvenile courts as performing a treatment function. Degradational change in status to a great extent inheres in the institutional setting itself, and is objectively manifested in the number of agencies and organizations which, through systematic recording of biographical data, practice exclusion of persons who have been processed by the juvenile court. At some point in processing by the juvenile court, depending on the individual and the court, we assume that deviation qualitatively changes in relation to the processing and to the impacts of the court and other agencies who take control over the child. Deviation becomes secondary in nature and, in a real sense, deviation begets deviation.[72]

[70] *Delinquency and Probation in California, 1960* (California: State Department of Justice, 1960), p. 19.

[71] Aaron Cicourel, "Adolescent Careers and the Legal Status of Juvenile Offenders" (manuscript).

[72] This was recognized quite early by Thrasher. See Frederick M. Thrasher, *The Gang* (Chicago: University of Chicago Press, 1927); see also David J. Bordua, "A Critique of Sociological Interpretations of Gang Delinquency," *Annals of the American Academy of Political and Social Science* 338 (1961): 120–36; Lee N. Robins, Harry Gyman, and Patricia O'Neal, "The Interaction of Social Class and Deviant Behavior," *American Sociological Review* 27 (1962); 480–92; Irwin Deutscher, "Some Relevant Directions for

While much of what has been said about active social control and deviation has referred to crime and delinquency, we believe that the generalizations are equally applicable to mental disorder, alcoholism, drug addiction, and other forms of deviation. This is most apparent when they emerge in a criminal or legal context, but also demonstrable in other settings, such as the armed forces, welfare organizations, health organizations, and corporations. Sociologists must be less concerned with the essential definitions of deviations like mental disorder and alcoholism than with the processes by which organizations recognize or do not recognize them as moral defect or disease, make them a basis for excusing or not excusing other deviant acts, or choose to assign or not assign benefits to those to whom the deviations are attached. While it is probable that such deviations assess certain minimal or universal "costs" to organizations in which they appear,[73] a variety of other values and costs having to do with their recognition as status modifiers must be seen as operating in decision-making.

CONCLUSION

The structural conception of deviation as developed by Merton has been criticized on the ground that it rests upon reified ideas of culture and social control. The associated ends-means schema, while it may be valid for the analysis of deviation in situations or societies with patterned values, is insufficient for this purpose in pluralistic value situations. Modern society, by reason of being more pluralistic than hierarchically ordered in regard to values, requires that valuation become a central concept in the explanation of deviation.

It will not escape the reader that Merton and the author concur on the primacy of goals in American social life. However, for Merton, "goal emphasis" is an initial assumption made by placing American culture at one extreme of a polar typology of cultures. For us, this prevalence on "ends sought" is derived from postulates concerning the preemptive nature of associations in American society, the multiple value claims made on individuals, and the underlying dynamics of modern technology. These make it possible to explain the problematical aspects

---

Research in Juvenile Delinquency," in *Human Behavior and Social Process,* ed. Arnold Rose (Boston: Houghton Mifflin, 1962), chap. 24.

[73] For a study showing how staff values affect the diagnosis of alcoholism in tubercular patients, see Joan K. Jackson, "Research on Alcoholism and Tuberculosis" (unpublished paper presented at California Tuberculosis and Health Association, April 1958).

of conformity as well as of deviation and to explain generic deviation, rather than mere differences in rates of deviation, without the necessity to invoke "inherent" qualities of whole cultures.

In accord with this line of thought we have proposed a risk-taking theory of deviation as an alternative to one emphasizing a single ends-means sequence. This makes deviation (or conformity) an outcome of several ends-means possibilities, with fortuitous factors and active social control being necessary to a complete explanation. This directs attention to the way in which human beings use chance in value conflict situations.

While class structure may be considered an important variable in deviation, equally important are technology, group interaction, socio-biological limits and psychic processes. Discussion of the latter two variables leads to the conclusion that secondary deviations, arising from the societal and subjective reactions to primary, or original, deviation, is one of the more important problems for analysis in modern society.

Meaning assigned to behavior in a context of constitutive norms is, for us, an inseparable part of deviation. Normalization, or conversely, assigning deviant meaning to actions, takes place in informal interaction or through formal agencies of social control. Agencies and agents of social control, actively seeking to advance or defend their values, define deviation and also assign deviant acts to individuals. This frequently, or characteristically in our society, reflects choice, valuation, and group interaction.

The most pretentious claim for our point of view is that it opens the way to subsume deviation in a theory of social change. Even more important, it gives a proper place to social control as a dynamic factor or "cause" of deviation, thus bringing into perspective a long line of thought beginning with the evolutionary theory of A. C. Hall and continuing, with varying degrees of explicitness, in the ideas of Jerome Hall, Walter Reckless, Vilhelm Aubert, Hermann Mannheim, A. K. Davis, and R. Nett.

3 THE CONCEPT
OF SECONDARY DEVIATION

In an earlier book [1] I proposed the concept of secondary deviation to call attention to the importance of the societal reaction in the etiology of deviance, the forms it takes, and its stabilization in deviant social roles or behavior systems. Sympathetic reception of the idea by a number of reputable sociologists and by unheralded teachers in the field has encouraged me to undertake further clarification of the concept and to articulate it with some of the newer ideas which have come out of sociological studies of deviance.

The notion of secondary deviation was devised to distinguish between *original* and *effective* causes of deviant attributes and actions which are associated with physical defects and incapacity, crime, prostitution, alcoholism, drug addiction, and mental disorders. Primary deviation, as contrasted with secondary, is polygenetic, arising out of a variety of social, cultural, psychological, and physiological factors, either in adventitious or recurring combinations. While it may be socially recognized and even defined as undesirable, primary deviation has only marginal implications for the status and psychic structure of the person concerned. Resultant problems are dealt with reciprocally in the context of established status relationships. This is done either through *normalization*, in which the

---

[1] Edwin M. Lemert, *Social Pathology* (New York: McGraw-Hill, 1951), pp. 75 f.

deviance is perceived as normal variation—a problem of everyday life—or through management and nominal controls which do not seriously impede basic accommodations people make to get along with each other.

Secondary deviation refers to a special class of socially defined responses which people make to problems created by the societal reaction to their deviance. These problems are essentially moral problems which revolve around stigmatization, punishments, segregation, and social control. Their general effect is to differentiate the symbolic and interactional environment to which the person responds, so that early or adult socialization is categorically affected. They become central facts of existence for those experiencing them, altering psychic structure, producing specialized organization of social roles and self-regarding attitudes. Actions which have these roles and self attitudes as their referents make up secondary deviance. The secondary deviant, as opposed to his actions, is a person whose life and identity are organized around the facts of deviance.

Parenthetically it needs comment that all or most persons have physical attributes or histories of past moral transgressions, even crimes, about which they are sufficiently self-conscious to have developed techniques for accepting and transforming, or psychologically nullifying, degrading or punitive societal reactions. Recognition of this compromised state of mankind led Goffman in his sensitive analysis of stigma to hold that secondary deviation is simply the extreme of a graded series of moral adaptations, found among "normal" persons as well as those with socially obtrusive stigma.[2] I believe, however, that this overlooks the fact that stigma involves categorical societal definitions which depict polarized moral opposites, and also that self definitions or identities are integral in the sense that individuals respond to themselves as moral types.

Moreover, whereas Goffman addresses himself to the question of how persons manage stigma and mitigate its consequences, secondary deviation concerns processes which create, maintain, or intensify stigma; it presumes that stigma may be unsuccessfully contained and lead to repetition of deviance similar or related to that which originally initiated stigmatization. Also, it does not exclude the possibility that stigmatized deviance may be strategic, willful, or readily accepted as a solution to problems of the person standing in a stigmatized position.

The way in which a person presents himself in public encounters, particularly in an attenuated, pluralistic society, does much to direct the kinds of reactions others make to him and by such means he protects cherished aspects of his identity. However, to dwell upon the cognitive, dramatic details of face-to-face interaction is to grapple with only part

[2] Erving Goffman, *Stigma* (Englewood Cliffs, N.J.: Prentice-Hall, 1962), p. 127.

of the thorny question of secondary deviance. Over and beyond these are macrocosmic, organizational forces of social control through which public and private agencies actively define and classify people, impose punishments, restrict or open access to rewards and satisfactions, set limits to social interaction, and induct deviants into special, segregated environments.[3]

Although the ideas of personal adaptation and maladaptation rest uneasily in a kind of sociological limbo, the conception of primary and secondary deviance inclines thought in their direction, or at least toward some comparable terms. Their consideration makes it clear that awareness of unenviable features of the self is a complex rather than a simple reciprocal of societal insults to identity, and, further, that adaptations can turn into maladaptations on the person's own terms.[4] This comes to light where efforts at validating the self are complicated by distinct feelings of hopelessness, entrapment, or loss of control over actions presumed to be volitional. These can be observed in certain forms of deviance best described as self-defeating; their peculiar, illogical manifestations speak of underlying difficulty or dilapidation in the communication process by which self and other are constituted.

THE SOCIETAL REACTION

The societal reaction is a very general term summarizing both the expressive reactions of others (moral indignation) toward deviation and action directed to its control. In broad purview the societal reaction often presents a paradox in that societies appear to sustain as well as penalize actions and classes of people categorized as immoral, criminal, incompetent, or irresponsible. The tendency of societies to sustain deviance was recognized quite early by Durkheim and by Marx, and recently in more explicit statements by Dentler and Erikson, and Coser.[5] Their line of thought emphasizes the functional necessity of deviance for promoting group solidarity, differentiating what is moral or goalworthy, and for keeping society's defense mechanisms at standby readiness. Their propo-

[3] John Kitsuse and Aaron Cicourel, "A Note on the Uses of Official Statistics," *Social Problems* 11 (1963): 131–39.

[4] On this point see Messinger's criticism of Goffman. Sheldon Messinger, "Life as a Theatre," *Sociometry* 25 (1962): 98–109.

[5] Emile Durkheim, *The Division of Labor in Society* (New York: Free Press, 1949), pp. 99–103; Robert Dentler and Kai Erikson, "The Functions of Deviance in Groups," *Social Problems* 7 (1959): 98–107; Lewis Coser, "Some Functions of Deviant Behavior and Normative Flexibility," *American Journal of Sociology* 68 (1962): 172–81. The reference to Marx is found in Coser's article.

sitions are commendable as general orientations to the study of deviance, but in my estimation do not account for secondary deviance and its variable emergence at different times and places. Explanations of the latter call for more detailed formulation of the processes by which societies create moral problems for deviants, define, and punish or reward the individual deviant's attempts to deal with such problems in a configuration of general life problems.

STIGMATIZATION

Stigmatization describes a process attaching visible signs of moral inferiority to persons, such as invidious labels, marks, brands, or publicly disseminated information. However, it defines more than the formal action of a community toward a misbehaving or physically different member. Degradation rituals, such as drumming the coward out of the regiment, administering the pauper's oath, diagnosing the contagious illness, and finding the accused guilty as charged may dramatize the facts of deviance, but their "success" is gauged less by their manner of enactment than by their prevailing consequences.[6] The point is commonly illustrated by the initial court appearance of the errant juvenile. The ancient ceremonial there may strike him with awe and fear, but if nothing much happens as a consequence, the memory fades or is retrospectively rationalized. Whatever the deviance, it remains primary.

An assertion, by no means new, is that for stigmatization to establish a total deviant identity it must be disseminated throughout society. Lecky spoke strongly on this point, contending that the solid front of public opinion against the "slightest frailty" among women in mid-nineteenth century England did much to add to the ranks of habitual prostitutes. To his view the "terrible censure" of opinion and the deep degradation of unchaste women caused the status of the prostitute to be irrevocable, and likewise contributed heavily to the associated crime of infanticide.[7]

Much the same thought was voiced by G. H. Mead, who first approximated a theory of criminal stigma in terms of the amount and kind of punishments inflicted upon law violators. His thesis, generically similar

[6] Garfinkel's article on the subject, while a succinct discussion of the requirements for successful denunciation of deviants, does not consider what happens or must happen afterwards. Harold Garfinkel, "Conditions of Successful Degradation Ceremonies," *American Journal of Sociology* 61 (1956): 420–24.

[7] William Lecky, *History of European Morals* (New York: George Braziller, 1955), pp. 282–86.

to Durkheim's, stressed the function of punishments in preserving group cohesion, but went further to show that deterrent punishments, conjoined with pursuit, detection, and prosecution, are incompatible with reinstatement of the criminal in society. Such a system, by suppressing all but aggressive attitudes toward the lawbreaker, effectively destroys communication and generates hostility in the criminal. Mead's conclusion, clearly a partial recognition of secondary deviance, was that a system of deterrent punishments not only fails to repress crime but also "preserves a criminal class." [8]

THE SENSE OF INJUSTICE

When scrutiny is narrowed to uncover the finer ways in which stigmatization fixes deviance and subjectively incorporates a deviant version of the self, the notion of total stigma gives some difficulties. Mead held that impartiality, maximization, and the *consistent* application of punishment, expressed in the "fixed attitude towards the jailbird," provoked intransigence and hostility in the criminal. He seemed to take it for granted that such reactive antagonism led to further crime. To emphasize this interpretation he cited the individualized justice of the newly developed juvenile court as an example of alternative corrective procedures most suited to avoid stigmatization and the recidivism otherwise likely to flow from deterrent punishments.

Standing in contrast if not opposition to Mead's conception of stigma are the views of later writers who assert that *inconsistent* imposition of punishments is the prime factor which sets youth in criminal careers, largely through the arousal of a natural sense of injustice. This idea was originally brought forward in obscure reports appended to some of the numerous crime surveys carried out in American cities between 1920 and 1930. Pound, Osborn, Chaffee, Jr., Stern, and Pollak severally and jointly noted the prevalent confusion in jurisdictions, procedures, and philosophies within or between law administering agencies, and they concluded that this could be vital in diverting occasional youthful offenders into habitual crime, primarily through engendering a sense of unfairness.[9]

[8] George H. Mead, "The Psychology of Punitive Justice," *American Journal of Sociology* 23 (1928): 577–602.

[9] See Roscoe Pound's summary in the *Cleveland Crime Survey* (Cleveland: Cleveland Foundation, 1922), pp. 585 ff; also Alfred Bettman, "Confusion of Concepts," *National Commission on Law Observance and Enforcement: Report of the Prosecution* (Washington, D.C.: Government Printing Office, 1931), pp. 161–66; the excerpt is from Zechariah Chaffee, Jr., Walter Pollak, and Carl Stern, "Unfairness in Prosecution," ibid., p. 268.

Not to be overlooked is the effect of unfairness upon the accused. Even if he is guilty there may be degrees of criminality which he may not have reached . . . but . . . if he feels deeply and justly that society . . . has behaved tyrannically and brutally . . . the natural effect of this emotion is to alienate him still further from the community and make him regard his criminal associates as the only ones who treat him decently. In consequence he may leave prison a bitter enemy of society, more willing than before to continue a criminal career.

Recent writers such as Cloward and Ohlin, and Matza, pursue much the same thought, but also show how "undue deprivation" and the sense of injustice support or reinforce a subcultural ideology of delinquency.[10] Matza holds the thesis, directly contradictory to Mead's that juvenile court procedure amounts to inconsistent punishment, that its very precept of individualized justice, when coupled with judicial arbitrariness and shifting group pressures reflected in court decisions, becomes from phenomenologi- cal perspective an affront to the charged youth's sense of the just.

The apparent contradiction that both consistency and inconsistency in the administration of punishments conduce to secondary deviance dis- solves if several dimensions of inconsistency or, better, incommensurability, in punishments are recognized: (1) inconsistency or disproportion between stigma or punishments and the deviant attributes or actions toward which they are directed; (2) inconsistent applications of stigma or penalties to the same person at different times or places; and (3) inconsistent penalties or stigma applied to persons in the same jurisdiction or by the same law officials.

The definition of stigmatization as a collective process which neces- sarily misrepresents what a person has done and attacks his integrity per- mits the deduction that it "naturally" arouses feelings of injustice.[11] The fact that a wide variety of deviants—the physically handicapped, stutterers, homosexuals, drug addicts, alcoholics, mental patients, as well as de- linquents and criminals—express such feelings turns empirical support to this hypothesis. But whether in fact a felt sense of unjust treatment at the

[10] Richard Cloward and Lloyd Ohlin, *Delinquency and Opportunity* (New York: Free Press, 1960), pp. 117–21; David Matza, *Delinquency and Drift* (New York: John Wiley, 1964), chapter 4; see also Allen Barton and Saul Mendlovitz, "The Experience of Injustice as a Research Problem," *Journal of Legal Education* 13 (1960): 24–39.

[11] For a discussion which derives the sense of injustice from natural law see Edmond Cahn, *The Sense of Injustice* (New York: New York University Press, 1949); whether natural laws need to be invoked is debatable. It is equally plausible to argue that a sense of justice is learned in primary group experiences, or that it reflects one of what Cooley called the primary group values.

hands of society in itself leads on to renewed deviance requires an order of assumptions many sociologists would be unwilling to make. Perhaps it is best regarded as a precipitating factor in some but not all forms of secondary deviance. It becomes one of the problems imposed by the societal reaction. More important is the expression and structuring of such feelings, and their reception by others. While subgroups and subcultural ideologies assume obvious importance here, I believe such subjective reactions are most profitably studied in a larger context of organized social control.[12]

SOCIAL CONTROL

The concept of stigma is burdened with certain archaic connotations suggesting tribal exclusion of unspecified provenience. These can be removed by starting with an updated version of deviance, more pertinent to contemporary society, as essentially consisting of problems of social control—an idea anticipated by Mead when he incidentally referred to the "modern elaborate development of the taboo." [13] The general principle at work is a simple one: when others decide that a person is *non grata*, dangerous, untrustworthy, or morally repugnant, they do something to him, often unpleasant, which is not done to other people. This may take shape in hurtful rejections and humiliations in interpersonal contracts, or it may be formal action to bring him under controls which curtail his freedom. The latter type of control has to have a rationale or a justification, but not necessarily to the entire society in which it occurs. In modern societies, where generalized public opinion and interest are absent, controls over deviants tend to be administered through welfare, punitive, or ameliorative agencies specially organized for the purpose. Justification of their actions devolves from larger moral ideologies, but it is more immediately derived from laws, policies, and administrative understandings. Versions of the deviant, his numbers in society, his putative characteristics, and his requirements become official, i.e., office-mediated.[14]

[12] It may be that the sense of distrust, or that one is a distrusted person, cuts across a wider population of deviants, and does more to explain their alienation. It indicates to the stigmatized person the ominous magnitude of his problem, not only the large number of social positions from which he is likely to be excluded, but also his difficulties of normalizing interaction.

[13] Mead, "The Psychology of Punitive Justice," p. 589.

[14] For a study of official commitments of the mentally ill in this vein, see Thomas Scheff, "The Societal Reaction to Deviance: Ascriptive Elements in Psychiatric Screening of Mental Patients in a Midwestern State," *Social Problems* 11 (1964); 401–13.

Among the requirements imposed on the deviant under some form of institutional restraint are that he accept or at least not threaten the dominant values of the responsible agency or the more specialized values of those strategically related to him within the organization. In order to become a candidate for reinstatement in society the deviant must give his allegiance to what is often an anomolous conception of himself and the social world, and try to live by rules, often rigorous in extreme, substituted for or added to those by which normals live.[15] Denials of the organizational ideology or violation of these rules become utilizable [16] confirmation for an official judgment that the deviant is "unreformed," "still sick," or "getting worse." It is in such special socio-psychological environments that the functional expression of stigma is concretized and a staging area set up for an ideological struggle between the deviant seeking to normalize his actions and thoughts, and agencies seeking the opposite.[17]

The stabilization of deviance resulting from the superimposition of official interpretations of the deviant's responses to restrictive management is readily seen in criminal persistence of the prisoner who has been denied parole because he has come to be defined as a "trouble-maker" within the institution. Even more revealing of second order deviance is the revocation of parole for drinking, for getting married without permission of the parole officer, or leaving the local area for any of a variety of reasons which would

[15] The ultimate example of these is found in prisons. In a list of forty punishable rule violations held to in one state prison only six corresponded to what would be misdemeanors or felonies outside of the prison. See Harry Barnes and Negley Teeters, *New Horizons in Criminology*, 3d ed. (Englewood Cliffs, N.J.: Prentice-Hall, 1959), p. 365; also, see an older discussion: Frank Tannenbaum, "The Professional Criminal," *The Century Magazine* 110 (1925): 581–82.

[16] I prefer the term "utilizable" because it favors a more dynamic view of the institutional environment. Rather than seeing the impact of an institution on inmates as "total," based on routinized interaction, it is preferable to look at its origins in the shifting, variable administrative, therapeutic, and custodial actions, keeping in mind that (1) conflict abounds among staff and custody people, and (2) staff and custody people have problems and are often defensively oriented. The important fact is that these people have total power if they decide it must be used. However, total power is qualified by the fact that no institutional system has ever been devised which can destroy informal communication of inmates. See Robert Sommer and Humphry Osmond, "The Schizophrenic No-Society," *Psychiatry* 25 (1962): 244–55.

[17] See Julius Roth, "The Treatment of Tuberculosis as a Bargaining Process," in *Human Behavior and Social Processes*, ed. Arnold Rose (Boston: Houghton Mifflin, 1962), chap. 31; Max Siporin, "Deviant Behavior in Social Work Diagnosis and Treatment," *Social Work* 10 (1965): 59–67; Sethard Fisher, "The Rehabilitative Effectiveness of a Community Correctional Residence for Narcotic Users," *Journal of Criminal Law, Criminology and Police Science* 56 (1965): esp. 192 ff.

be deemed entirely normal or good for other, unstigmatized persons. Additional illustrations come from the juvenile court where in some areas a youth may be judicially reclassified and sent to an institution not because he has committed criminal acts but because he has flaunted an order of the court or probation officer.

The history of the treatment of the insane furnishes equally revealing illustrations in which deviance emerges as an artifact of its control. During the period when, among other indignities, demented persons were chained to walls, it was assumed that chains were necessary to prevent maniacal attacks on others or self-destruction. With the rise of moral treatment in the early nineteenth century it began to be appreciated that excerbations of insanity in large part derived from the restraints themselves and their animalistic implications for the patient. An early English medical man sympathetic to Pinel's new philosophy, cogently referred to the asylums of his day as "nurseries of madness," specifically charging that the means of institutional control were those by which madness was made permanent.[18]

> There is ground to apprehend that fugitive folly is too often converted into a fixed and settled frenzy, a transient guest into an irremovable tenant of the mind: an occasional and accidental aberration of the intellect into a confirmed and inveterate habit of dereliction: by a premature and too precipitate adoption of measures and methods of control.

Deeper insights into the nature of the interaction associated with then-current methods of control are provided by a Quaker physician of the era, who was impressed by the way in which it weakened self control.[19]

> They who are unacquainted with the character of insane persons are very apt to converse with them in a childish, or, which is worse, in a domineering manner . . . the natural tendency of such treatment is to degrade the mind of the patient, and to make him indifferent to those moral feelings which . . . strengthen the power of self restraint . . . and . . . render coercion in many cases unnecessary.

[18] John Reid, "Essays on Insanity, Hypochondria and Other Nervous Afflictions" (London: Longmans, Green & Company, Inc., 1816), cited in Richard Hunter and Ida Macapine, *Three Hundred Years of Psychiatry* (London: Oxford University Press, 1963), p. 724; the philosophy of moral treatment originated with Phillipe Pinel, *A Treatise on Insanity*, trans. D. D. Davis (1806), cited by Hunter and Macapine, *Three Hundred Years*, pp. 602–10.

[19] Samuel Turk, "Description of the Retreat, an Institution near York, for Insane Persons of the Society of Friends" (1813), cited in Hunter and Macapine, *Three Hundred Years*, p. 696.

It is, of course, not difficult to transpose such ideas into the context of secondary deviance. Mentally disordered persons ordinarily enter or are committed to a hosiptal because their expressive behavior has made problems for others as well as for themselves. If this is assumed to reflect an inner struggle to retain self-control it can be seen why the mental hospital, which imposes a kind of moral orthodoxy with shifting criteria of compliance, makes it more rather than less difficult to normalize expressive behavior. Feelings of hostility or deep frustration which may be entirely appropriate to a situation in which a person is abandoned by his family, incarcerated, and compelled to live by a completely new or different set of rules can be expressed only at the risk of validating the deviant definition already placed upon the patient. Even more defeating is the official suspicion of the conforming patient, that he may be shamming, or that his is only an "institutional cure." [20]

Modern observations and research on the psychic impacts of mental hospital environments, while heedful of the demoralizing effects of degradation or "mortification of the self," have disclosed the frequent occurrence of a functional analogue to the inconsistent punishment theory of criminal recidivism. Here I have in mind studies showing that conflicts and faulty communication among staff and custody people often are followed by an increase of disturbed behavior among patients and a rise in suicide attempts. This has been called "cognitive dissonance." It may be interpreted several ways, one of which is that the confusion of uncertainties coming in the wake of institutional crises bring an "end of hope" in patients. Another way to see such phenomena is that they fracture the tenuous interpersonal ties on which patients must rely in their efforts to build some meaning into what to them is a meaningless world. If it is correct that normalization of the patient's actions requires relationships of trust with others, then the difficulties of normalizing interaction are implicit in the hospital situations. Staff people and attendants at best can offer verbal assurances of trust because administrative expediency and internal conflicts periodically destroy its substance.[21]

[20] A superintendent of a midwestern mental hospital once commented ruefully in the presence of the writer, "These damned patients feign sanity."

[21] See Ezra Stotland and Arthur Kobler, *Life and Death of a Mental Hospital* (Seattle, Wash.: University of Washington Press, 1965); William Caudill, *The Psychiatric Hospital as a Small Society* (Cambridge, Mass.: Harvard University Press, 1958); R. Boyd, S. Kaegles, and M. Greenblatt, "Outbreak of Gang Destructive Behavior on a Psychiatric Ward," *Journal of Nervous and Mental Diseases* 120 (1954): 338–42; Jack Brehm and Arthur Cohen, *Explorations in Cognitive Dissonance* (New York: John Wiley, 1962).

SUB-CULTURE AND SECONDARY DEVIANCE

Most sociological research on mental hospitals deals with formal organization and staff-patient interaction, whereas sociological interest in prisons
has concentrated on informal organization among the inmates and on the
"prison community." Herein is met the difficulty of sociologically assessing
the general importance of groups and subcultures in the growth of
secondary deviance. That they are of undoubted significance has long been
recognized, harking back to Vidocq's Memoirs,[22] which is threaded with
comments on the unsought consequences of imprisonment in the form of
"moral contamination" and education in crime. In their survey of American prisons, Beaumont and de Tocqueville emphasized the extent to which
the "corrupting discipline" of prisons had become a central issue in early
nineteenth-century penology.[23] By the end of that century the belief that
reformatories spawned by the "institution craze" in England and the
United States converted many less sophisticated youthful offenders into
hardened criminals had strong partisans.[24]

There is much to be found in the considerable accumulation of research and theory on inmate social systems and socialization in prison
which supports the conclusion that incentives to rehabilitation and social
reintegration advocated in American penal programs tend to be self-
defeating.[25] Explanations for this have featured status degradation, which
many indications show to be unavoidable—even in the best treatment-
oriented prisons.[26] This is held to account for the growth or preservation of
a deviant subculture within the prison. Administrative logistics favor this
by determining that recidivists are more likely than others to be sent to
institutions. There they dominate the prison world, control communication
with staff and custody people, and successfully propagate an ideology that
"you can't make it on the outside." To the newcomer without prior prison
experience, old inmate ways and views not only operate as pressures to
conform to the system but also offer predictable means of salvaging some
dignity and self-respect from situations where they are in short supply.

[22] Vidocq, Memoirs, ed. and trans. Edwin Rich (Boston: Houghton
Mifflin, 1935).

[23] Gustave de Beaumont and Alexis de Tocqueville, On the Penitentiary
System in the United States and its Application in France (Carbondale, Ill.:
Southern Illinois University Press, 1964), chap. 2, esp. p. 55.

[24] William Tallack, Penological and Preventive Principles (London:
Wertheimer, Lea and Co., 1896), pp. 342–48.

[25] Richard Cloward, "Social Control in Prison," in Theoretical Studies in
Social Organization of the Prison, Pamphlet 115 (New York: Social Science
Research Council, 1960), p. 28.

[26] Gresham Sykes and Sheldon Messinger, "The Inmate Social System,"
ibid., p. 13.

Yet when all of this has been said, questions remain as to the relationship between inmate socialization and subsequent criminality on discharge from reformatories and prisons. Does new deviance spring from a continuing sense of injustice, which is reinforced by job rejections, police cognizance, and strained interaction with normals on the outside, or is it due to an acquired ideological view that this is what the world will be like when reentered? Does the latter, in turn, build into sensitivity and cause a projection of deviance expectancy in interaction, or does it lead discharged criminals to seek out companionship of delinquents, criminals and ex-convicts like themselves? On such questions research is less enlightening than it is on workings of the prison system.[27]

While the enumerated possibilities are all attractive explanations for secondary criminal deviance, they do not readily apply to cases of "lone-wolf" criminals, such as systematic passers of bad checks, who at most are only marginal participants in prison or criminal sub-cultures. Moreover, at the more general level of explanation, heed must be given to forms of deviance other than criminal, in which small group interaction and sub-culture are comparatively unimportant in the self-transformations of secondary deviance. The insane do not form groups, nor do stutterers, alcoholics, certain kinds of sex offenders, epileptics, or the poor. Further complication arises in the larger picture of drug addiction, in which some drug users participate in a criminal subculture but others, namely physician addicts, do not. The former tend to regard themselves as criminals, the latter do not. Yet both classes of drug users have no illusions about their status as addicts.[28]

Obviously the nature of the deviance merits a par value with groups and culture in seeking the explanation of secondary deviance. The form of the deviance indicates a good deal about the necessity for deviant group formation and participation, whether it be a means to an end, or whether the necessity is expressive as an "end in itself." Groups become instrumentally important in those forms of deviance which require for their systematic or continued activation goods and services provided by others through specially organized relationships. Prostitution in modern society well illustrates such deviance,[29] as do gambling, confidence games, and political radicalism. Homosexuality, although practicable through seducing normals, generally requires partners of similar inclinations. Armed robbery, or the "heist," can be carried out single-handed, but it is done most

[27] For a beginning of research and discussion on this general problem see Stanton Wheeler, "Socialization in Correctional Communities," *American Sociological Review* 26 (1961): 697–712.

[28] Charles Winick, "Physician Narcotic Addicts," *Social Problems* 9 (1961): 174–86.

[29] James Bryan, "Apprenticeships in Prostitution," *Social Problems* 12 (1965): 287–97.

efficiently and profitably in groups created for the purpose.[30] In contrast to these forms of deviance, the stutterer can and does have his speech spasms in any audience, and an alcoholic can surreptitiously find ways and means to pursue his drinking in a wide variety of conventional groupings. Finally, the pauper, the sick, and the physically handicapped find their means of survival through legitimatized organizations established by society.

Whether the expressive needs of deviants require specialized group participation and subcultural definition is more difficult to determine. The case seems strongest for certain kinds of criminals, such as con men, whose high degree of technical differentiation sets them apart from other criminals as well as from society. Prostitutes frequently experience conflicts about their identities, which appear to be most easily solved through relationships with pimps, or, in some instances, through homosexual relationships. Political radicals also seem to require association with like persons as audiences to validate the "ideological purity" important to differentiating or culturing their identities.[31] However, at the other extreme are the mentally disordered, who, outside of hospitals at least, tend to be threatened psychologically by the presence of others with a comparable stigma. Subgroups are irrelevant to stuttering because stutters are usually unable to express themselves consistently to their own satisfaction in any group.

THE POSITIVE SIDE OF NEGATIVE IDENTITIES

That which may be overlooked in the discussion of deviant identities is the way in which they can be assumed and sustained through antagonistic or degrading interaction with agents of respectable society as well as by accommodations and solidarity with deviant associates. A fuller consideration of the former points to various situations or conditions where negative identities, i.e., those generally stigmatized, may offer temporary or relatively stable solutions to life problems despite the fact that they represent a lower order of human existence. This makes it important to examine more closely the ways in which a deviant status or role gives access to rewards and satisfactions.

If effective stigmatization imposes penalties and circumscribes access to conventional means of life satisfactions, it may also provide new means to ends sought. Thus becoming an admitted homosexual ("coming out")

---

[30] Everett DeBaun, "The Heist—The Theory and Practice of Armed Robbery," *Harpers* (February 1950), pp. 65–76.

[31] Egon Bittner, "Radicalism and Radical Movements," *American Sociological Review* 28 (1963): 928–40.

may endanger one's livelihood or his professional career, but it also absolves the individual from failure to assume the heavy responsibilities of marriage and parenthood, and it is a ready way of fending off painful involvements in heterosexual affairs. To be sent to a camp for delinquent boys is degrading and a career threat, but at the same time it may be an avenue of escape from an intolerable home situation where degradation is greater. To be committed to a mental hospital is a blot on one's reputation, but it may be one sure way of stopping a divorce action by a straying spouse, the outcome of which would be even more intolerable.[32]

THE LIMITS OF DEGRADATION

There are at least two salient reasons why stigmatized persons may seek and find gratifications as well as having to endure painful humiliation and frustrating restrictions associated with a deviant status. One has to do with the dialectical qualities of cultural values, public policy, laws, and social control, the other with the complex ways in which personal evaluations are made of things and experiences objectively represented as rewarding or punishing.

A wider view of many forms of deviance shows that they frequently tend to be integrally connected with cultural dilemmas in which generic forms of human action potentially lead to either social approval or social disapproval or both. Among these, for example, are sexual provocativeness in females and sexual aggressiveness in males, both of which are culturally approved or encouraged as the means by which high-order values of the family, religion, or property are conserved. However, such sexuality is disapproved when it results in illegitimate births, prostitution, incest, spread of disease, or internal conflict and demoralization within tightly integrated functional groups. Although the consequences of the latter must be condemned and their participants stigmatized for conservative reasons, the persons involved cannot be ignored socially thereafter. The unwed mother and her bastard child must be supported, and the diseased prostitute treated, if for no other reason than to protect society from further evil consequences. Hence, private or public organizations come to their aid or succor. The effects of this are to assign them definitive status and to validate a claim on the services of others, or more simply, to make possible a way of life. While transition to such status may be initiated by moral condemnation, social rejections, and penalties, it is completed by charitable justifi-

---

[32] This has been referred to as a "psycho-social moratorium." More simply it is a form of delaying action not an uncommon resort in human affairs. See Harold Sampson, Sheldon Messinger, Robert D. Towne et al., "The Mental Hospital and Marital Ties," *Social Problems* 9 (1961): 141–55.

cation, acceptance, and provision of the material prerequisites of survival.[33]

Dual moral ideologies, combining rejection with rehabilitative actions directed to social reinstatement, also mitigate public reactions to alcoholics, drug addicts, criminals, physically handicapped persons, and the poor. The accretion of special meanings which attach to ameliorative services, and their subversion to ends other than those intended, often explain why deviant statuses may be more amenable than they are or than can be officially represented. Organized social control of deviance, as with social control in general, at most has a marginal influence on the interactional processes which give it existential meaning. Collective efforts to organize systems of rewards and punishments to repress deviance and promote reformation along expected lines are always subject to vicissitudes of interpretation, diversion, and cooptation of agents of authority at their points of intervention in social interaction.

LAW, POLICY, AND SOCIAL CONTROL

The idea that society's efforts to alleviate social problems of deviance through the establishment of public policy may aggravate or perpetuate the problems is by no means novel. The adverse consequences of the corn laws in early Roman society in producing "sloth" and further poverty did not escape the notice of such commentators as Cicero, and beginning with sixteenth-century England, the idea that pauperization and dependency were largely the hedonistic consequences of public policy set by the Poor Laws came to be widely accepted by critics.[34] Much of the succeeding history of public and private charity to the present time has turned on the issue of how, in institutional terms, to "insure that people who are not provided for by the usual economic arrangements of society shall be maintained and yet not incapacitated for future participation in the organized economic system." [35]

[33] See Kingsley Davis, "Illegitimacy and Social Structure," *American Journal of Sociology* 45 (1939): 215–33.

[34] See J. R. Prettyman, *Dispauperization* (London: Longmans, Green, 1878), sections I-III.

[35] Helen Witmer, *Social Work, An Analysis of a Social Institution* (New York: Farrar, Straus and Giroux, 1942) p. 128. Generally it has been held that the poor laws had a direct effect of creating and perpetuating poverty by discouraging thrift and encouraging marriage and reproduction. However, the poor law study reports reveal much emphasis placed on intervening factors, such as lack of clarity in the laws, their inconsistent interpretation, and corrupt administration. For example, publicans elected to Boards of Guardians sometimes insisted that outdoor relief be given to habitueés of their houses. See *Report of the Royal Commission on the Poor Laws and Relief of Distress* (London: Wyman & Sons, 1909), chaps. 1–6.

While the nineteenth-century hedonistic explanations of pauperism are unacceptable from a sociological perspective, nonetheless the possible importance of calculational factors cannot be summarily set aside in a sufficient analysis of secondary deviance—particularly in those problems of deviance which have identifiable economic features. This stands out in sharpest relief where a demand is created for illegal goods and services, illustrated on the grand scale by public prohibition of the consumption of alcoholic beverages, and to a lesser degree in current legal repression of prostitution, gambling, and the unlicensed use of narcotic drugs. Stringent enforcement of laws against these forms of deviance, called crimes without victims by one writer, can be presumed to make the forbidden goods and services more difficult to secure and also to raise their costs. This in turn lays a basis for the growth of an entrepreneurial subculture offering opportunities of status and income for criminal deviants. At the same time problems are built up for the customer seeking a supply of the goods or services; he has to participate in the criminal subculture for his purposes, and he may have to expend time and money ordinarily allocated to established or conventional claims on his budget. If he is strongly motivated, as with persons addicted to alcohol, drugs, or gambling, he may neglect his family, alienate his friends, and beyond this, engage in outright criminal activity to finance his costly habit.[36]

A good deal has been written on the contribution which repressive laws make to the "problem" of narcotics in the United States, especially as sources of illegal traffic in drugs and the commission of crimes by addicts in order to supply themselves with drugs. Yet it remains to be shown that the laws themselves cause addiction; more plausible are the assertions that laws and policy determine access to drugs, their forms of use, the attributes of the addict population, their degree of contact with criminals and other deviants, their involvement in other deviance, and the particular kinds of self-conception held by addicts.[37] From these must be teased out the more generic factors which underlie or sustain addiction. Needless to say, after this has been done, it would be totally unrealistic to ignore the peculiar physiological effects of the drugs in the making of an addict. Furthermore, in this and other forms of deviance there remains a knotty problem of assigning relative weights to the factors assumed relevant, determining their mutual effects and the order in which they occur. The solution for this methodological problem traditionally has been held by many sociologists to lie in the concept of process.

[36] Edwin Schur, *Crimes Without Victims* (Englewood Cliffs, N.J.: Prentice-Hall, 1965); Alfred Lindesmith, *The Drug Addict and the Law* (Bloomington, Ind.: University of Indiana Press, 1965).

[37] Alfred Lindesmith and John Gagnon, "Anomie and Drug Addiction," in *Anomie and Deviant Behavior*, ed. Marshall Clinard (New York: Free Press, 1964), p. 159.

PROCESS AND SECONDARY DEVIANCE

The most general process by which status and role transitions take place is socialization. As it has been applied to the study of deviants the concept has been further circumscribed to designate such processes as criminalization, prisonization, "sophistication," "hardening," pauperization, addiction, conversion, radicalization, professionalization, and "mortification of self." All of these speak in varying degrees of a personal progression or differentiation in which the individual acquires: (1) morally inferior status; (2) special knowledge and skills; (3) an integral attitude or "world view"; and (4) a distinctive self-image based upon but not necessarily coterminous with his image reflected in interaction with others.

The earliest descriptions of deviant socialization current in sociology came from Shaw's documents on delinquent careers. These were likened to natural histories and so titled, but their descriptive content was derived from the delinquent's "own story," as related to an interviewer.[38] From a present-day perspective these studies appear to have been colored by Shaw's unconcealed interest in reform and the probable interest of the respondent in supporting Shaw's views. Valuable as the stories were and still are for certain purposes, they carried unavoidable overtones of nineteenth-century entrepreneurial ideology in reverse, resembling "sad tales," or reminiscent of Hogarth's *Rake's Progress*, or early moral propaganda tracts which portray prostitution as the "road to ruin."

The deviant career concept also has been linked with or partly derived from an occupational model, examples of which are found in the descriptions of criminal behavior systems, such as thieving, and the marginal deviance of dance musicians.[39] The occupational parallel, of course, can be demonstrated in the professionalization of some types of thieves, prostitutes, political radicals, vagrants, bohemians (beatniks), beggars, and to some extent the physically handicapped. In contrast to these, however, there is little indication of an occupational orientation among alcoholics, mentally disordered persons, stutterers, homosexuals, and systematic check forgers.

[38] Clifford Shaw, *The Jack Roller* (Chicago: University of Chicago Press, 1930). Goffman uses the concept "moral career" as a broad orientation to changes over time basic and common to persons in a social category. He regards it as a two-sided perspective which shifts back and forth between the self and its significant society. Erving Goffman, "The Moral Career of the Mental Patient," *Psychiatry* 22 (1959): 123–42.

[39] E. H. Sutherland, *The Professional Thief* (Chicago: University of Chicago Press, 1937); Howard Becker, *Outsiders* (London: Free Press, 1963), chaps. 5, 6; C. Cambor, Gerald Lesowitz, and Miles Miller, "Creative Jazz Musicians: a Clinical Study," *Psychiatry* 25 (1960): 1–15; Raymond Mack, "The Jazz Community," *Social Forces* 38 (1960): 211–22.

Closer examination of the career concept suggests that its application to deviance should be guarded. I doubt, for example, that the notion of "recruitment" of persons to most kinds of deviance can be any more than a broad analogy. While learning specialized knowledge from other deviants is a condition of some deviance, it is not so for all, and the notion that deviants serve an "apprenticeship" may be more figurative than literal where it is applicable. A career denotes a course to be run, but the delineation of fixed sequences or stages through which persons move from less to more serious deviance is difficult or impossible to reconcile with an interactional theory. Furthermore, no incontrovertible evidence has yet been marshaled to justify the belief that prodromal signs of deviance exist— either in behaviors or in personality syndromes such as "predelinquent," "prepsychotic," or "addiction-prone." The flux and pluralism of modern society make concepts of drift, contingency, and risk far more meaningful in deviance than inevitability or linear progress.

A more defensible conception of deviant career is that of recurrent or typical contingencies and problems awaiting someone who continue in a course of action, with the added notion that there may be theoretically "best" choices set into a situation by prevailing technology and social structure. There is some predictive value of a limited or residual nature in concepts like "turning points" or "points of no return," which have been brought into the sociological analysis of careers. These allow it to be said that persons having undergone certain changes will not or cannot retrace their steps; deviant actions act as social foreclosures which qualitatively change meanings and shift the scope of alternatives within which new choices can be made.[40] Even here a caveat is necessary, for alcoholics, drug addicts, criminals, and other deviants do sometimes make comebacks in the face of stigma, and an early history of deviance may in some instances lead to success in the conventional world.

DRIFT, CONTINGENCY, AND DISCOVERY

While some fortunate individuals by insightful endowment or by virtue of the stabilized nature of their situations can foresee more distant social consequences of their actions and behave accordingly, not so most people. Much human behavior is situationally oriented and geared to meeting the many and shifting claims which others make upon them.[41] The loose

[40] See Lemert, *Social Pathology*, chap. 4; also Becker, *Outsiders*, chap. 2; for a careful evaluation and critique of attempts to predict delinquency, see Jackson Toby, "An Evaluation of Early Identification and Intensive Treatment Programs for Predelinquents," *Social Problems* 13 (1965): 161–75.

[41] The concept of drift comes from Matza, *Delinquency and Drift*, chap. 1, esp. pp. 27–30.

structuring and swiftly changing façade and content of modern social situations frequently make it difficult to decide which means will insure ends sought. Often choice is a compromise between what is sought and what can be sought. Finally, even more important, situations and the actions involved often are defined after they occur, or late in the course of interaction when formal social controls intrude. Where deviance is a possible contingency, delayed definition is more likely than early.

All of this makes me believe that most people drift into deviance by specific actions rather than by informed choices of social roles and statuses. Each of such actions has its consequence and rationale and leaves a residual basis for possible future action depending on the problems solved or the new problems brought to life. From the societal side, repetition of deviant action may be ignored or normalized by those who are thereby threatened, or it may be compounded through patronage of associates who have something to gain from it. The pimp may encourage his new female conquest in her belief that she is entertaining men for pay because she "loves him so." The family of the heavy-drinking man erects perceptual defenses against seeing his action as alcoholism because they, like him, are distressed by this ascription of meaning. The ideological gulf between stereotypes of good and bad, acting in concert with prevalent medical conceptions of deviance as the symptom of a defective or "sick" personality strengthens such normalizing tendencies by inhibiting recognition of similarities between the primary deviant and stigmatized persons. Meantime they allow the drift to deviance to go on.

This may proceed from one of two kinds of psychological states: in one the individual has no prior awareness that such actions are defined or definable as deviant; he must learn or must apply the definitions to his attributes or actions.[42] In the other the person already has learned the definitions but progressively rationalizes or dissociates them from his actions. Unequivocal perception of a deviant self comes when the person enters new settings, when supportive (normalizing) interaction with intimates becomes antagonistic, or when contact is made with stigmatizing

[42] Lindesmith, of course, has held that opiate addiction depends upon learning that withdrawal symptoms can be alleviated by taking more opiates. Alfred Lindesmith, *Opiate Addiction* (San Antonio, Tex.: Principia Press, 1947). A study of teen-age drug users in New York found that lack of deterrent information was a factor in willingness to try heroin. However, shift to regular use was explained on the basis of a need. In some cases youths began regular use after one shot, saying in effect, "This is what I have been waiting for all my life." While such a person might be "hooked" in a figurative sense, the full social and physiological implications of addiction come later when he becomes a "frantic junkie." Isidor Chein, Donald Gerard, Robert Lee, and Eva Rosenberg, *The Road to H* (New York: Basic Books, 1964), chap. VI.

agencies of social control. In other cases internal changes or changes in the feedback of meanings from the actions themselves bare the new self.[43]

Whether the imputation of self-characteristics, or "labeling" in itself, initiates or causes deviant acts is something of a moot point. The possibility cannot be arbitrarily ruled out, but it moves onto questionable grounds where social reality is made coterminous with ideas and symbolic representations. Erik Erikson, not to be designated as an idealist, speaks of changes from positive to negative identities which result from societal diagnosis by the "balance of us." This is illustrated by the mother who constantly berates her daughter as "immoral," "no good," or "tramp." The girl in time may yield to the derogatory self-image because it is nearest and "most real" to her. Yet Erikson is careful to say that this may be only a final step in the acquisition of a negative self-image, and he also refers to the necessity of confirming changes in identity.[44] I take this to be a way of saying that there must be some basis for validating a degrading self-conception in prior acts, to which I would add that it also needs subsequent overt acts to clothe it with social reality. Such acts may be fortuitous or they may be deliberate in origin, but in any case they conclude with some manner of interpersonal involvement or commitments. More complete data collected in actual cases similar to the hypothetical case in question often disclose that the girl takes some precipitant action, such as running away from home, is then arrested and handled in a way to confirm the mother's expectation. Even more tangible confirmation transpires if, as may happen, she is picked up by strange men who take her in charge and exploit her sexually.

While an abiding deviant self demands validation and reinforcement in social interaction, it overdraws the social to insist that self-discovery always has immediate antecedents in participant social interaction drama-

[43] Tannenbaum, whose early ideas came close to a statement of secondary deviance, believed that delinquency was the outcome of a hardening process observable in conflict of youthful gangs with police and with other gangs. In the process, new definitions get placed on their actions. This, of course, was a forerunner of the subcultural, learning conception of delinquency. Frank Tannenbaum, *Crime and The Community* (New York: Columbia University Press, 1957), esp. pp. 19–22; More recent views, such as those of Sykes and Matza, direct attention to the coexistence of conventional as well as criminal values, in the delinquent youth, his ambivalence, and resolutions of the ambivalence through a process of neutralization. Gresham Sykes and David Matza, "Techniques of Neutralization: A Theory of Delinquency," *American Sociological Review* 22 (1957): 664–70; David Matza and Gresham Sykes, "Juvenile Delinquency and Subterranean Values," *American Sociological Review* 26 (1961): 712–19.

[44] Helen Witmer and Ruth Kotinsky, eds. *New Perspectives on Delinquency*, Washington, D.C.: U.S. Department of Health, Education, and Welfare, No. 56 (1956): 1–23.

tizing good and evil. Revelations may be little more than solitary moments of disenchantment, points at which a fabric of rationalizations collapses in the face of repeated contradictions from cumulative experiences. The alcoholic looks at his dirty clothes, shabby hotel room with a scattered array of empty bottles, and realizes the pretense that he is "between jobs," or still the best auto salesman in town is just pretense and nothing more. The check forger finally throws away a book listing his victims and with it the idea that he will someday repay the sums he has carefully noted by their names. The form of the deviance, the situation, and the flow of meaning in face-to-face interaction undoubtedly have great importance in normalizing action and supporting perceptual defenses against the slow stain of deviation, but the logic of self-discovery is an inner one.

THE SECONDARY DEVIANT

Devaluation of the self on society's terms ordinarily has a sequel of internal or psychic struggle, greatest where the sense of continuity of the self is massively threatened. Some persons never move beyond this state, overtly striving to conform at times, at others entangling themselves with deviance. Terms like "unorganized" or "transitional" deviance may be apt descriptions of their actions for certain purposes. Assuming that the person moves further toward deviance, the abatement of his conflicts usually follows discovery that his status as deviant, although degraded is by no means as absymal as represented in moral ideologies. The blinded war veteran learns that blindness is not a stark tragedy but more like a "damned nuisance," and that life is possible, particularly if a lot of "charitable" people would leave him alone. The prostitute soon realizes that her new life is sometimes rough and unpredictable, and that arrest is a hazard, but it is not a life of shame. Having discovered the prosaic nature of much of his life under a new status, the deviant, like other people, usually tries to make out as best he can.[45] What happens will be conditioned by several factors: [46] (1) the clarity with which a role or roles can be defined; (2) the possession

---

[45] This may be likened to playing a game with new and not very favorable rules. Tannenbaum described it in connection with the professional criminal; "After a while he accepts it (the game) as a matter of course. He bargains upon the amount of freedom he may have, hopes for escape, for total freedom from arrest, but bargains with fate and gives hostages to freedom, calculates his chances and accepts the inevitable with stoicism." Frank Tannenbaum, "The Professional Criminal," *Century Magazine*, p. 584.

[46] I am indebted for these ideas to William Robinson who some years ago in a seminar at UCLA suggested them as a parsimonious summary of Leonard Cottrell's article, "The Adjustment of the Individual to His Age and Sex Roles," *American Sociological Review* 7 (1942): 617–20.

or acquisition of attributes, knowledge, and skills to enact, improvise, and invent roles; and (3) the motivation to play his role or roles.

A great deal can be said, mostly illustrative, about the first two items. Confidence men, for example, have clearly defined occupational roles in a criminal world, but not many persons are recruited to the roles because they lack the requisite skills and knowledge for this exacting form of thievery. In decided contrast, there are few or no specialized roles available to stutterers, save perhaps that of a clown or an entertainer. Fashioning their own roles is difficult because effective speech is a requirement for most social roles. Consequently they are reduced to filling conventional occupational roles usually below their educational or skills level, becoming, in a figurative sense, ridiculous or strangely silent hewers of wood and haulers of water. Somewhere between the two extremes of confidence men and stutterer is the drug addict, most of whom in our society are excluded from conventional occupations and tend to be excluded from professional or organized criminal pursuits. However, they may elect to be petty thieves, burglars, prostitutes, hustlers, stool pigeons, or choose to peddle drugs to other addicts.

While the social roles available to deviants vary in number, kind, and degree of stigmatization, there is always some basis for adaptation or a modus vivendi open to the deviant. Moreover, attributes can be faked or concealed and some measure of skills and knowledge learned, whether they be means of filling the leftover, low-status roles of conventional society or those more explicitly defined as immoral or criminal. Such conclusions furnish the more pertinent one that secondary deviance to a large extent becomes a phenomenon of motivation.

MOTIVATION AND LEARNING

If motivation to exploit the possibilities of degraded status and to play a deviant role are critical aspects of transition to secondary deviance, then analysis is pushed toward some form of learning theory, preferably one which accounts for the variable social meanings of satisfactions, rewards, and punishments. This enters an area little trod by sociologists and to some extent looked upon as an alien if not sterile preoccupation of psychologists. Yet notwithstanding the criticism that the laws of learning have been largely formal and devoid of content, the outlook is less bleak than sometimes pictured—particularly where efforts have been made to bring together dynamic personality theory and ego-psychology with newer formulations of the learning process.

If nothing else, common sense dictates that some variant of the law of effect be made part of the explanation of secondary deviance. This is true even in the face of the formidable task of specifying what is rewarding or punishing to human beings, whose actions in contrast to those of the rest of the animal world are complicated by symbolic learning and delayed gratification. Restated and applied to deviance, the law of effect is a simple idea that people beset with problems posed for them by society will choose lines of action they expect to be satisfactory solutions to the problems. If the consequences are those expected, the likelihood that the action or generically similar action will be repeated is increased. If the consequences are unsatisfactory, unpleasant, or make more problems than they solve, then the pattern of action will be avoided.[47] The fact that anticipation of satisfactions or expectation of punishments is a cognitive process based upon symbolic learning as well as experience does not vitiate the principle of effect; it only reasserts the longstanding need to show how individuals evaluate their own responses in a world where the accommodations of others become means to ends. The absence of any well worked-out theory for doing this leaves the field open to several propositions which may be suitable for further study of the process of evaluation connected with secondary deviance.

1. Defining one's self as deviant is instrumental in seeking out means of satisfaction and mitigating stigmatization. The redefinition of self leads to reinterpretation of past experiences, which in turn reduces inner tensions and conflict. Ends and means are more easily sorted out, and personal accommodations established necessary to utilize available alternatives.

2. The value hierarchy of the degraded individual changes, in the process of which ends become means and means become ends. Conventional punishments lose their efficacy with loss of status. Experiences at one time evaluated as degrading may shift full arc to become rewarding. The alcoholic is an example; deeply ashamed by his first stay in jail, he may as years go by come to look upon arrest as a means of getting food, shelter, and a chance to sober up.

3. Persons who renounce conventional status are less affected by the promise of remote satisfactions and more by those within their immediate ken. This is related to the degree of degradation, and also to incarceration or hospital sojourns which determine the point in personal life cycles at which evaluations are made. Deprivation and long experience with highly specific systems of sanctions within control institutions reinforce a world view of the attainable over the achievable.

4. Once deviance becomes a way of life the personal issue often be-

[47] The law of effect was originally stated by the psychologist, E. L. Thorndike. For a discussion of his principle and learning theory in general, see O. Hobart Mowrer, *Learning Theory and Behavior* (New York: John Wiley, 1960), chap. I.

comes the costs of making a change rather than the higher status to be gained through rehabilitation or reform. Such costs are calculated in terms of the time, energy, and distress seen necessary to change.

SELF-DEFEATING DEVIANCE—THE NEUROTIC PARADOX

Thus far I have offered a sociological brief for some form of neohedonistic theory of secondary deviance. Baldly reduced, it says that persons become secondary deviants because they manage to find more satisfactory solutions to their problems through deviance than through nondeviance; the nature of their problem solving differs because degradation and newly perceived contingencies change their conceptions of what is satisfying. Maintenance of deviance once established is explained in much the same way, with the added observation that perceived costs of change introduce elements of conservatism into the processes of evaluation. The impression is left that secondary deviance ensues from problem-solving action which is complicated by status loss and changes in value hierarchies but still not generically different from other human problem solving.

There are, however, some forms of recurrent deviance which reflect disturbances in the problem-solving and perceptual process itself, in which irresolution rather than solution of problems emerges as the key factor in deviance. In such deviance there is no easily discoverable or even inferable balance of pains and pleasures; indeed, there is much in the self-initiated actions of the individual which continually generates pain, hardship, defeat, and degradation, with little compensatory satisfaction. These are kinds of self-defeating, self-perpetuating behaviors, whose persistence defies common sense logic, whose baffling manifestations led Freud to several revisions of his thinking, and which present a discomfiting challenge to learning theory partisans.

The deviant patterns in question range from ordinary "bad habits," through vices and addictions of those which get labeled or formally diagnosed as neurotic or psychotic. Those singled out for a basis of discussion here are stuttering, systematic check forgery, alcoholism, and drug addiction. They are marked by the almost total absence of any durable pleasure in the persons involved. Instead their lot is one of gnawing anxiety, pain, unhappiness, and despair, in some cases ending with deterioration or suicide. Some writers have referred to such deviance as vicious circles in that they repeat a continuous chain of cause and effect, beginning with deviance and ending with deviance. Seen in this way they readily qualify as classic cases of secondary deviance.

The earliest speculations on self-defeating deviance dealt with what can be described as a hiatus, blocking, or constriction of the cognitive process. Even before Freud had spoken in English on the subject, F. M.

Alexander, an obscure practitioner concerned with psychic aspects of disease, postural abnormalities, and speech defects, had theorized that they were aggravated or preserved by faulty ideas of causation; consequently efforts of afflicted individuals to eliminate their bad habits became the very means by which they were kept alive or made worse.[48] John Dewey generously credited Alexander for several important ideas which he took to form his well-known functionalist thesis that bad habits (idling, gambling, and addiction to drugs and alcohol) are not merely negative failures to act according to social norms but rather are functional responses sustained through interaction in social situations. Efforts to break out of vicious circles become integrated parts of the habits themselves and act as trigger mechanisms.[49]

> The hard drinker who keeps thinking of not drinking is doing what he can to initiate the acts which lead to drinking. He is starting with the stimulus to his habit.

Both Freud and Adler were aware that a social context with access to rewards had a part in preserving ways of living they considered neurotic. Adler spoke of rewards which motivate "neurotic invalidism," [50] and Freud discerned a similar phenomenon which he designated "advantage through illness." In so doing he used language strongly reminiscent of the concept of reinforcement.[51]

> When such mental organization as the disease has persisted for a considerable time, it displays something like a self-preservative instinct. It forms a kind of pact, a modus vivendi with other forces in mental life, even those fundamentally hostile to it, and the opportunities can hardly fail to arise in which it once more manifests itself as useful and expedient, thus acquiring a *secondary function* [italics mine] which again strengthens its position.

Freud's biological orientation, however, made the reality principle something less than social; he assigned only marginal significance to that which I have called secondary deviance, preferring to treat its expressions as products of irrational symptom formation and not "real" solutions. In so

---

[48] F. M. Alexander, *Man's Supreme Inheritance* (London: E. P. Dutton, 1910).

[49] John Dewey, *Human Nature and Conduct* (New York: Modern Library, 1930), p. 35.

[50] Alfred Adler, *Understanding Human Nature* (New York: Greenberg Publishing, 1927), pp. 200–207.

[51] Sigmund Freud, A *General Introduction to Psychoanalysis*, trans. Joan Riviere (New York: Garden City Publishing, 1943), p. 334.

doing he inaugurated confusion between stabilized deviance and the neurotic paradox. At the same time he obscured his own vision by pursuing only the inner dynamics of "symptoms." [52]

It is not by chance that one of the more challenging efforts to elevate symptoms of inner conflict to their proper level of importance in the study of self-defeating deviance should come from the pen of a leading student of speech disorders. Here I refer to Van Riper's deeply insightful analysis of adult stuttering, which in many respects represents the "pure case" of secondary deviance.[53] I say this because stuttering thus far has defied efforts at causative explanation. It appears to be exclusively a process-product in which, to pursue the metaphor, normal speech variations, or at most, minor abnormalities of speech (primary stuttering) can be fed into an interactional or evaluational process and come out as secondary stuttering.[54]

Van Riper contends, in essence, that symptoms, which Freud set to one side, stand for an important segment of the self. In stuttering they are neurotic mannerisms which originate as defensive reactions to the penalties which our culture imposes upon those individuals whose nonfluency is excessive. It is the stutterer's efforts to avoid his own defensive actions, i.e., the stuttering self, which feed back into and maintain the disordered speech. So long as he keeps trying to be what he knows he isn't—a normal speaker—his problems continue. Only by equating the self with the stuttering symptoms can change be brought about.

In more detail, Van Riper shows that stuttering is both rewarding and punishing to the person, and characteristically it generates ambivalence, or "approach-avoidance" [55] reactions to speaking; efforts to speak are accompanied by a rising level of anxiety which phases into panic when

[52] Actually, Freud's illustration of advantage through illness—the crippled workman who becomes a beggar and accepts a dole—nicely outlines the problem of secondary deviance in social terms. He observes that the beggar's position is supported by that which destroyed his old life. To remove the disability would remove his livelihood and leave the question as to his ability to resume his old work. Freud, "General Introduction."

[53] Charles Van Riper, "Symptomatic Therapy for Stuttering," in Handbook of Speech Pathology, ed. Lee Travis (New York: Appleton-Century-Crofts, 1957), chap. 27.

[54] Wendell Johnson, "Perceptual and Evaluational Factors in Stuttering," Handbook of Speech Pathology, chap. 28; C. S. Bluemel, "Primary and Secondary Stammering," Proceedings of the American Speech Correction Association 2 (1932): 295–302; Charles Van Riper, "The Growth of the Stuttering Spasm," Quarterly Journal of Speech 23 (1937): 70–73.

[55] See Joseph Sheehan, "Theory and Treatment of Stuttering as an Approach-Avoidance Conflict," Journal of Psychology 36 (1953): 27–49; also Sheehan, ed., Stuttering: Research and Therapy (New York: Harper & Row, 1970).

the speech blocks occur. Termination of the blocks, which stutterers can predict, are rewarding because they put an end to the anxiety. However, the rewarding sense of relief also reinforces the blind struggle actions or specific acts immediately preceding their end. These, of course, are the very actions which distort the speech rhythms.

This analysis has much in common with more recent statements of learning theory, such as Mowrer's "two factor" process, which separates problem solving from the effective consequences of the attendant action.[56] From a broader overview it indicates that human beings, ordinarily purposeful agents exercising an endowment of choice within the limits of their culture, get manoeuvered or manoeuvre themselves into cyclical impasses in which acute anxiety takes command, constricts the cognitive, self-defining processes and ephemerally reduces learning to a desperate hedonistic level.

There is much here that is applicable to other forms of self-defeating deviance, particularly if the concept of phases or cycles in which punishment and rewards alternate is seen in various time dimensions. A related view of cycles in the drinking of alcoholics develops similar ideas. Thus intoxication is both rewarding and punishing; and it proceeds from ambivalence, with a surrender to drinking following rising anxiety. Intoxication becomes an immediate reward through reducing the anxiety, but as it continues it begins to produce highly painful episodes or frightening illness. The end of a drunk is rewarded in a number of social situations which have a common effect of protecting the alcoholics from "aversive stimuli." [57] Social support at this time also rewards expressions of guilt and remorse and purely verbal adaptations such as good resolutions, which leave the cognitive aspects of self and action untouched, or they provide new facets to a complicated system of rationalizations relied upon by the drinker to deny his alcoholic self.

Elsewhere in this volume I have included a chapter on the cyclical changes in the actions of the systematic check forger, which seeks to enlighten the dynamic relationships between role enactment, anxiety, and identity in perpetuating the curious self-defeating features of this pattern of crime. While Lindesmith and Strauss have seriously questioned the applicability of learning theory to the explanation of drug addiction,[58] nevertheless, a study of cycles of abstinence and relapse in drug addicts offers some data which seem entirely amenable to the general kind of

[56] Mowrer, *Learning Theory*, esp. chaps. 3, 9.

[57] Elaine Kepner, "Application of Learning Theory to the Etiology and Treatment of Alcoholism," *Quarterly Journal of Studies on Alcohol* 25 (1964): 279–91.

[58] Alfred Lindesmith and Anselm Strauss, *Social Psychology*, rev. ed. (New York: Dryden Press, 1956), pp. 361–65.

analysis which I have urged here.[59] In time, more detailed ethnographic studies of the daily patterns of life of drug addicts, touching on sequences and timing of activities such as "copping," "hustling," "scoring," and "shooting," may bring into better focus the interplay of satisfactions and penalties in patterns of drug use. A beginning of this kind of research has already been made in investigations of drug addiction in certain areas of New York City.[60]

DEVIANCE AS IDENTITY PROBLEMS

The most telling objection to learning theory which seeks for constant or direct referents of human choice in social experience is that inner urgencies, strivings, "emitted behavior," and autonomous motives extrude themselves in human action. In the process, rewarding actions may be discontinued, and unrewarding or even punishing ones are pursued in blind folly. Grand examples are the forewarned missionary who rashly treads on sacred beliefs and customs of alien natives until he is ignominiously killed and his body desecrated, or the dictator who wages war hopelessly until he pulls his nation down in a crashing Wagnerian finale.

A more immediate or microcosmic analogue of the Wagnerian epic may be reenacted by the alcoholic who repeatedly downs whiskey only to have it come up as vomit, and who feels no relief, and even sicker, when he finally gets some to remain in his angry stomach. It is also mimed by the drug addict who continues with drugs even though acquired tolerance eliminates the possibility of any longer achieving a "high," or who is using so much heroin that he can no longer hope to beg, buy, or steal a supply sufficient for his "habit." The check forger adds to the piece when he mechanically cashes his bogus checks knowing that arrest and prison are only a step away.

It can be said that the alcoholic and the drug addict have endogenous cravings, and that the bad check artist has a compulsion which drives him, or even that the stutterer has a need to stutter.[61] Be this as it may, I prefer to believe that cravings are inferable functions of social reality at least in part. I judge them to be related to (1) the degree of personal involvement in deviance and (2) the duration of such involvement. The totally long-involved drug addict is illustrative; he has in the course of time introduced

[59] Marsh Ray, "The Cycle of Abstinence and Relapse Among Heroin Addicts," *Social Problems* 9 (1961): 132–40.

[60] Isidor Chein, Donald Gerard, Robert Lee, and Eva Rosenfeld, *The Road to H* (New York: Basic Books, 1964), chaps. III, VI.

[61] Lee Travis, "The Need for Stuttering," *Journal of Speech Disorders* 5 (1940): 193–202.

narcotics into all or most facets of his life; he has used them night and day, at home and at work, on foot and in automobiles, and in many toilets of the land. He has injected arms, legs, knees, and other parts of his body, and he has sniffed and swallowed drugs. When this has gone on for years in countless social situations, the administration of narcotics, their imagery, and their concomitant feeling states become, to employ a common sense term, "second nature." This means that narcotics have become bound up in complex, intermeshing ways with his physiological, psychological, and social reactions which in the large form a supplementary self. In the same way it is possible to discern an alcoholic self, a stuttering self, or a check artist self, identified with the body, material artifacts, and surroundings, as well as the social environment.[62]

Cravings or compulsions by definition are only observable in persons who have been deprived, and, I would add, in ways significant for the self. Those living for some time in alien cultures are known to experience feelings of loss of identity, and they also periodically crave food, drinks, movies, newspapers, and other appurtenances to their former daily routines of existence which anchored them to their native identities. If the sober alcoholic, the abstaining drug addict, the stutterer in remission, and the check criminal "going straight" are seen as akin to persons living in an alien culture or foreign psycho-social environment, their cravings and compulsions lose some of their mystique. They become the cumulations of irritability which grow with new responsibilities or problems confronted without old accouterments of the self. Alcoholics speak of the strain of staying sober, drug addicts of the crankiness and meanness of their "off drug" personality, the check writer of his boredom with humdrum workaday life while on parole.

A net conclusion from what has been said is that self-defeating deviance at times must be understood as the complex consequences of an identity crisis. In phenomenological language the crisis is the outcome of a dialectic between two major self-systems, the "true" self and a "false" self.[63] The adaptive devices making up the false self-system have an ephemeral "pay off" or allow the deviant to "get by," but the satisfactions, or perhaps protection, gained thereby are compromised or tainted by an accompanying sense of bad faith, insincerity, and unjustified or undeserved gains. Conversely it may be that false self-systems interfere with the experiencing of guilt arising from real as opposed to phantasied transgressions, and prevent

[62] So-called plastic involvement of the self was once illustrated for the writer by an ex-addict who told of the scene preceding his marriage. He had put his "works" (spoon, eyedropper, pin) on the table in his room to which he had asked his bride-to-be. Asked if she knew what that was she said yes. He replied, "Well, that's me, and if you marry me, you marry that, too."

[63] R. D. Laing, *The Divided Self* (Baltimore: Penguin Books, 1965), chapter 6.

restorative actions (restitution) which would help to structure the self in social interaction and reduce some of the acute anxiety which underlies self-defeating deviance.

While a considerable amount has been written on the subject of identity problems, much of it has been in a phenomenological or existential mode of thought. Searching out the referents of such problems in social situations and social structures is mandatory if the concept is to have utility for sociological studies of deviance. In a general way it can be shown that modern mass society is characterized by a shrinking inventory of life situations in which identities can be stabilized. The demands and expectations of others increasingly tend to get defined in terms of mere overt conformity or the appearance of such. Along with this, opportunities for substantiating rewards through interpersonal action diminish, as do those for venting moral indignation. Finally, the practice of restitution declines and gives way to public protection or insurance, and the expiation of sins or wrongs done others has become archaic, or is replaced by impersonally organized treatment of deviants as sick people exempt from blame. Beyond these observations, however, lies a more arduous sociological assignment of specifying the situational and structural contingencies related to identity crises in particular kinds of deviance.[64]

CONCLUDING COMMENTS ON SECONDARY DEVIANCE

The concept of secondary deviance unavoidably strikes a strong conservative note in contemporary sociology. It is more than a little reminiscent of the dour philosophy of William Graham Sumner, in that it starts with a jaundiced eye on collective efforts of societies to solve problems of deviance, particularly when this work of social control is propagandized as primarily in behalf of the deviants. As such, "secondary deviance" may be a convenient vehicle for civil libertarians or young men of sociology to voice angry critiques of social institutions.

In part the underlying issue is the old one of rights of individuals versus necessities of collective life, aggravated and sharpened by the great power delegated or preempted by the state and the jumbo organizations in modern society. The coexistence of older philosophies and procedures of punishments with a positivistic, psychiatric ideology enjoining treatment of social deviants sanctions the use of power both arbitrary and all-inclusive; it makes possible a kind of scientific tyranny in which social control is

[64] The distinction between the status problem in secondary deviance and the identity problem and relation of the latter to "problems implicit in paternalistic mission culture" is admirably documented by Earl Rubington, in "Grady Breaks Out: A Case Study of an Alcoholic's Relapse," *Social Problems* 11 (1964).

justified less by an individual's demonstrable threat to society than by someone's authoritative judgment of his potential menace. One result is that persons whose moral infractions have been minor can face indentured public servitude of indefinite termination.

Perhaps all of this means that a high energy society mediated by a delicately integrated technology can ill afford to risk granting unqualified statuses to persons of doubtful integrity or competence. Fortunately there are trends which counter this stringent conception of societal necessities and promise reallocation of power to individuals. One of these is the renewed interest of social scientists in social control as such, which conceived as a marginal intrusion into human affairs, must raise questions of the advisability of such intervention, the when and the where of intervention, and its consequences, sought and unsought.

Another reassuring counterdevelopment has come from high-court decisions, which on one hand have sanctioned large grants of power to public organizations, but on the other have made it unequivocally clear that abridgment of freedom of individuals by state or private organizations shall meet procedural requirements designed to equalize powers of contestants at the points where the decisions are made.

Finally, the preservation of civil libertarian values has been furthered by federal and state clarifications of rules of administrative law. In this area, little known to sociologists, it is possible to see the early growth of a more functional kind of morality, especially where it embraces the licensing and regulation of business, professions, and occupations. While moral turpitude implied by criminal conviction and apparent disabilities of mental disorder, alcoholism, and drug addiction can be legislated into prima facie evidence for disqualifications of status, the procedural tendencies in administrative adjudication have been to require demonstration on a functional basis that past deviance does or will effectively threaten welfare of particular public clienteles served by the deviant. In time such administrative judgments may crystallize a wider democracy for deviants and evolve organizational devices for hedging the process by which degradation is translated further into denials, suspensions, and revocations of the right to follow one's livelihood.[65] Hopefully, there may come the time when a larger class of degraded persons will have the right to appeal from nonfunctional stigmatization by organizations. Sociologically this means that amplification of deviance handicaps at the level of status will be diminished. Whether the identity problems of deviants can be approached through comparable organized activity or legal change is doubtful.

[65] See Lawrence Friedman, "Freedom of Contract and Occupational Licensing, 1890–1910: A Legal and Social Study," *California Law Review* 53 1964): 487–534.

II

deviation
and
social control

4 LEGAL COMMITMENT AND SOCIAL CONTROL

Elsewhere the writer has advanced a simple, hypothetical system for the analysis of social control situations.[1] The system conceives social control in terms of (1) deviation—the difference between the objectives of control and the behavior of the groups or persons being controlled; (2) the differential in power between controllers and controlled; (3) the means of control; and (4) the forms of control. This article suggests the further application of these concepts to the legal commitment of mentally diseased persons. Here, however, discussion will be confined to some considerations of deviation and the power differential as they affect this process.

One of the greatest fallacies in many discussions of social control has been the Sumnerian assumption of automaticity in the control process, the assigning of reified coercive qualities to the mores, social norms, and social laws, with a consequent ignoring of the dynamic aspects of the process.[2]

Reprinted with permission from Sociology and Social Research 30 *(May–June 1946): 370–78.*

[1] Edwin M. Lemert, "The Grand Jury as an Agency of Social Control," *American Sociological Review* 10 (1945): 751–58.

[2] Pitirim Sorokin, *Contemporary Sociological Theories* (New York: Harper & Row, 1928), pp. 699–700; Daniel Katz and Richard Schanck, *Social Psychology* (New York: John Wiley, 1938), p. 21; Edwin M. Lemert, "The Folkways and Social Control," *American Sociological Review* 7 (1942): 394–

That the process is a highly variable one in this instance is apparent from the estimate that only 50 per cent of mentally diseased persons are ever institutionalized.[3]

It would probably be agreed by most psychiatrists, psychiatric social workers, clinical psychologists, and trained observers of mental disease that psychotic deviation as described in formal psychiatric categories is not in itself the basis of commitments to mental hospitals. Rather it is the deviations of the psychotic person from customary role expectancies which increase his social visibility and put strains upon others that provide the impetus to insanity proceedings. It seems sound to argue in general that different types of psychoses have different degrees of social visibility and potentialities for strain upon family and community organization. For example, it has been suggested that the manic-depressive will be apparent in almost any social context, in contrast with at least certain types of schizophrenia.[4] The speeded-up, group-disruptive behavior and occasional suicidal attempts of the manic are much more likely in our type of culture [5] to lead to hospitalization than the seclusive behavior of the schizophrenic.

However, broad generalizations about the relevance of certain psychotic symptoms to culture are probably of less value than an intimate knowledge of how they relate themselves to expectancies based upon age, sex, marital status, and occupational, ethnic, and locality affiliations. The combinations and interaction of these are often extremely complicated and make generalizations difficult. One apathetic schizophrenic man may escape institutionalization as a result of routine employment under close supervision; another with comparable symptoms may fail in his role because he has a job calling for sustained attention and synthesizing adjustments. A schizophrenic woman without children may be tolerated or pampered by her husband, but the care of children may throw an intolerable strain on the husband or other family members. It is also true that community agencies have a stake in these cases.[6] The tolerance of

---

99; also the critical comment on A. B. Hollingshead's concept of social control by Rupert Vance, "Toward Social Dynamics," *American Sociological Review* 10 (1945): 128, 129.

[3] Carnay Landis and James D. Page, *Modern Society and Mental Disease* (New York: Farrar, Straus and Giroux, 1938), pp. 19–38; Henry B. Elkind, "Are Mental Diseases on the Increase?" *Psychiatric Quarterly* 13 (1939): 165–72.

[4] Mary B. Owens, "Alternative Hypotheses for the Explanation of Some of Faris' and Dunham's Results," *American Journal of Sociology* 47 (1941): 49 ff.

[5] The higher readmission rates for the manic depressives are suggestive here. Landis and Page, *Modern Society and Mental Disease*, p. 130.

[6] In one case investigated by the writer a mother was unable to purchase and keep accounts of groceries and utilities; she mislaid money; her house was

groups for the disruptive behavior of psychotic members finds expression in variable institutionalizing tendencies or preferences, or, perhaps better, in a tolerance quotient.[7] As has been pointed out, such a tolerance quotient will vary with status or role indicators. It will also have time-space dimensions.

The two main groups involved in commitment are the family and the community in its more formal collective capacities. The equilibrium in which the psychotic person has status may be quite unstable. Commitment may be a sign of changed tolerance for the deviant rather than of an exaggeration of his psychotic behavior. Often an unbalanced family member is tolerated only through some attenuated dyadic relationship, and when this is broken commitment follows. An illustration is a case in which a mother cared for a demented daughter for many years until her own health failed; since the brother and sister refused to provide the necessary care, hosiptalization had to be sought. Common cases in recent years are those where growing family responsibilities cause children to be unable to care for senile parents, most obvious in urban areas, perhaps, where old persons become traffic hazards or add to housing difficulties. Old people often become serious fire hazards, especially in rural areas, but even such a simple thing as overtaxing the laundry facilities of a growing family by incontinent elders may be the social break leading to hospitalization. In a sociological time-analysis of the phenomena of institutionalization it is clear that the tolerance quotient must be related to such things as family life cycles and linear or cyclical changes in community life.

The question of the spatial distribution of institutionalized cases of mental disease probably hinges on the differences between the tolerance quotients of families in general and those of community agencies. Perhaps a more significant and more generally operating variable is the degree of primary contacts in various areas.[8] It is the writer's impression from

---

filthy; and she often let clothes soak for as long as six weeks in the tubs. However, it was her failure to feed the children regularly, clothe them properly, and get them to school that was the culminating stress leading to her commitment.

[7] This problem has been tentatively discussed in connection with criminal deviation. "It is . . . maintained that the sociologically important aspects of behavior along the various vectors of deviation from normal or approved conduct may be expressed in terms of a quotient which is a ratio between the behavior in objective terms and the community's willingness to tolerate it, with a critical point for each case where the community in its corporate capacity goes into action." Courtland C. Van Vechten, "The Tolerance Quotient as a Device for Defining Certain Social Concepts," *American Journal of Sociology* 46 (1940): 35–42.

[8] M. B. Owens suggests that the differences in the spatial distribution of catatonic schizophrenia and paranoid schizophrenia in urban areas (Chicago) might be explained in terms of such a difference ("Alternative Hypotheses," pp. 49, 50).

approximately 100 interviews with relatives of persons committed to a Midwestern state hospital that families will tolerate extreme deviation on the part of psychotic members, seeking legal commitment only with great reluctance and show of guilt, and after exhausting all other resources. Isolated or rural communities also seem to show broad tolerances for psychotic persons. An estimate supplied by the local physician in an isolated community in the Great Lakes region placed the number of nonhospitalized psychotics at 40, out of a total population of 600, somewhat more than 6 per cent of the whole. There can be little doubt but that the greater familism of rural people and the tendency of smaller communities to handle problems informally is involved here.[9]

In large urban communities it is pertinent to know whether the family or the formal control agencies in the community show greater tolerance for comparable psychotic behavior. Unfortunately there are almost no studies that shed direct light on this question. There can be no doubt, however, that families and community agencies seek hospitalization of psychotics for widely different reasons. A comparative study of cases committed by families and by police in Peiping, China, showed that police tended to take action in more cases which involved attacks, violence, confusion, and general disorderly conduct, whereas family cases were more numerous with delusions, hallucinations, "restless" behavior, physical complaints, and suspected physical complaints. The greatest differences were in the cases of general disorderliness and confusion, in which police cases were three to five times as numerous as family cases. The greatest preponderance of family over police cases came in the category of delusions.[10]

The second factor involved in the commitment of mentally ill persons is significant where commitment occurs before a critical point is reached in the tolerance ratio and where a critical point is reached but no commitment follows. Here are seen the convergent effects of behavior

[9] This is particularly true of some of the sex deviations associated with the menopause and senile disturbances in men. Police in one small midwestern community confided to the writer that they frequently made only perfunctory efforts to apprehend "window peepers" even when they had a good idea as to who they were, preferring that neighbors catch such persons and give them a beating.

[10] Francis L. K. Hsu, "A Brief Report on the Police Cooperation in Connection with Mental Cases in Peiping," in Neuropsychiatry in China, ed. R. S. Lyman, V. Maeker, and P. Liang (Peking: H. Vetch, 1939). The writer's impressions, based upon case histories, interviews with relatives, and hospital ward contacts, would tend to bear out these facts. One case investigated revealed that the patient had lived in a rooming house in Chicago for more than a year, during which time he called the police several times as a result of visual and auditory hallucinations. Each time the police told him he had been drinking too much and not to bother them. Later, when he returned to his family home in a small town, his relatives sought his commitment after a short period.

aberrations and power struggle. Often serious psychiatric symptoms are present without much social visibility or strain, so that commitment is sought as an incident of intra- or intergroup struggle. Perhaps the term "spurious deviation" [11] is appropriate to describe situations of this sort. Ordinarily commitment struggles are between factions of relatives in the family group, based upon property considerations, the custody of children, or simply on general hostility. In other cases community cleavages are expressed symbolically in commitment proceedings. Neighbors, local business establishments, employers, insurance companies, welfare agencies, physicians, lawyers, probate court members, even the staff of the mental hospital itself may inject considerations of status into the otherwise perfunctory process of legal commitment.

It is precisely at this point that our conventional, mechanistic social control concepts fall down and the need for an understanding of the more dynamic aspects of control becomes apparent. A case history investigated by the writer clearly illustrates what has been said thus far and perhaps provides clues for further elaboration of concepts for testing.

S——— was a boy of 18, a member of an isolated Polish family living in a sparsely populated township in a mid-western state. Most of his life he was mentally retarded, this being explained by the mother as the result of an accidental head injury at an early age. Neighbors generally thought the boy queer but not particularly dangerous. A nearby nurseryman gave him occasional work, which he was able to carry on under the close supervision of his brother.

A pronounced ingroup-outgroup cleavage existed between a group of the neighbors and the boy's family, hostility being directed at the whole family group instead of any one of its members. Attention of the investigator was called to such things as the father's terrific temper and beating of the boys and to the mother's refusal to talk to people and her habit of gathering pebbles along the road. Credence was given stories that the family did not eat together at a table in their home, supported in part by the uncouth manners of the boys when they ate in neighbors' homes. Hostility grew out of the feeling of S———'s brother that they were exploited by farmers for whom they worked; ultimately they refused such work. Many farmers termed them lazy.

When S——— reached 18 his brother got a job in a nearby town, and the work of S——— became less dependable. He was rejected for military service as mentally deficient. One day he was in the company of a group of boys in front of a ramshackle old house owned by a senile man who lived in a lean-to affixed to the rear. This man was considered by many

[11] Not to be confused with the folk concept of "railroading." Cases of commitment of normal persons are probably so rare that they can be dismissed from consideration.

neighbors to be more peculiar than the boy. He had been something of a nuisance to the Polish family. The boys made joking threats to hurl stones through the sagging, half-broken windows of the house. S——— went further and actually threw the stones, making wild threats to "blow the house into the sky with dynamite."

The boy was taken into custody on complaint by the old man. In the course of an examination it was revealed that the boy habitually engaged in autoerotic practices. On this discovery a woman recently moved into the neighborhood became much concerned for the safety of her daughters. The sheriff also was much impressed by this fact. Over strong resistance of the mother and later of the father, the boy was committed to the state hospital for the insane, where a psychiatrist tentatively diagnosed him as schizophrenic. When the father carried his complaint to the governor of the state, there was a tendency for some of the staff to consider him demented.

This case seems a clear illustration of some of the concepts here defined, bringing out the precarious nature of the neighborhood equilibrium in which S——— participated, the changing social role expectancies associated with S———'s attainment of maturity, and the changing tolerance quotient as the structure of the neighborhood and family groups was modified. Perhaps even more significantly indicated is the part played by overt hostility based upon culture conflict. There is little doubt that the isolated position of the Polish family heightened the social visibility of S———'s deviation, in spite of the fact that, as one hired hand said, "He didn't do nothing any other boy wouldn't have done." A study of mental disorders in urban areas shows that commitment rates are higher for ethnic groups living in areas not predominantly inhabited by persons of their own nationality.[12] A point missed or ignored by the authors in their interpretation of this phenomenon is that breakdowns in social communication have a two-way effect. They not only weaken the personal integration of the individual and thus increase the likelihood of incidence of certain types of mental disorder,[13] but also change the tolerance quotient of the group. The putative facts of "spurious deviation" are a reciprocal of deviation by the isolated individual.

Another line of reasoning suggested here is that isolation relates closely to the organizational basis of power. Being on the group margins, the isolated individual has little call upon the loyalties of others to resist

[12] Robert E. L. Faris and H. Warren Dunham, *Mental Disorders in Urban Areas* (Chicago: University of Chicago Press, 1939), p. 177.

[13] The proposition that manic-depressive insanity represents such gross social deviation (as opposed to psychiatric) that the power differential seldom operates would have to be tested in order to validate more completely the type of analysis that has here been suggested.

institutionalization. In this case it was obvious that the elective sheriff and probate judge were not influenced by considerations of possible political repercussions of their action.

Although studies of the social etiology of mental disorders may not be vitiated by being based upon data for hospitalized cases, more modesty and care in phrasing conclusions in such research are indicated. If the arguments here have any validity, then such data are only a crude measure of the incidence and perhaps an unreliable measure of the variety of mental deviation. They are at least as much a measure of the aspects of social control.

5 ALCOHOL, VALUES, AND SOCIAL CONTROL

A general analysis of alcohol and social control deals with the universal qualities of alcohol, the values and costs of its use, the distribution of power in social structures, the available means of control, the probabilities of resistance, and patterns of values in cultures and individuals. These concepts are designed for a kind of "action analysis," being oriented to research into problems of alcohol use which have emerged from the impact of rapid technological change in Western societies and from the spread of modern technologies and ideologies to nonliterate and "underdeveloped" societies of the world. Central to this analysis is the hypothesis, well grounded in empirical findings of alcohol research, that values are crucial factors in the social control of alcohol use.

THE ATTRIBUTES OF ALCOHOL AND VALUES

The values which have been assigned to alcoholic beverages throughout the world partially rest upon their physical qualities and certain of their recurrent or universal physiological effects. It has been pointed out that alcohol is distinctive for the ease and cheapness of its preparation. Other physical properties permit it to be stored for long periods and transported with facility.[1] In many societies alcohol is valued as a food, as a promoter of digestion and sleep, as a protection against cold and fatigue, and as a medicine to relieve pain or to treat specific illnesses. This is not to say that alcohol metabolism determines symbolic associations among human beings. It should be emphasized that the ascription of values to alcoholic beverages diverges from and transcends their demonstrable physiological functions.[2]

The more important symbolic associations of alcohol derive from its function as a behavior modifier. Mild to severe intoxication promotes the expression of a variety of idiosyncratic values in the individual and a large measure of socially shared and communicable values. Perhaps the most important of the former is the relief or relaxation from fatigue, tension, apathy, and the sense of isolation.

The social values facilitated by the consumption of alcoholic drinks spring from a recognition of their function in diminishing social distance and strengthening group bonds. These values revolve around fellowship, social amity, and group morale. Often these values are expressed through rituals which symbolize the solidarity of kin groups and work groups or the collective willingness of warriors and soldiers to die for a leader or a cause. Alcohol is further valued for its ritual functions in symbolizing status changes at birth, marriage, coming of age, and bereavement. Alcohol also finds an important place in some societies in the specialized culture of ecstasy and in Dionysian communion with gods. A number of societies have institutionalized groups in which drinking and drunkenness are terminal rather than mediating values.

There are other positive values of alcohol use, less concerned with interpersonal interaction, which come to the fore in larger nation-state–type societies. One of these is the recognized ease with which revenue for state purposes can be raised through taxing alcohol production. This, of course, is a more specialized valuation of alcohol held by political or administrative elites. Closely related to this is the recognition of the value of induced dependence upon alcohol as a means of social control. This can be seen in connection with contract labor and peonage, in connection with sex behavior, and in connection with diplomacy and power struggles between ruling elites. Finally, there is a set of sharply defined values attached to

---

[1] H. W. Haggard and E. M. Jellinek, *Alcohol Explored* (Garden City, N.Y.: Doubleday & Company, 1942); Donald Horton, "The Functions of Alcohol in Primitive Societies: A Cross-Cultural Study," *Quarterly Journal of Studies on Alcohol* 4 (1943): 199–319.

[2] Function in this article means operation or process; value is an object or a state which is desired. Functions may or may not be valued.

alcohol by those whose economic livelihood and occupational status rest upon the production and distribution of alcoholic beverages.

There is a tendency, perhaps universal, for valuations of alcoholic beverages to become polarized. At one extreme, liquors, wine, and beer are glorified in song, poetry, and drama as keys to ecstasy and sublimity; at the other extreme, they are viewed as perverters of human morality and the chief causes of the ills of society as well as the sorrows of individuals. This imparts a marked ambivalence to attitude and opinion concerning the proper place of alcohol in social life.[3] In part this ambivalence stems from an awareness that satisfactions brought by imbibing alcohol not infrequently have a spurious quality. What seemed to be love to the intoxicated maiden turns out in sober retrospect to have been sex exploitation. The comradeship of the college reunion in afterthought is seen realistically as largely inspired by the martinis rather than by common interest long since gone.

A more important ingredient of this ambivalence toward alcohol comes from the perception of its previously mentioned function as a behavior modifier. Modifications in human behavior brought by intoxication are socially and personally destructive as well as socially integrative. The same object which makes human pleasures makes human pain and unhappiness. Although this can be said of many other objects used by human beings, alcohol is distinctive in that it is difficult to predict which will be the consequences of its consumption.

THE COSTS OF ALCOHOL USE

It is a reasonable assumption that there is some kind of hierarchy in the values held by human beings. This signifies that in a hypothetically free situation with unlimited means at hand there is an order in which values are satisfied. However, this order is imperfectly manifested in actual choice-making by individuals because the environmental situation limits choices, often excluding opportunities for satisfying some values and allowing only a partial or compromised satisfaction of others. The cost of a value, stated most simply, is the degree to which other values must be sacrificed in the process of its satisfaction.[4] Generally speaking, the cost of a value is estimable in terms of time, energy, and the amount of discomfort expended to satisfy it.

Indulgence in alcohol, while promoting fulfillment of previously

[3] Abraham Myerson, "Alcohol: A Study in Social Ambivalence," *Quarterly Journal of Studies on Alcohol* 1 (1940): 13–20.

[4] W. Fred Cottrell, *Research for Peace* (Amsterdam: North Holland Publishing, 1954).

mentioned values, frequently does so at the cost of others. This is most apparent in the tendency for intoxication to encourage or "release" aggression and deviant sex behavior.[5] Intoxication also impairs physiological functions, making for the neglect or inadequate performance of roles as well as accidents. The values commonly sacrificed by drunkenness are respect for person, life, property, health, longevity, family integrity, parental responsibility, regularity of work, and financial dependability. Apart from these general or universal costs chargeable against intoxication are countless others which are more variable and understandable only in relation to a particular sociocultural system.

The strictly economic costs of drunkenness and alcoholism in our society have been subject to estimates and can be considerable.[6] The theoretical limits to such costs can be only speculative. Adam Smith[7] stated that "there is no risk that nations will destroy their fortunes through excessive consumption of fermented liquors." However, the production of alcohol may take place at the cost of necessary commodities and services, as happened in the Hawaiian Islands at one time.[8] The mutineer colony of Pitcairn Island came perilously close to annihilating itself through drunkenness and conflict over women.[9]

It is possible that rapid social change in the last 150 years, which has been strongly felt in Western societies and is emergent throughout the world, has enhanced the values of alcoholic intoxication. Such things as culture conflict, stress, and "anomie" may have grown to such proportions that alcohol in many societies is increasingly valuable as a social reagent and as a sedative for personality conflicts.[10] This hypothesis is a large one and, with the present state of sociology, a difficult one to test.

Modern technology changes the costs of satisfying values even though the order of the values may remain unchanged. This is to say that technological and related cultural changes very definitely affect choice-making behavior in relation to social control. As applied to alcohol consumption,

[5] Horton, "The Function's Alcohol in Primitive Societies."

[6] Benson Y. Landis, "Some Economic Costs of Inebriety," *Alcohol, Science and Society* (New Haven, Conn.: Journal of Studies on Alcohol, 1945), pp. 201–21.

[7] Adam Smith, *The Wealth of Nations* (London: Methuen, 1950), pp. 456–57.

[8] "Translation of the Laws of the Hawaiian Islands Established in the Reign of Kamehameha III" (Honolulu: Hawaiian Missionary Children's Society Library, 1842), Manuscript.

[9] Charles B. Nordhoff and J. N. Hall, *Pitcairn's Island* (Boston: Little, Brown, 1934).

[10] Selden D. Bacon, "Alcohol and Complex Society," *Alcohol, Science and Society* (New Haven, Conn.: Quarterly Journal of Studies on Alcohol, 1945), pp. 190–93.

this means that intoxication and drunkenness levy critically higher costs in certain contexts of technologically mediated, interdependent, high-speed, high-productivity, health-oriented societies. Thus to older, more universal, costs of drunkenness are added death and injury from traffic accidents, lowered productivity and absenteeism in industry, disease, disturbances of public order, crime, and weakening of military discipline. Furthermore, with the growth of statism and welfare values, costs of policing and treating the chronically inebriate population must be reckoned in the overall economy of alcohol use.

VALUES AND POWER ELITES

It should not be concluded that policies or lines of action or inaction followed by societies in relation to the control of drinking result from a simple summative economy of values and costs. For this reason serious questions have to be raised about the sufficiency of research into such things as "basic personality," "themes," "cultural patterns," and "national character" in order to predict the course and results of social control. Social action and control usually emanate from elite power groups who have their own systems of values, which differ from those of the general population, from those of other groups, and even from those of individual members of the elites. The organizational values of such elites and their rules of procedure also have a strong bearing on controlling events. Furthermore, elites are limited by the amount of power they exercise, the kinds of alliances they make, and the means of control available to them to reach their goals.

The position of groups and individuals at the point of their inter-action in a social structure is of great significance in predicting the resultant action taken by a society or government to control or decontrol alcohol consumption. Groups and individuals whose values are being sacrificed by intoxication and drunkenness may have no structure to formulate their vaguely felt dissatisfactions. On the other hand, minorities, because their programs are defined and their power is organized and well-timed, more readily have their values cast into the emergent pattern of social action.[11]

RESISTANCE

Action by groups or whole societies to change the drinking behavior of a population necessarily alters the costs of satisfying values that have been

[11] Cottrell, *Research for Peace*.

sought directly through the medium of alcoholic beverages. At the same time other costs may be assessed through modification of laws and re-organization of the political and socioeconomic structures required to institute the new controls. Many of these costs are likely to be unanticipated and to carry the risk that resistance will follow. A consideration of the amount, the duration, and the form of the resistance must be part of the study of social action to control drinking.

If resistance arises, decisions must be made as to how it will be met and dealt with by control agencies. Such choices may be constricted by social structures and generalized values which make some means of control available but exclude others. For example, coercion may be an acceptable sanction in some societies but not in others. The organization of power in space and time may prevent the application of coercive controls to resisting populations, even where they are morally and legally permissible.

A special factor complicating the choice of controls over drinking is the irrationality of the intoxicated person and his unresponsiveness to symbols which limit the responses of sober persons. Added to this is the fact that socially deleterious behavior of the drunken person is often followed by acceptable or even praiseworthy behavior. While the inebriated person is nowhere regarded as mentally disordered, some societies have sought to solve this problem by treating him as irresponsible. However, this is not a solution in the sense of control.

THE ABSENCE OF SOCIAL CONTROL—LAISSEZ FAIRE

A substantial number of societies appear to exercise little or no social control over consumption of alcoholic beverages; they approximate a condition of laissez faire. In these societies there is no organized public opinion unfavorable to drinking or drunkenness. With respect to the drunken person the attitude seems to be *caveat socius* rather than *caveat potor*—let society beware of the drinker rather than the reverse. Efforts at control in such societies are directed to avoiding the costly consequences of drunkenness rather than to controlling it. Speeches are made prior to feasts or drinking sprees, or rituals are performed urging drinkers to avoid quarreling and fighting or to "have a good time." Sober persons are told to stay away from quarrelsome drunks and even blamed for not doing so if they are injured. In extreme cases, fighting drunks may be separated and passively restrained. They may be tied to trees or, as in a case familiar to us among Salish Indians of British Columbia, placed in cooking retorts ordinarily used to pack canned salmon. When the drunken person passes out he may have a pillow placed under his head or be covered with a blanket or wrapped in a hammock pending his return to sobriety.[12]

The apparent tolerance and lack of direct control of the inebriated persons in such societies are attributable in part to the high value placed upon intoxication by individual members. The attenuation of control is also consistent with the fact that the integrating functions of drinking for society are perceived and collectively valued. When urgent and persistent needs are met thereby, drunkenness may assume institutionalized form, as it did among Northwest Coast Indians.[13] Correspondingly, losses from drunkenness in these societies may be relatively low. Consuming beverages of low alcoholic content, such as beers, may mitigate the drunkenness or shorten its duration. The presence or absence of toxic congeners in the beverages and adulteration are additional variables predictive of unwanted consequences of intoxication.

Even when drunkenness is widespread and destructive at the time, its occurrence in the form of sprees or festivals following or preceding planting, harvest, hunting, and fishing seasons minimizes interference with economic activities.[14] If the production of food is carried out by isolated families, the costs of drunkenness will not be felt by the whole community. Finally, in those societies living close to a subsistence level, the withdrawal of labor from the food quest tends to be a self-limiting phenomenon. With all of these facts to consider, it is probably correct to say that many primitive and rural societies adjust to rather than control intoxication and drunkenness. In all cases there are costs, but they seem to be written off or absorbed.

The gemeinschaft qualities of many primitive and isolated rural societies make them ill-adapted to take action toward drunkenness even though the costs are substantial and are realistically perceived. Their dependence upon locality and kinship groups as units of control does not seem to work well because they are bound together on an intensely personal basis. This happens because the aggression and aberrant sex behavior released by intoxication come from impulses in the drunken person which were never fully integrated in social interaction with family

[12] Horton, "The Functions of Alcohol in Primitive Societies."

[13] Edwin M. Lemert, Alcohol and the Northwest Coast Indians, Publications in Society and Culture, No. 2 (Berkeley; University of California Press, 1954), pp. 303–406; Edwin M. Lemert, "The Use of Alcohol in Three Salish Indian Tribes," Quarterly Journal of Studies on Alcohol 19 (1958): 90–107.

[14] In a hunting society where hunting is a continuous necessity rather than seasonal, drunkenness may be more disruptive than in an agricultural society. This seems to have been true of Eastern Woodlands Indians. M. Kelbert and L. Hale, The Introduction of Alcohol into Iroquois Society (unpublished manuscript, Department of Anthropology, University of Toronto, n.d.).

members, companions, and neighbors.[15] The latter people seem to sense this, and, furthermore, they realize that they must "live with" the drunken person for years to come. This fosters ambivalence and deters forceful action, a condition which exists in families and neighbors of drunken persons even in modern urban societies.

When societies are organized into clans, a drunken person may be an especially vexatious problem because attempts to restrain him may backfire and lead to demands for damages or they may trigger warfare. When this is combined with a diffuse kind of authority in leaders and the absence of supraclan or "super-ordinate" organization, control over the drunken person may be at a minimum.[16] Wives, who often bear the heaviest costs of drunkenness, have low status in most primitive and rural societies and often are products of outgroup marriages. Hence, the values they hold are more easily sacrificed.

RITUAL AND DRUNKENNESS

Evidence from several societies indicates that notwithstanding a high tolerance for drunkenness, serious difficulties are created when drinking coincides with ritual performance. Efforts to integrate the two may be made, but they are seldom successful. The Snohomish of Puget Sound say that intoxication spoils their spirit dancing. Likewise the Kwakiutl of Kingcome Inlet in British Columbia and the Bella Coola farther north say that drinking is contrary to the sacred value of their potlatch dances.[17] Yet attempts at control on these ritual occasions more often than not were completely absent or at best they were token efforts. The Pomo Indians of California on one occasion decided that a four-day winter ceremonial dance had been spoiled by drinking. No one, however, was reprimanded or punished. Instead the entire ritual was repeated.[18]

To the degree that basic values of a society are widely expressed in ritual, drunkenness becomes more costly to the community. It is quite possible that the detailed, complicated, and interlocking ceremonial life of the Zuni Indians, in which all feel a sense of participation, may explain why they went through the experience of first accepting then re-

---

[15] Clyde Kluckhohn, *Navaho Witchcraft*, Papers of the Peabody Museum, Vol. 22, No. 2 (Cambridge, Mass.: Harvard University Press, 1944): 52–54.

[16] Horton, "The Functions of Alcohol in Primitive Societies."

[17] Edwin Lemert, "The Life and Death of an Indian State," *Human Organization* 13 (1954): 23–27; T. F. McIlwraith, *The Bella Coola Indians*, II (Toronto: University of Toronto Press, 1948).

[18] Clement Meighan, Personal Communication, Department of Anthropology and Sociology, University of California, Los Angeles, 1952.

jecting alcoholic beverages.[19] The high degree of organization of Pueblo societies seems to have prepared them better to establish policing agencies and to use authoritative controls than was true for most other American Indians. Their response to temperance propaganda was more broadly based, and early nineteenth-century temperance societies among them were less a missionary implant and more an indigenous growth.[20] Yet some accounts suggest that the problem of drunkenness was not completely solved by the Pueblo peoples.[21]

CONTACT AND INTERACTION WITH WHITE SOCIETY

The relation of social structure to the deficiency of social control over intoxicating drinks comes into clearest focus in American Indian societies which experienced direct and continuing contact with white explorers, traders, missionaries, settlers, and soldiers. The introduction of strong liquor into these societies was accompanied by a great deal of social disruption, destructive behavior, and demoralization.[22] None of these societies was able to take effective action in the matter. Chiefs and high-ranking Indians in a number of tribes clearly appreciated the social costliness of immoderate liquor consumption, and they themselves sometimes showed restraint. In several instances, in the territories of the Iroquois and the Shawnee, efforts were made to install prohibition but without success.[23]

The problem, while obviously concerned with values, hinged also upon the importance of clans and kin groups as agencies of control in these societies and upon the need for complete unanimity of public opinion

[19] Ruth Benedict, *Patterns of Culture* (New York: New American Library, Mentor Books, 1958), pp. 78–82.

[20] Ernest H. Cherrington, *Standard Encyclopedia of the Alcohol Problem* (Westerville, Ohio: American Issue Publishing, 1925), pp. 5–7, 37–39.

[21] Leslie White, *The Pueblo of Santa Ana*, Memoir Series, 44 (Menasha, Wis.: The American Anthropological Association, 1942): 69.

[22] F. W. Howay, "The Introduction of Intoxicating Liquors Amongst Indians of the Northwest Coast," *British Columbia Historical Review* 6 (1942): 157–69; William C. MacLeod, *The American Indian Frontier* (London: Kegan Paul, French, Trubner, 1928), chap. III; Emile Salone, "Les Sauvages du Canada et les Malades Importées de France au XVIIIe Siècle: La Picote et l'Alcoolisme," *Journal de la Société des Américanistes* 4 (1904): 1–17.

[23] MacLeod, *The American Indian Frontier*; Peter Wraxall, *An Abridgment of the Indian Affairs*, Contained in Four Folio Volumes, Transacted in the Colony of New York, From the Year 1678 to the Year 1751, ed. Charles H. McIlwain (Cambridge: Harvard University Press, 1915).

before taking action.[24] The typical way in which nobles and chiefs sought to influence the behavior of others—through precept and example—also proved to be a poor technique for restraining those—often younger men—who chose to get drunk or enter into dealings with liquor sellers.

Looming over the immediate situation was a larger context in which American Indian societies were caught in conflicts of power between imperialistic nations of Europe, especially France and England. Jealous colonial governments and rival fur trade companies gave added dimensions to these struggles. Later the United States became a party in the conflicts. In some cases warring nations deliberately used rum or brandy as a means of weakening Indian tribes allied with their enemies.[25] The few agreements reached by competing fur companies to curtail the sale or trading of liquor to Indians quickly fell into disuse.[26] Many colonial governments and, later, states and Canadian provinces passed prohibition laws, but their history has been one of evasions and unenforceability.

Although missionaries tried to aid the American Indians in their struggles with liquor, their policies and methods were not readily accepted. The price they demanded in return for the Christian sobriety they promised was one the Indians could not afford to pay, being more or less a complete repudiation of deeply cherished values as well as their culture-sustaining rituals. Thus, drunkenness often took on a reactionary virtue—becoming a means of resistance and of discrediting the "missionary way" and at the same time reaffirming older values.[27]

While control and, indeed, the idea of control over drinking, as we have shown, have been weakly developed or absent in many societies,[28] other societies, particularly those of the Western world have followed a much more positive course of action. They have recognized drinking and its consequences as a problem to be solved or as a threat to the integrity of society itself which calls for removal. This has been undertaken through decrees, passage of laws, and the indoctrination of special ideologies. A variety of control systems and methods have been devised: specialized agencies and organizations have been instituted and given responsibility

[24] Margaret Mead, "Public Opinion Mechanisms Among Primitive People," *Public Opinion Quarterly* 1 (1937): 5–16.

[25] MacLeod, *The American Indian Frontier.*

[26] Hiram Chittenden, *The American Fur Trade of the Far West,* Vol. 1 (New York: Harper & Row, 1902), chap. IV.

[27] Lemert, "The Use of Alcohol in Three Salish Indian Tribes."

[28] It is not intended to claim here that lack of control over drinking is a characteristic of primitive societies in general. Indeed, recent research has revealed the existence of reasonably successful "disciplined" drinking in certain Polynesian societies. See Edwin M. Lemert, "Alcohol Use in Polynesia," *Tropical and Geographic Medicine* 14 (1962): 183–89.

for control over alcohol consumption. To discuss all of these in the detail they merit is impossible here; at best we can examine a few of the salient ideas around which they have been built.

FOUR MODELS OF SOCIAL CONTROL

A reasonable working assumption is that the objective of social control over alcohol use generally is to minimize the costs of intoxication and drunkenness. For purposes of determining whether and how such an objective can be reached, it is helpful to formulate a number of hypothetical models of social control. These are drawn from the experiences of whole societies and also from the ideologies and programs of power elites which at different times and places have actively sought to bring alcohol use under control.

Model I

The costs of intoxication and drunkenness can be reduced by a system of laws and coercive controls making it illegal to manufacture, distribute, or consume alcoholic beverages.

This, of course, is a familiar model—prohibition. It has been tried in several forms, for long and short periods of time, in Aztec society, ancient China, feudal Japan, and Polynesian Islands, Iceland, Finland, Norway, Sweden, Russia, Canada, and the United States. The well-documented failures of the model can be attributed to its high costs, the instability of power elites favorable to prohibition, the limitations of power and available means of control, and the growth of resistance unresponsive to coercion.

The prohibition model in effect sacrifices all of the values of moderate drinking as well as those associated with intoxication, plus the vested values of those who earn a livelihood or receive investment returns from the production and distribution of fermented drinks and liquor. In order for such high costs to be willingly paid a large number of power elites must either see positive value gains in prohibition laws or see them as a means of protection against threatened value losses.[29] Consequently the prohibition model most likely can be established only through a social movement during periods of rapid social change, culture conflicts, conquest, or nationalistic movements.

Reform movements, from which prohibition springs, tend to be

---

[29] Alfred Lee, "Techniques of Social Reform: An Analysis of the New Prohibition Drive," *American Sociological Review* 9 (1944): 65–77.

ephemeral in nature because new issues supplant the old, undermining or destroying the alignments of elites supporting them. Disillusionment of their individual adherents and defection of groups through changing policies are speeded by difficulties of enforcement and consequences of resistance.

Resistance can be predicted for any model of control requiring the abandonment of values deeply held by large segments of population. In the case of prohibition the problem of enforcement is augmented because it is a form of sumptuary legislation which affects the more personal aspects of human behavior and individual choice-making in intimate or private behavior. In the absence of a reinforcing public opinion the application of coercive controls seldom has succeeded. Even the most severe punishments, such as death among the Aztecs and exile to Siberia in Russia, failed to abolish bootlegging in those societies.[30]

In large, complex societies a control model which prohibits a highly desired item increases its scarcity value and also the probabilities that collective enterprise will grow up to supply it. The large variety of foods which can be converted into alcohol and the ease and cheapness of its production and its movement make bootlegging and smuggling inevitable. The costs to the state of discovering and stamping out such illegal industry can reach a point where governing elites are unable or unwilling to pay them. The organization of evasion poses threats to other values such as respect for property and life, and even the value of government under law. This contributes further to resistance and reaction against prohibition.

The power of a given state to enforce prohibition may be insufficient if the economic and political values of other states are threatened thereby. In 1841, France intervened under threats of bombardment and compelled the reigning monarch of the Hawaiian Islands to end prohibition there.[31] France, Germany, Russia, and Spain at different times variously applied pressures to Finland, Norway, Iceland, and Turkey in order to prevent interference with liquor imports and smuggling.[32]

It may be more profitable to speculate on the conditions under which the prohibition model can succeed rather than to inventory the reasons for its failure. Probably it would require conspicuously high costs of drunkenness on one hand and on the other a positive replacement of

[30] Edwin M. Lemert, "An Interpretation of Society's Efforts to Control the Use of Alcohol," in *Alcoholism—Society's Responsibility* (Berkeley, Calif.: California State Department of Health, 1958).

[31] Lauren A. Thursten, "The Liquor Question in Hawaii . . ." (Manuscript Collection, University of Hawaii Library, n.d.).

[32] George Catlin, *Liquor Control* (New York: Holt, Rinehart & Winston, 1931).

the drinking values or substitution of new means for achieving the old values. A precondition of this would be relatively complete geographic isolation, similar to that found on islands, where behavior deviations have a high visibility. A social structure in which power is concentrated and little affected by public opinion or is upheld by supernatural sanctions perhaps would make for successful prohibition. Needless to say, condition such as these are increasingly anomalous in the world of the present.

Model II

The costs of intoxication and drunkenness can be reduced by a system of indoctrination of information about the consequences of using alcohol—thus leading to moderate drinking or abstinence.

The assumption behind this control model is that a causative relationship holds between controlled presentation of information and change in attitudes and values. The general idea is favored by some research on attitudes in specified areas of behavior. The findings, however, are not altogether consistent and where giving information has been found to modify attitudes and values the change is not always in the anticipated direction.[33] In general it would be hard to say whether exposure to information leads people to change specific values or whether the reverse is true—that is, whether the adherence to certain values stimulates people to inform themselves of pertinent facts. Currently there is no conclusive research from which judgments can be made about the kinds of information or educational content best calculated to achieve the goals of abstinence or moderation in drinking.

In the absence of data, the content of alcohol education has tended to be influenced by values and policies of temperance groups. This has been especially true of alcohol education in the schools of countries where forms of this model have been tried. Those whose values are more directly involved—parents—are not inclined to resist the inclusion of special curricula on alcohol education in the schools because many believed that some guidance is needed, especially in the United States where education is apotheosized as a solution for social problems. On the other hand some evidence from England and America speaks of indifference to or lack of sympathy with the alcohol curriculum on the part of teachers who do not subscribe to temperance values. This may reflect a failure to reconcile religious and scientific orientations in the recommended curricula.[34] Resistance from these sources, of course, need not necessarily be fatal to the working of this model.

[33] Hubert Bonner, *Social Psychology* (New York: American Book Company, 1953), pp. 185–92.

[34] Hermann Levy, *Drink: An Economic and Social Study* (London: Routledge & Kegan Paul, 1951), pp. 136–41.

A more serious flaw in the educational model of alcohol control lies in the probability that values surrounding drinking and embedded in drinking patterns are primarily shaped by experiences in the family and in peer groups rather than by formal educational agencies.[35] No problem is created for the society relying upon the educational model if it is homogeneous with reference to its drinking or abstinence habits. In the absence of such homogeneity, educators are faced with discontinuity between the learning process in the schools and what goes on in primary groups outside. Examples set by parents at home or pressures to conform in friendship groups easily cancel out the abstinence or moderation precepts of the school.

Education for restraint in drinking might be directed to parents instead of youth, through agencies outside or peripheral to the school. Yet prospects for this kind of enlightenment are not promising. Family-life education generally considered has yet to prove its worth.[36] Other programs, such as those promoted by state mental hygiene departments or by local alcoholism committees, or by citizens' committees as in Russia, are still largely untested by research or extensive empirical trial. In some places it has been shown that mental hygiene education can have effects opposite to those intended.[37]

The means which can be made to work for alcohol education have not been well adapted to the ends sought. Pamphlets, charts, movies, and lectures which dwell upon the results of excessive drinking often seem to run afoul of the ambivalence underlying popular reactions to alcohol. The arousal of fears, implied warnings, or threats as to what will happen if one drinks too much have been noted to provoke avoidance reactions toward further propaganda. There also seems to be an unwillingness of audiences to particularize such propaganda. This is very apt to be true if the educational materials are pointed to alcoholism as an end result of drinking.

Research into the factors which account for the long history of Jewish sobriety makes it fairly certain that the indoctrination of values is significant. It has not yet been settled what the values are, nor whether they are generalized or specific in nature. Furthermore there is a good

[35] Levy, *Drink*; Sakari Sariola, *Drinking Patterns in Finnish Lapland* (Helsinki: Finnish Foundation for Alcohol Studies, 1956); Robert Straus and Selden D. Bacon, *Drinking in College* (New Haven, Conn.: Yale University Press, 1953), chaps. 6, 9.

[36] William J. Goode, "Social Engineering and the Divorce Problem," *Annals of the American Academy of Political and Social Science* 272 (1950): 86–94.

[37] Elaine Cumming and John Cumming, *Closed Ranks: An Experiment in Mental Health Education* (Cambridge, Mass.: Harvard University Press, 1957); Kingsley Davis, "Mental Hygiene and Class Structure," *Psychiatry* 1 (1938): 55–65.

possibility that such values may be functional only in a special context of ongoing social control represented by the Jewish community.[38] Comparable research into drinking by Italian Americans and Italians concludes that valuation of wine as a food is an important part of their relative sobriety.[39] Yet this scarcely seems to be a complete explanation, and even if it were, there are no investigations to clarify the process by which such a value is inculcated or maintained in the ethnic population.

A final necessary comment on the educational model of control is that in a mobile, culturally diversified society which changes rapidly it becomes difficult to predict what pattern of values indoctrinated in children will best serve to adjust them as adults. To the extent that drinking is a response to situations, to adventitious groupings, and to stresses generated by role conflicts or social isolation, reliance upon a preconceived pattern of drinking values to control excessive use of alcohol may fail. Attention must be directed to the controls functioning in the drinking situation.

Model III

The costs of intoxication and drunkenness can be reduced by legal regulation of the kinds of liquor consumed, its pecuniary cost, methods of distribution, the time and place of drinking, and its availability to consumers according to age, sex, and other socioeconomic characteristics.

This model rests upon the conviction that the state or its agencies can determine what amounts and what forms of drinking have costly consequences. In most comprehensive form the model defines drinking as a privilege which, if abused, can be withdrawn from the individual; corollary to this is withdrawal of privileges, such as that of driving an automobile, which are affected by drinking. Archetypes of this model are found in the history of Scandinavian countries—particularly Sweden, home of the Gothenberg and Bratt systems of liquor control. Examples also come from the temperance orders of medieval Germany, possibly including the apocryphal *jus potandi*, the drinking code of orders given to heavy drinking.[40]

---

[38] D. D. Glad, "Attitudes and Experiences of American-Jewish and American-Irish Male Youths as Related to Differences in Adult Rates of Inebreity," *Quarterly Journal of Studies on Alcohol* 8 (1947): 406–72; Charles R. Snyder, *Alcohol and the Jews* (New York: Free Press, 1958).

[39] Giorgio Lolli, et al., *Alcohol in Italian Culture* (New York: Free Press, 1958).

[40] James Samuelson, *The History of Drink* (London: Trubner and Company, 1878), chap. VIII.

Government regulation of alcohol consumption grew up historically largely from nonmoral considerations. Among these were popular agitation that governments make fermented beverages equally available to localities and demands that the quality of such drinks be insured against fraud. The willingness of populations to accept taxes on alcohol production as a revenue measure has been an enticing path to regulation for financially hard-pressed governments.[41] This last possibility has caused a persistent dilemma for governing officials who have to choose between raising money the "easy way" and at the same time taking steps to diminish heavy drinking, which has the effect of decreasing revenue. The dilemma has been conspicuous in the history of Russia, where, under the Tzar's kabak system, and subsequently under the "farming out" system of vodka monopoly, the government abetted or encouraged widespread drunkenness.[42] The dilemma still lives today in muted controversies over the respective merits of licensing versus monopoly and trust systems of alcohol distribution.

Effective alcoholic beverage control may strike heavily at the economic values of producers and distributors even when it does not threaten drinking values of the population. If these elites are numerous and well organized, their resistance may well nullify efforts at regulation. A well-documented case in point is France, whose parliaments passed a series of regulatory laws after the First and Second World Wars. Yet the great power of the wine industry there has prevented anything beyond token enforcement of the laws. The presence of approximately a third of the electorate who are either workers in the wine industry or their family members does much to explain this phenomenon.[43] The so-called *bouillers de cru*, home distillers, who are entrenched in certain areas of France seem to defy regulation openly, protecting their traditional privileges largely through sheer power of numbers at the polls.

In the latter part of the nineteenth century, in some countries pressures from temperance groups exerted a mounting influence on government regulation. The result has been that regulation more and more reflected a power conflict between temperance organizations and those of the liquor industry. Regulations formulated by legislative bodies have been the incorporation less of consistent policy and designed control than of compromises, special concessions, exceptions, and arbitrary requirements.

[41] Catlin, *Liquor Control.*

[42] Vera Efron, "The Tavern and Saloon in Old Russia: An Analysis of I. G. Pryshov's Historical Sketch," *Quarterly Journal of Studies on Alcohol* 16 (1955): 484–505; W. E. Johnson, *The Liquor Problem in Russia* (Westerville, Ohio: American Issue Publishing Company, 1915).

[43] André Mignot, *L'Alcoolisme: Suicide Collectif de la Nation* (Paris: Cahiers des Amis de la Liberté, 1955), pp. 83 f.

The atmosphere of mutual distrust between the two power alignments, of which these have often been the products, is not conducive to enforcement.

As other power elites, such as health, welfare, and law-enforcement people, researchers, and tax officials, become more professionalized and articulate, their values and regulatory laws can become more symmetrical. Administrative rule-making also permits a more rational adaptation of means of control to ends. If the regulatory model is to work efficiently, however, conflicting elites must be able to believe that their values can be realized or preserved through regulation. Those persons and groups who have to bear the heaviest sacrifice of values must be able to find alternatives.

The organization and jurisdiction of regulatory agencies present as yet unsolved problems of this control model. In large, heterogeneous societies like our own and perhaps that of Russia, a high level of uniformity in regulations coupled with centralized control over alcohol use carries a strong probability of resistance. On the other hand extreme decentralization of control and dependence upon purely local agencies invite connivance and circumvention of rules where they deviate from local drinking customs or run counter to interests of local power elites.

Although this model is not designed to liquidate values associated with drinking or even drunkenness, it may nevertheless have this effect through regulations which significantly alter the form or pattern of drinking. In areas where public opinion does not support such regulations or the actions of the enforcing agencies, the result often is simply to add extraneous behavior to the form of drinking without appreciably modifying it. Thus a rule specifying that children and youth may not enter a liquor establishment unless food is served there may do nothing more than cause proprietors to install a bare minimum of restaurant equipment. Requirements that wine and liquor can only be served with meals may simply have the effect of adding the cost of a meal to the liquor bill.

Where lawyers or legal-minded elites set the policies of regulatory agencies there may be little understanding of the functions and values of drinking groups and related institutions. Historical studies and research reports both have shown a significant relationship between drinking groups and the persistence of primary groups' values.[44] Ignorance or disregard of such facts easily vitiates regulation. In this country many states have regulations against extending credit in bars and taverns. Yet frequently the success of such a place depends upon personal ties between customers and barkeepers. Hence many of the latter put drinks "on the tab" or

---

[44] John H. Kolb, *Emerging Rural Communities* (Madison: University of Wisconsin Press, 1959), pp. 60 f; Levy, *Drink*, pp. 25 f.

"hold" personal checks as a means of giving credit. Not only does the regulation often fail in its purpose, but it also plays a part in many bad-check offenses.

The chief means of implementing regulatory rules are suspensions and withdrawal of distributors' licenses or, in the case of monopoly systems, manipulating the number of outlets and their hours of sale. Along with these are the withdrawal or ration cards or "buyer surveillance," [45] techniques aimed at errant individual drinkers. Behind all of these is the possibility of police action for persistent and flagrant violators.

Distributors and retailers unquestionably can be hurt economically and made more receptive to rules by suspension or revocation of licenses. Furthermore, experiments in rural Finland have shown that placement of sales outlets does have some limited effects upon the kinds of alcoholic beverages consumed in certain population categories.[46] No workable methods yet have been invented to control the individual drinker or drinkers who want to "beat the system." If motivation is strong enough such persons will find ways of circumventing the regulations. Furthermore, controls focused upon the excessive drinker often inconvenience or alienate persons who comply with the form and meaning of the regulations. Even in Scandinavian countries, where a strong tradition of government paternalism prevails, ration cards and "buyer surveillance" have not been popular.[47]

This underscores the importance of public opinion in securing cooperation necessary for regulatory control. The cooperation of local law-enforcement officials is equally important. A broad area of responsibility for dealing with consequences of drinking must always remain with the local community because it must deal with disturbances of public order, offenses against the family, and juvenile offenses, which in varying degrees involve drinking and drunkenness. Legal procedures and coercive controls, such as fines and jail sentences, are poor methods for handling such cases because the consequences of punishment often are worse than the offense.

Model IV

The costs of intoxication and drunkenness can be reduced by substitution of functional equivalents of drinking.

[45] K. E. Lanu, *Control of Deviating Drinking Behavior* (Helsinki: Finnish Foundation for Alcohol Studies, 1956).

[46] Pekka Kuusi, *Alcohol Sales Experiment in Rural Finland* (Helsinki: Finnish Foundation for Alcohol Studies, 1957).

[47] Lanu, *Control.*

This model has received most attention in England where it has been the subject of investigation under the heading of "moderating influences" and "counter attractions."[48] It has interested those who see excessive drinking as a symptom of some kind of "deprivation" of human beings due to defects or omissions in social structures.[49] It carries the assumption that values satisfied through drinking or drunkenness can be fulfilled through other activities. It calls for an engineering-type reorganization of community life so that time, money, and interests devoted to drinking will be redirected into sports, games, gardening, radio listening, motion picture, travel, and similar diversions. Improved housing to make family life more attractive and building of community centers also are envisioned as part of this model.

In certain kinds of internally controlled or isolated community situations where boredom and apathy or social isolation have reached critical proportions, diversionary activities may very well decrease the extent of drunkenness. This has been observed in military encampments and isolated outposts.[50] Comparable data are also at hand in the history of a missionary system of control among Salish Indians of British Columbia where religious pageantry organized by Catholic Oblates for a time, at least, successfully replaced whiskey feasts and decreased other forms of drunkenness.[51]

It is, of course, naïve to expect to convert urban communities into analogues of military camps or missionary societies. Short of this the best that can be done is to introduce new programs, such as recreation, into situations where many other variables cannot be controlled, and to look for changes in the amount and forms of drinking. This is a crudely empirical procedure and can be very costly. Where heavy economic costs must be met, as in housing developments, business and governing elites will not easily support the programs.

Despite these reservations this model may have usefulness in many situations which occur in contemporary societies. Here we think of logging camps, long-term construction projects in sparsely settled areas, technical research teams, and diplomatic corps in foreign countries, as well as of military installations throughout the world. Wherever there are situations in which centripetal social integration operates, manipulation of social participation may be significant in reducing drunkenness.

[48] Levy, *Drink*.

[49] Robert F. Bales, "Cultural Differences in Rates of Alcoholism," *Quarterly Journal of Studies on Alcohol* 6 (1946): 482–98; Jean Poirier, "Les Sources de L'Alcool," *Alcool en Oceanie* No. 66 (Paris: Mission des Iles, 1956).

[50] Merrill Moore, "The Alcohol Problem in Military Service," *Quarterly Journal of Studies on Alcohol* 3 (1942): 244–56.

[51] Lemert, "The Life and Death of an Indian State."

This model has an appeal to the researcher because in the kinds of situations which have been specified it may lend itself to rigorous testing. An important task in such research would be to ascertain whether in given cultural contexts drinking is inescapably associated with attaining certain value satisfactions. The obverse of the question is whether drinking or drunkenness is symptomatic for societies in the same way that some psychiatrists hold it to be for individuals. This also merges into a query about the influence of values on the selection of narcotics, stimulants, and sedatives by societies, similar to the problem of "symptom choice" in psychiatry.

CONCLUSION

As yet, no model of social control has been evolved which has been greatly effective for diminishing the costs of excessive drinking. Research is complicated by the fact that the adoption of control programs and a decline in drunkenness both may be functions of changes in larger value systems. In general, those societies and groups which place a high value on sobriety and a low value on intoxication do not have a need for extensive social control. This is subject, however, to the qualification that drunkenness among a small number of persons whose roles express basic values of the society or drunkenness at vulnerable junctures in an industrial system magnifies the need for control. Presumably the necessary controls are more easily established under such conditions.

Societies which place a high premium upon the pleasures of drink and which have the greatest need for control are inclined to reject programs of control or to sabotage them if they are established. Members of these societies who do not share the drinking values or who perceive their high costs may be unable to make their voices heard in the arena of government or in community councils. If they do, they risk unpopularity and ostracism. France is an almost classic example of this situation.

Large societies with mixtures of ethnic minorities, diverse locality, and occupational groups make it unlikely that any one model will suffice to eliminate socially harmful drinking. The problem of choice of a model is complicated by the fact that drinking may be, in turn, a culture pattern, a symptom of psychic stress, a symbolic protest, or a form of collective behavior. Yet a technologically oriented society inexorably demands that drinking, whatever its form, not be permitted to disrupt crucial social integrations which cut across many groups. Formulation of these requirements in the areas of industry, communications, health, and family life probably can only be done by controlling elites "from above." Achievement of these minimum conformities in drinking behavior can best be implemented at the "grass roots" level in particular groups where resources for control at the level of informal interaction can be tapped and brought into play.[52]

An example of the possibilities in such a process was the decision of English labor groups and associations in the nineteenth century to remove their meetings from public houses. According to some writers,[53] this was important among other influences bringing about a decline in drunkenness during this period. Returning to our present-day situation, there is little hope that state officials or police can directly control such indigenous cultural growths as office parties at Christmas time, New Year celebrations, "martini luncheons," "beer-bust" picnics, and general weekend and holiday drinking behavior. It does seem possible, however, that employers' groups, professional groups, unions, clubs, and civic associations which are close to drinking phenomena can assume a larger share of responsibility for such control.

The problem of establishing communication between these groups and responsible control agencies is formidable, and it requires more than legal instrumentation. When drinking takes place adventitiously or when it is a form of protest or alienation from society—as with much teenage drinking and with "bottle gangs" in Skid Row—control through the cooptation of groups is difficult if not impossible. It is here that direct regulation, unsatisfactory though it may be, must be applied.

Control of any kind is a marginal influence in social and cultural change—a consideration no less true of action to reduce the costs of intoxication and drunkenness. Control cannot create behavior *de novo*, but it can strengthen existing tendencies by articulating unspoken values and by organizing the unorganized dissidents in a population. Further, it can define programs of action in a way to minimize resistance or gain the support of otherwise opposed or indifferent groups. Whether this can be done at the local, regional, or national level is a question best left to research and open-minded experimentation.

No effort has been made here to devise and discuss a model of control for the addictive drinker. Models suitable for limiting drunkenness in whole societies most assuredly will not apply to the alcoholic. The nature and ordering of values in these persons is such that they usually are unmoved or even made hostile by symbols of control which have an effect upon other drinkers. The extreme tensions under which they labor and their disturbed social interaction distort their value systems in complex ways which preclude the communication necessary for control. Such pathological drinkers presumably can be made responsive only through specially invented therapeutic models of control.

[52] Lanu, *Control.*
[53] Samuelson, *The History of Drink.*

6 THE LIFE AND DEATH OF AN INDIAN STATE

The Gulf of Georgia Salish tribes—the Homalthko, Tlahoose, Sliammon, and Seschelt—which are subjects of this report, present a challenging problem in Northwest Coast acculturation for the following reasons: (1) the almost complete sloughing-off at a relatively early contact period of their ceremonial culture (that is, of the potlatches and dancing rituals that are generally accepted as the main integrating features of Northwest Coast Indian cultures); (2) the relatively complete Catholicization of the tribes within a very short period of time, under the aegis and control of Bishop Durieu's "system"; and (3) the abrupt decay of this system of social control under the impact of external changes affecting the Indian communicants, and internal changes in the personnel and policy of the missionary order responsible for its origin and administration.

Space limitations here—and the oversight of Northwest Coast ethnographers—preclude a concise summation of the pristine culture of the four missionized tribes, other than to indicate that their Salish traits seemed to have had a recent overlay of Southern Kwakiutl culture, most pronounced in the Homalthko at the Bute Inlet but continuing down the mainland of British Columbia to the Seschelt.[1]

Reprinted by permission of the Society for Applied Anthropology from Human Organization 13 (1954): 23–27.

[1] Homer G. Barnett, "Notes on the Coast Salish of Canada," *American Anthropologist* 40 (1938): 118–41.

The Homalthko, Tlahoose, and Sliammon were bound together through a common language, intermarriage, and common winter ceremonials. Less frequent intermarriage and occasional mutual potlatching created tenuous ties between these three tribes and the Seschelt.

The first direct contact between these mainland Salish tribes and missionaries occurred in 1860 when two priests of the Oblates of Mary Immaculate made a brief reconnaissance of the Seschelt and, significantly, were driven away because the Indians "knew what white men are." [2]

Two years later a delegation from the same tribe arrived at New Westminster entreating the Oblate Fathers to establish a mission among them. A small chapel was promptly constructed at the Pender Harbor potlatch grounds to serve as a focus for mission activities. At first only a small nucleus of the converted Seschelt met for confession, mass, and guidance, but progress in conversion was so rapid that by 1871 the sacrament of confirmation was administered to the entire Seschelt tribe.[3]

So far as can be ascertained this set a record for proselytization on the Northwest Coast, from the standpoint of priority and universality of native response, that we believe to be unequalled—even by the much-heralded performance of Bishop Duncan among the Tsimshian at Metlakatla.[4]

Further, it can be affirmed accurately, if somewhat facetiously, that the belated claims for the Catholic entry into the historical missionary competition do not rest upon a tissue of baptismal records. The ritual confirmations of the Seschelt produced substantial changes in individual behavior, as well as a high degree of discontinuity in cultural form. The documentation of these points emerges with undeniable clarity in the description of Bishop Durieu's system.

THE SYSTEM

The model of the autarchic moral and economic order forged among the Seschelt, and later extended to the Squamish on the South and to the Homalthko, Tlahoose, and Sliammon on the North, bore unmistakable resemblances to the Jesuit mission prototype in seventeenth century

[2] Rev. George Forbes, "Origins of the Archdiocese of Vancouver" (unpublished, undated paper, from author's files).

[3] Rev. William Brabender, "Mission de Seschelt, Ses Penibles, Ses Epreuves, Ses Succès," *Missions des Missionaires Oblats* 253 (1935): 37–41.

[4] Homer G. Barnett, "Applied Anthropology in 1860," *Applied Anthropology* 1 (1942): 19–32.

Paraguay.[5] That the latter was Father Durieu's probable inspiration seems amply evidenced by his initial step when, in 1868, he brought together the five existing Seschelt tribes on what is now known as the Seschelt Peninsula, and by his later abortive attempt to communalize the Homalthko, Tlahoose, and Sliammon near Powell River. Danger and difficulty of travel, the shortage of missionaries, and habit rigidities born of spatial associations were practical considerations reinforcing the decisions behind these removals. A new spatial context, with a church and modern-type houses, proved as important to the socio-religious reconstitution of the Seschelt as it was to the Tsimshian at Metlakatla.

Father Durieu (later Bishop Durieu) initiated his zionistic project with the several propositions that:

> The Indian is weak in heart and mind . . . and must be ruled by religious motives. . . . He must be protected against himself and against evil-doers. . . . He must be paternally guided (for). . . . Indians are only big children . . . and hence (have) need for other than regular white law and control. . . .[6]

In retrospect, the system erected upon these articulate premises has, quite candidly, been designated by clerical commentators as an Indian State, with the Bishop, missionaries, or one or two resident priests acting as supervisors over instituted tribal theocracies. The functionaries at the local level included chiefs, subchiefs, watchmen, policemen, catechist, chanters, and sextons. However, not all of the tribes had the same complement of officials, nor were their functions comparable from one village to the next. The more complex differentiation occurred at Seschelt, where there were four chiefs, each with his own captains, watchmen, and policemen. In other villages, authority rested with two chiefs, one appointed by the government and the other by the supervisory priest, the latter being known as the "real" or eucharist chief. Some villages had two catechists, one for girls and another for boys. Watchmen served as truant officers to insure attendance at religious instruction meetings which, in early days, included adults as well as children; they also reported instances of misconduct and helped maintain old taboos, such as entering houses where there were pubescent girls or using property without the owner's permission. Chanters had the task of publicizing wrongdoing by reading

[5] Gabriel Dionne, "Histoire des Méthodes Utilisées Par Les Oblats de Marie Immaculée Dans L'Evangélization des Indiens Du 'Versant Pacifique' au Dixneuvième Siècle" (M.A. thesis, University of Ottawa, 1947), p. 150.

[6] Rev. E. M. Bunoz, "Bishop Durieu's System," Etudes Oblats 1 (1942): 193–209.

aloud a community inventory of sins prior to confession. The sexton was official bell-ringer, or "ting-ting" man, as an old French priest has quaintly called him.

Social control under the system resided with the local chief and two others who acted as judges in case of misbehavior, with the priest reserving the right to preside over hearings. The watchmen became the eyes of the court; the judges passed down punishments and native policemen carried them out. Final and effective authority, of course, flowed into this structure from the presence and direct intervention of the priests.

The positive compliances sought through this system of social control covered such things as learning prayers, catechism and hymns, observance of the Sabbath, and participation in church ritual. Important among its secular goals were the preservation and strengthening of aboriginal patterns of early marriage, incest rules, and respect for elders. Apart from these, the priests encouraged native communicants to build new houses and keep them painted and washed periodically with disinfectant, to plant gardens and fruit trees and, later, to construct water and lighting plants. The erection of monolithic white churches that loomed along the coastline over the smaller Indian homes in many ways became the primary focus of the social and economic life of these Salish Indian communities.[7]

In the early period of missionization, behavior to be avoided or "given up" received explicit and rigorous definition. Proscriptions largely concerned traditional ceremonial complexes and practices standing in a direct competitive relationship to Catholic dogma and ritual. Thus Bishop Durieu held uncompromisingly to four requirements: (1) the Indians must give up all primitive dances; (2) they must give up the potlatch; (3) they must cease all patronage of the shaman; and (4) they must give up drinking intoxicants and gambling. All of these proscriptions came to be included under a generalized concept of "temperance." The term symbolized a new way of life based upon a whole series of abstinences, rather than standing more narrowly for alcoholic abstinence as it did with Protestant missionaries.[8]

As might be expected from the nature of social control in aboriginal Salish society, in areas of behavior falling within the Bishop's rigorous code the local chiefs proved to be somewhat unsubstantial and vacillating surrogates of priestly authority. Consequently, direct sanctions were imposed by the priests themselves, who punished whole villages by omitting to visit them, in some cases for as long as two years. Errant individuals were brought to conformity by more familiar threats of excommunication,

---

[7] Ibid.

[8] Dionne, "Histoire des Méthodes."

withholding of baptism, communion, and the right to burial in consecrated ground. Civil penances supplemented and reinforced ritual penances. Thus drunkenness drew fines which went for the upkeep of the church and also unpleasant assignments of manual labor such as clearing fields of rocks. The more stringent penalty of flogging, involving forty lashes with arms outstretched, was kept for those who shirked church attendance and for cases of adultery. Adulterers also had their shame made public by having to stand side by side in front of the church during services.

If something has begun to sound familiar to the reader the impression will be extended by the nature of the sermons delivered by the priests, which bore directly and forcefully upon persons and events and, in many particulars, echoed the dramatic denunciations and foreboding sermons of John Cotton and Cotton Mather in seventeenth century New England. Thus epidemics of disease became grim evidence of God's punishment of wrongdoing by the Indians, or of their "scandals" as early priests preferred to term them.[9] The frequency of such cataclysms during the naissance period of Bishop Durieu's system indirectly became a source of continuing power for his priests.

The success of this system is most objectively measured against the objectives of the system itself or, perhaps, against those of the larger Catholic Church. While there is not sufficient space here to chronicle this success in the detail it merits, the documentary sources and our own unrewarded efforts to discover any substantial incidence of functioning aboriginal ritual in these tribes within the past fifty years leave it unquestioned. That the success of the system transcended its religious objectives is apparent from secular evaluations of the "Roman mission" at Seschelt made by travelers, Indian agents, and newspaper editors around the end of the century. The appellations of "moral" and "industrious" applied to the missionized natives in these independent assessments cue us to the cultural renovations finding favor with the essentially Protestant and nonreligious population of the Province.[10]

Some factors operating in the realization of Bishop Durieu's Indian State suggest themselves rather obviously; others are of a more subtle variety. They are as follows: (1) the relevance of the Oblate priests' leadership to the culture crises confronting the Seschelt, Homalthko, Tlahoose, and Sliammon at the end of the fur trade era; (2) syncretisms both intended and unintended; (3) the planned development of religious pageantry in keeping with the basic personality structure of the natives;

[9] Rev. P. E. C. Chirouse, "Missions Dans le District de St. Charles" (unpublished letter, 1879, from author's files).

[10] *Annual Report of the Department of Indian Affairs*, Dominion of Canada, Ottawa, 1880.

and (4) counterbalancing cultural innovations and residues of informal traditional culture.

That the fur trade period was one of crisis for Indian societies on the Northwest Coast few will deny; the real problem is to factor out aspects of the crisis which were most significant in the regional and local acculturative processes. Whereas missionaries have preferred to castigate cohabiting white men and alcoholic liquor as "demons of the piece," an equally good or superior case can be made for epidemic disease and increments of weath as the more disruptive elements. Impressive evidence can be marshaled to demonstrate that recurrent epidemics and high death rates struck crippling blows to the primitive societies in the culture area, undermined the faith of the Indians in their own institutions, and engendered widespread apathy among them. Less apparent but no less real was the strain imposed upon their social systems by the embarrassment of riches flowing from the fur trade.[11]

It is important that the Oblate priests were the only persons in the terminal fur trade period who concerned themselves with the plight of the Salish tribes under discussion. They traveled hundreds of miles through dangerous coastal waters to disease-prostrated villages no one else would enter, vaccinated thousands of Indians, dispensed medicines, and otherwise sustained them at the cost of no small personal discomfort and risk. In this connection, the special dedication and tight discipline of the newly-organized Oblates stood in sharp contrast to the missions of secular priests working elsewhere on the Coast.

Apart from these ministrations the Oblate priests gave the Indians hope, however specious it appears in retrospect, and they concretized this hope with new goals and activities. Specifically they organized church and house building, and other projects which gave both old and new meaning to the expenditure of money earned through trapping, fishing, and the logging industry.

The social structure superimposed by the Oblates allowed preexisting status differentials within the Salish tribes to be recognized; they ascribed roles with a moderate amount of prestige to chiefs and others whose loss of status otherwise might have been highly disruptive. It is probable that the limited number of somewhat spurious substitute roles with differentiated status sufficed for the Salish where they would not have for the Kwakiutl, for example, because the Salish lacked an elaborate system of chiefs and precisely delimited statuses that had to be reconciled with the new order. Continued recognition of hereditary status differences among the natives was made possible by special commendations and

---

[11] Irving Goldman, "The Alkatcho Carrier of British Colombia," in *Acculturation in Seven Indian Tribes,* ed. Ralph Linton (New York: Appleton-Century-Crofts, 1940).

titles bestowed by the missionaries for outstanding religious piety. Wealth could still be used to signify high status by making sizeable contributions of money for the construction and maintenance of church buildings and, at Seschelt, for the residential school. Although potlatches drew stern disapproval from the priests, feasts still could be used as status-symbolizing devices, subject only to slight modification. Likewise the aboriginal marriage custom of paying money to the parents of the bride survived, perhaps because it was not entirely alien to the French concept of a dowry.

Bishop Durieu had sufficient insight to perceive that what he and his missionaries proposed to do would badly fracture the native way of life and that, in effect, if important segments were pulled out of a social system something had to be put back. Consequently, although he was adamant that potlatching, winter ceremonials, and gambling be abandoned, he was equally insistent that they be replaced by church festivities and pageantry calculated to "capitalize on the Indian's love of display." It is precisely here, in the introduction of elaborate religious gatherings attended in some instances by thousands of Indians from the Coast and the interior, that we see the more unique contribution of Bishop Durieu that distinguished his system from the one at Metlakatla and from missionary programs in other coastal areas.

No complete description of these can be given, other than to specify services held in huge brush tabernacles with costly, decorated altars, long foot processions adorned with banners and torches of bengal fire, nocturnal canoe processions lighted by Japanese lanterns, pyrotechnic displays, and tableaux of the Passion Play presented by Indian actors, usually the Seschelt. The fervor and histrionic versatility with which the Salish peoples participated as actors and spectators in these activities amazed even the priests, and leave little doubt of the psychic usefulness of this pageantry to the natives. Although the gatherings were mass spectacles, tribal identities remained intact, with competitive participation and honorific expenditures figuring conspicuously in the interaction.[12]

It would be incorrect to contend that the reorganization of the various Salish societies in line with Bishop Durieu's grand design took place uniformly or without event and strain. Early and more complete conformity came at Seschelt, whereas the geographically removed Homalthko and Tlahoose seemed more reluctant to renounce their "scandals" —perhaps aided and abetted by their boisterous and unreconstructed Kwakiutl neighbors. The system created its deviants, particularly among those who disliked the petty espionage of the watchmen and among those subjected to severe punishments. The attenuation of the status of

[12] "Indian Gathering at St. Mary's," *The Month* 1 (1892): 188–90.

the chiefs and their intermediary position created further stress and unintegrated tensions.

The twin to revolution is reaction born of stresses and strains, and our data show no immunity of the Salish to these contingencies of discontinuous cultural change. But in their case, reaction took contrapuntal rather than destructive form. Episodic continuity with the past was maintained through informal interaction in the small group situation of the feast, and in the drinking or homebrew party, which one way or another became integrated with the new social system. The semi-clandestine drinking party that evolved out of the flagrant drunkenness of the fur trade period became an arena for the reaffirmation of old culture forms and values, expressed in drinking songs, feast songs, myth telling, ecstatic indulgence, and verbal tirades which kept alive old kinship rivalries. This interpretation is the application of an hypothesis we have developed and documented elsewhere as part of a more general analysis of the function of inebriation in Northwest Coast Indian cultures.[13]

In this case we can merely caption those data by pointing to the importance attached to the proscription of intoxication in Bishop Durieu's quadralogue of Indian sins. What we are suggesting is that this clerical disapproval arose less from Protestant temperance motives than from the early perception of the Oblates that whiskey feasts and drinking parties had become an integral part of the winter ceremonials of the Salish; to destroy the latter necessitated destruction of the former. This would explain the omnibus moral connotation of *la temperance*, to which reference has already been made.

DEATH OF THE SYSTEM

Bishop Durieu's system, like many species with an ephemeral life cycle, matured only to die. The first dramatic portent of its death came in 1892 with the arrest, trial, and conviction of a highly regarded Oblate priest, Father Chirouse, for his acquiescent role in the double flogging of an adulteress in one of the interior villages of the Lillooet Indians where the system also had been instituted. The trial was widely publicized and its effect was to damage seriously and weaken the entire social control system of the priests by removing its underlying sanction of force and coercion. The shadow of secular power inexorably cast itself across that of the priest.

However, more insidious forces had already been at work. By 1890 the geographic isolation of the four Salish tribes had begun to give way in the

---

[13] Edwin M. Lemert, *Alcohol and the Northwest Coast Indians* (Berkeley: University of California Press, 1954), pp. 303–406.

face of a steady infiltration of white settlers from the South and the East, expedited by the completion of a transcontinental railroad at Vancouver. Many of the natives soon learned English and when they did they promptly disregarded the chinook-speaking and other priest-designated authorities within the villages. This precipitous decline of delegated native leadership presently extended to an erosion of priestly authority, as the skepticism, agnosticism, and anti-Catholic attitudes of white loggers, fishermen, and others were communicated to the Indians.

In time a kind of anti-clericalism arose among the Salish in this area, vague at first, but centering with increasing clarity upon economic, educational, medical, and other intrusive problems with which the priests could give them little real assistance. Today, this anti-clericalism is most articulate among Indians between the ages of 45 and 60, some of whom speak with unrestrained bitterness of early days when the "French priests filled suit-cases with dollar bills to hoard and take back to France," or of priests who "kept them from going to school and held them back until it was too late." Easily aroused and frenetically expressed is the claim of these older Indians that "it was our money which built the church and the school —not the priests."

Some of the aged Indians still remain loyal to the symbols of the old system but nevertheless voice their discontent through invidious comparisons between the pioneer and present-day priests who, they complain, fulfill their duties in a perfunctory fashion and "always have their hand out for money." This special facet of anti-clericalism, reflecting the altered image of the priest, dates from approximately 1910, and has a realistic reference in erosive changes within the Oblates Order. And here is a rare convergence of the organic analogy with sociological fact, for literally as well as figuratively Bishop Durieu's system died with the death and retirement of its French and Belgian personnel. The Bishop's fond hope of recruiting a native priesthood never materialized and the Oblates failed to dispatch more missionaries from France. By 1910 a shortage of missionaries left a number of Salish reserves without priests.

Subsequently, English-speaking Oblates, largely of Irish origin, replaced the older generation of priests, tokening a shift in ethnic alignments within the order, or perhaps the outcome of a power struggle within the larger American Catholic Church. Whether the Church hierarchy grew fearful of the autonomous power of Bishop Durieu's Indian State is conjectural; no open rupture ever appeared as it did between Duncan and the Church Missionary Society over the proprietorship of the Indian colony at Metlakatla in 1877. However, in certain Church circles the tenets and practices advocated by Bishop Durieu have been criticized and to a large extent repudiated, at least tacitly, as a form of the heresy of Jansenism. This French sectarian movement had long been condemned for having "erred" in the direction of moral rigorism and overemphasis upon the forms of the mass, to the neglect of feelings and heart behind the ritual.[14] In other words, Bishop Durieu apparently was too much of a puritan for Catholic comfort, a judgment his own priests, who dared not drink wine in privacy, undoubtedly must have shared at times.

The other factors finalizing the decay of Bishop Durieu's system need little elaboration: increasing contacts with a brawling, bruising, largely male, white population; direct encroachments of Dominion, Provincial, and local governments on the authority and power of the chiefs and priests; institutional schooling of the young and their hospitalization for tuberculosis; and growing mobility and urbanization by taxi, motorboat, steamboat, and airplane. In terms of social control, the immediate repercussions of these changes were the breakdown of exogamous marriage rules, patrilocal residences, segregation of the sexes, and, most importantly, loss of respect of the young for their elders. In terms of deviant behavior the manifestations of change were more varied: Indian-white cohabitation, detribalization of women, illegitimacy, prostitution, thievery, off-reserve drunkenness, and highly destructive intrafamily and interfamily conflict.

Today there is little left of Bishop Durieu's system beyond pathetic coteries of a few elderly Salish who still follow the lead of two old former watchmen, one a Homalthko the other a Tlahoose, and an ancient bell-ringer at Sliammon. Middle-aged Salish observe an uneasy truce with the Church for the purposes of baptism, marriage, and burial. A number of the younger men openly rebel against the priest as well as against their parents, pointedly refusing to do his bidding in such things as attending church, marrying at an early age, and remaining sober. This year for the first time in their history a group of the Homalthko got drunk while the priest was visiting their reserve, an indignity ordinarily reserved for the Indian agent.

For the perspective of the student of social organization and social control, the social systems of the early Salish can be seen as resting upon a fabric of cues and symbols which limited individual responses and ordered overt actions into appropriate spheres. Bishop Durieu's system was a generically similar alternative in that it too was implemented by moral prescription and by external rather than internal controls. However, the shift from one system to the other was largely at the level of overt behavior.

The failure of the missionary system to induce changes at the level of attitudes, sentiments or "latent" culture was recognized and commented upon by the priests themselves. Specifically the priests inveighed against the obvious disposition of the Indians to lie in their public confessions. This

---

[14] St. Cyres, "Jansenism," in the *Encyclopedia of Religion and Ethics*, ed. James Hastings (New York: Scribner's, 1951).

reluctance to publicly admit misconduct, particularly by higher-ranking persons, is quite understandable in the light of the sensitivity to shame indoctrinated in the individual in Northwest Coast cultures. The other area of failure of the system had to do with attitudes toward communion. Apparently, the priests never were able to inspire fear of the communion ritual that typically is manifested by white Catholics. Durieu commented a little ruefully that the natives looked upon communion as a pleasant experience and would take it every day if it were offered.[15]

In actuality neither the native control system nor its religious successor had the potentialities for survival in a society that demands more flexible adjustments and a creative intelligence from its members.

[15] Dionne, "Histoire des Méthodes."

III

some forms
of
deviance

7 AN ISOLATION AND CLOSURE
THEORY OF NAIVE CHECK FORGERY

The research on forgery we report here is inspired by the methodological dissent from older formulations in criminology—formulations
which incorporated generalizations covering all crime and all criminals. At
the same time our report is a part of that dissent. As such it seeks to build
in a cumulative way upon the work of Hall and Sutherland, who have insisted that criminological research will best advance through the study of
sociologically defined units of criminal behavior.[1] Over and beyond this,
ready justification for the inquiry rests in the paucity of descriptive data
available on the crime of forgery itself and the almost complete absence of
efforts at its systematic analysis.[2]

Reprinted by special permission of The Journal of Criminal Law, Criminology and Police Science, *copyright © 1953 by the Northwestern University
School of Law, 44, No. 3 (September–October 1953): 296–307.*

[1] Jerome Hall, *Introduction to Theft, Law and Society* (Indianapolis:
Bobbs-Merrill, 1935); E. H. Sutherland, *Principles of Criminology*, rev. ed.
(New York: Lippincott, 1947), chap. 13.
[2] While there are incidental data on forgery scattered through the
literature on crime, we note only two descriptive articles exclusively devoted to
forgery: I. A. Berg, "A Comparative Study of Forgery," *Journal of Applied
Psychology* 28 (1944): 232–38; David Maurer, "The Argot of Forgery," *American Speech* 16 (1941): 243–50; some attempt at the analysis of the forger's
behavior will be found in John Gillin, *The Wisconsin Prisoner* (Madison: Uni-

In the process of collecting and analyzing our data it soon became apparent that the invocation of many of our more generalized theories of crime provided only minimal insight into the cases which came under our purview. Culture conflict, delinquency area background, emotional conflict, and others proved either to be completely irrelevant or nondiscriminating theories so far as causation was concerned. While Sutherland's concept of differential association appeared as a necessary factor in the explanation of professional forgery it was found to be unrelated in any important way to the class of forgery cases we chose to consider, namely, naive check forgeries. Hence, a considerable amount of innovating became necessary in order to explain and interpret our research findings. A preliminary of our theoretical formulation was the definition of the behavior unit subsumed under naive check forgery.

In terms of generic or common law, forgery is thought of as the false signing of a legal instrument which creates a liability. This holds even if or when the entire legal instrument if false and only gives the appearance of legality. Thus defined, forgery covers a wide variety of acts, such as forging wills, public documents, sales slips, and prescriptions for narcotic drugs. It is not our purpose to propound a theory subsuming all such acts but rather one for check forgeries only. This includes all acts commonly charged as forgery, fictitious checks, issuing checks without sufficient funds, and uttering and passing falsified checks. The theory cannot without further research be applied to forgeries arising out of mail thefts or out of the theft and the raising of money orders.

The concept of naive forgery was devised to indicate forgeries committed by persons who have had no previous criminal record and no previous contact and interaction with delinquents and criminals. It is designed to exclude forgeries which are incidental to the commission of other crimes, and forgeries which are retrogressive or progressive phases of an already established criminal career. Common examples of the types of forgeries eliminated would be those of burglars who come onto a drawer full of checks in burglarizing a business office and often—not too wisely—cash them. We also exclude the forgeries committed by embezzlers, as well as the occasional forgeries of con men, chiefly because they are incidental or alternative techniques by which their crimes are committed. The embezzler is further distinguished from the forger by his being in a position of trust.

The validity of our delimitation of the class of forgeries about which

---

versity of Wisconsin Press, 1946), p. 167; an informal historical treatment of the subject is at hand in Henry T. F. Rhodes, *The Craft of Forgery* (London: John Murray, 1934).

TABLE 7–1. *Prior Record of 1023 Persons Convicted for Forgery in Los Angeles County 1938 and 1939.*

Nature of prior record	Number	Percent
No prior record	306	29.9
Prior forgery only	189	18.5
Prior forgery plus other crimes	211	20.6
Other crimes only	317	30.9
Total	1023	99.9

we seek to generalize may be questioned on the grounds that it narrows excessively the universe of crimes and correspondingly decreases the usefulness of our generalizations. The answer to any such question we hold will be found in the nature of the prior records of those convicted of forgery. From the following tabulation we can make several important observations on this point. First we see that almost one-third of the forgers had no prior record whatsoever and almost one-half were either in this class or had committed only prior forgeries. In the other two categories there are included substantial numbers of persons convicted on petty theft or grand theft charges which in actuality were forgeries but which for legal reasons were prosecuted otherwise. Also there was a sizeable number of persons whose records involved forgeries plus drunkenness or drunkenness only, which cases we may regard as involving persons essentially without criminal sophistication. Finally there was a fair number of cases such as those of sex offenders, offenders against family laws, desertions from the armed forces, and certain federal offenses (illegal entry, impersonating an officer) which do not presume criminal associations or learning. Altogether we would be inclined to add another 27 percent of the cases to our general category of naive forgeries, thus raising the total to 75 percent for which our theory is pertinent.

Our theory of naive check forgery as delimited above can be stated in terms of (a) the characteristics of the crime; (b) the person; (c) the situation; and (d) the sociopsychological process. The hypothesis in general is that naive check forgery arises at a critical point in a process of social isolation, out of certain types of social situations, and is made possible by the closure or constriction of behavior alternatives subjectively held as available to the forger. We will attempt to show how the four enumerated factors operate both directly and in interaction with one another to produce the crime.

THE CHARACTERISTICS OF CRIME

A number of crimes such as robbery, assault, rape, certain forms of theft, and burglary are high visibility crimes in that they are either objectively apparent to others or subjectively perceived by their perpetrators as crimes prior to or at the time they are committed. In contrast to these, check forgeries, especially those committed by first offenders, have low visibility. There is little in the criminal act or in the interaction between the check passer and the person cashing the check to identify it as a crime. Closely related to this special quality of the forgery crime is the fact that while it is formally defined and treated as a felonious or "infamous" crime it is informally held (by the legally untrained public) to be a relatively benign form of crime.[3] The combined effect of these two factors, we will show, facilitates the subjective acceptance of a particular criminal solution to the crisis situation.

THE PERSON

The concept of person is used here simply as a way of delimiting the class of people most likely to commit forgery when situational and socio-psychological factors are present and operate in certain sequence. Generally speaking, forgers tend to be native white in origin, male, and much older than other criminals when they commit their crimes—somewhere in their very late twenties and early thirties. Their intelligence is much higher than that of other criminals and they equal or surpass the general population in the number of years of education they have completed. The occupational classes contributing disproportionately to the population of forgers are clerical, professional, and skilled or craft workers. More particularly, salesmen within the clerical group have a greater-than-expected representation among persons convicted of this crime. Some forgers come from prestigeful, wealthy families in which siblings have achieved considerable social eminence. A large percentage of forgers for many years have been residents of the community in which their crimes are committed. According to comparisons we have made between the past records of forgers and those of burglars and robbers the former are less likely to have a record of juvenile delinquency. From this and the data of our interview sample we are convinced that very few forgers have originated from the so-called delinquency areas of their communities.[4]

---

[3] This inconsistency has a long history. See Rhodes, ibid., p. 22.

[4] The data for this paper consist of statistical materials compiled on 1023 cases of forgery in Los Angeles County for 1938 and 1939 and a sample

The description of forgers in terms of temperament and personality tendencies is a much more hazardous academic task than their demographic characterization. Nevertheless, we will suggest certain differentials of this sort, chiefly because of their rather uniform occurrence in the interview data. The most obtrusive of these appeared as a distaste or sense of repugnance toward forms of crime other than forgery. In case after case come the unsolicited "I could never hurt anyone," or "I wouldn't have the nerve (or guts) to rob anyone or to steal." While all criminals tend to rationalize their crimes somewhat in the prison situation, evidence that we were confronted with real differentials came from other sources, namely, the experience of detectives, who say they seldom if ever have trouble arresting a forger; often they are waiting for the police to come, or they voluntarily give themselves up. Guns are very rarely found in the possession of persons arrested on forgery charges and when they are it is usually a case of some other type of criminal casually turned to check passing. It is also true that inmates of prisons recognize a temperamental difference of forgers, sharply distinguishing them from men in the so-called heavy rackets.[5]

Detectives who have dealt many years with forgers depict them generally as people who are personally likeable and attractive, who easily ingratiate themselves and who have a facile grasp of the arts of convincing others. They are people who like to live well and fast, being able to con a merchant or "snow a dame under" with equal dispatch. As one burglar (nonforger) put it: "Forgers are guys who like to pretend to be someone they ain't." In addition it has been observed that an element of impulsiveness seems to thread through the behavior of forgers, being detectable even among professionals, who, for example, have expressed to the writer their dislike for con games because of the slow "buildup" involved.

Because the observations we record above refer to sophisticated forgers as well as to naive forgers it is difficult to say to what extent such personal tendencies exist in nascent form in the previous histories of forgers and how far they have been the function of the life a forger must necessarily pursue once committed to his check passing. However, it is hard to escape the idea that some sort of precriminal personal differentiae are present in the winsomeness and tempo of behavior shown by persons who resort to check forgery.

of 29 forgers interviewed by the writer at the Los Angeles County Wayside Honor Rancho. Interviews lasted from 45 minutes to two hours. We are indebted to the Los Angeles County Sheriff's department and especially to Captain Harold Stallings for making available facilities and permission to conduct the interviews. In general what we have said thus far about the population of forgers is corroborated by the findings of Berg, "A Comparative Study."

[5] Berg, "A Comparative Study."

In summary at this point it can at least be stated that forgers come from a class of persons we would ordinarily not expect to yield recruits to the criminal population. By definition, of course, naive forgery is a crime of persons who are unacquainted with criminal techniques; but aside from this the persons involved would appear to have acquired normal attitudes and habits of law observance. It follows that naive forgery emerges as behavior which is out of character or "other than usual" for the persons involved. In the act of forging an ephemeral personal reorganization occurs in response to situational interactors which may be recognized as a special symbolic process conceived to cover aspects of motivation, feeling, emotion, and the choice of adjustment alternatives. The personal differentiae we have set down here are the original broad limits within which a certain class of situations can impinge upon the person with the possibility of emergent forgery.

THE SOCIAL SITUATION

That the social situation is a dynamic factor in naive check forgery is obvious from even the most cursory reading of case history materials, and it has been commented upon widely by probation officers, judges, social workers, and others who have come into contact with forgers. Such contingencies as unemployment, business failure, gambling losses, dishonorable discharge and desertion from the armed forces, alcoholic sprees, family and marital conflict, and separation and divorce all figure prominently in the case histories of naive check forgers. Yet to set down such critical experiences as "causes" of forgery is only indicative and not discriminating, because many people similar in background to naive forgers confronted by similar crises do not seek a solution by forgery. A more discriminating factor was suggested by the unusually high rate of divorce and separation among married forgers and the high incidence of family alienation and repudiation among single forgers. The very high rates of marital disruption for our cases can be seen in Table 7–2. Even when allowances are made for the somewhat higher divorce rate to be unexpected in a middle-class group such as our forgers it will be appreciated that the rate remains inordinately high.

Examination of case history documents and our interview materials revealed that the marital breakups of the persons who later became forgers often were exceptionally rough, and usually grossly traumatic experiences, particularly from the view of their subjective impact. The marital ruptures quite frequently were followed by continuous drunkenness, job inefficiency, occupational detachment, and occupational mobility, often in decided contrast to the predivorce history. This, of course, is not to say that the

TABLE 7–2. *Marital Status of 473 Persons Convicted of Forgery and 53 Persons Convicted of Grand Theft in Los Angeles County 1938.*

	Forgery No.	Forgery Percent	Grand Theft No.	Grand Theft Percent	Los Angeles City Population, Percent
Single	118	24.9	16	30.1	30.8
Married	172	36.3	25	47.1	54.9
Divorced, Widowed or Separated	183	38.6	12	22.6	15.3*
Totals	473	99.8	53	99.8	100

* Includes divorced, widowed, and "wives not present in home." *United States Census,* 1940, pp. 182, 190, Tables 8 and 11.

marital breakups always initiated the social isolation, for in some cases it was a non-marital crisis which led to excessive drinking, sexual promiscuity, or loss of earning, which, in turn, resulted in separation and divorce. However, in nearly all cases the isolating experiences tended to be progressive and mutually reinforcing.

Among the forgers with no marital experiences, isolation was perceived as alienation from the parental family, with the concept of "black sheep" being fairly expressive of the family status involved. We also noted among both the single and married forgers a number of persons who had begun their adult lives with social status from which social isolation could be inferred; here we refer to persons with physical handicaps, members of ethnic minorities, orphans and step-children, and the occasional homosexual. In all 29 of our interview cases we were able to find at least one measure of social isolation and in most of them, multiple measures.[6] This may be seen in the accompanying table.

[6] Specifically: *occupational isolation* was taken as unemployment, job instability (some cases had as many as 20 or 30 different jobs per year), or conditions of work separating the person from his customary association; *marital isolation* was taken as divorce, separation, or alienation of spouses; *family isolation* was taken as an invidious position in the parental family due to educational, occupational, or economic inadequacy; *ethnic isolation* was taken as isolation due to race or national status, i.e., a rural Negro migrant, a second generation Portuguese in conflict with parents and his neighborhood, a Jew who due to bankruptcy and sexual immorality was alienated from other Jews as well as gentiles; *physical* and *"other" isolation* was that of physically handicapped persons, homosexuals in conflict, and the deviants we mention in the text above; *subjectively felt isolation* was taken as a sense of isolation expressed in response to direct questions on the subject.

TABLE 7–3. *The Frequency of Occurrence of Measures of Social Isolation in 29 Cases of Naïve Check Forgery, Los Angeles County, 1951.*

Case No.	Measures of Isolation			Ethnic, Physical, "other"	Subjectively Felt Isolation	Case Frequency
	Occupational	Marital	Family			
1	X		X	X		3
2			X	X		2
3	X		X	X		3
4	X			X	X	3
5	X	X				2
6	X	X		X	X	4
7	X			X		2
8	X	X	X			3
9	X			X		2
10		X		X		2
11	X		X		X	3
12	X	X		X	X	4
13			X	X	X	3
14	X	X				2
15	X		X	X		3
16		X	X	X		3
17	X	X			X	3
18	X		X	X	X	4
19		X			X	2
20			X		X	2
21	X	X			X	3
22	X					1
23			X			1
24	X	X	X		X	4
25		X			X	2
26	X	X				2
27	X		X	X	X	4
28			X	X		2
29	X	X		X		3
Totals	20	14	14	16	13	77

Assuming we have established situational isolation as the more general prerequisite for the commission of naive check forgery it is still necessary to factor out more specific situational factors conducive to the crime. These we believe are found in certain dialectical forms of social behavior, dialectical in the sense that the person becomes progressively involved in them. These behaviors are further distinguished in that they make imperative the possession of money or money substitutes for their continuance or fulfillment. They are objective and identifiable and once a person is committed to them the impetus to "follow through" with them is implicit. A quick example is that of a man away from home who falls in with a small group of persons who have embarked upon a two- or three-day or even a week's period of drinking and carousing. The impetus to continue the pattern gets mutually reinforced by interaction of the participants, and tends to have an accelerated beginning, a climax, and a terminus. If midway through such a spree a participant runs out of money the pressures immediately become critical to take such measures as are necessary to preserve the behavior sequence. A similar behavior sequence is perceived in that of the alcoholic in a bar who reaches a "high point" in his drinking and runs out of money. He might go home and get clothes to pawn, or go and borrow money from a friend, or even apply for public relief, but these alternatives become irrelevant because of the immediacy of his need for alcohol. Another example, fairly common during the late war, is that of the individual who impersonates a high-ranking army officer or public official and get increasingly involved in a whole set of reciprocal obligations, which, when his money is exhausted he must implement with false credit or worthless checks. Otherwise he must expose himself or put an end to the whole fraudulent business by leaving town, as he often does.

We encountered several cases in which forgeries occurred around Christmas time, and the evidence seems strong that the institutionalized, cumulative social pressures to engage in buying behavior at this time (symbolized in newspaper box-scores of the "number of shopping days left before Christmas" and "getting the Christmas spirit") were real factors in building up a sense of crisis leading to forgeries. The sense of social isolation among the forgers detached from their families also was intensified during this holiday period. It was our further impression that many of the type situations more specifically leading to forgeries—gambling, borrowing, and "kiting" to meet debts and business obligations, desertion, and escaping authorities, and being the bon vivant tended to be dialectical, self-enclosed systems of behavior in the sense that the initial behaviors called for "more of the same." While making the possession of money critically necessary they also reinforced or increased the social isolation of the indulgee; many forgers admitted that at the time such behavior was perceived as having a "false structure" to it.

THE SOCIOPSYCHOLOGICAL PROCESS—CLOSURE

Thus far we have spoken of the election of check forgery as a behavior alternative in relation to the general social isolation of the person and in relation to his involvement in collective or institutionalized behavior dialectics directly dependent upon the use of money or symbolic substitutes for money. It is also necessary to note the way in which the socio-psychological processes in the person interact with them to produce check forgeries. The special process is one of closure. This we take to mean a process whereby the tension initiated by a situation is resolved and the configuration (whether of behavior or of mental process) tends to be as complete or "closed" a condition as the circumstances permit. The concept denotes a "demand for meaning" as well as a fitting or selection from alternative modes of behavior to resolve a critical situation.[7] As it operates in check forgery it is a total behavioral response, more frequently impulsive and unverbalized than deliberative or narrowly perceptual.

The significant fact to account for in our data was the apparent contradiction of well-educated, often gifted, and certainly otherwise law-abiding persons electing a criminal alternative as a solution in this closure process. A second fact to explain is why they selected the particular crime of check forgery. Beginning with the second fact we can say rather simply that the class of persons committing naive check forgery do not have the skills nor are they in a position to carry out or "close on" most other forms of crime. Furthermore, in contrast to many other types of crime no special skills or knowledge are needed in order to manufacture and pass worthless or even forged checks. In thus commenting upon what may be an obvious fact we digress somewhat to discuss the importance of prior learned behavior in commission of this crime.

The first thing to be said in this connection is that forgery (excluding actually imitating other people's signatures) is very simple to perform; it is probably the easiest major crime to commit that we have. Most people in their everyday transactions have occasions to cash personal or payroll checks and hence encounter all the precautions business uses to prevent the making and uttering of bad checks. From this it is arguable that the criminal defense measures adopted by business become in effect an inverted education in the simple essentials of forgery. We can also hold with good reason that in a competitive society which modally creates aggressive temperament they become a challenge to contrive workable evasions of the protective devices. We see this in the resentment shown by "honest" customers at having their checks questioned and in the gamelike characteristics of many of the techniques invented and employed by forgers.

The point we dwell upon here was demonstrated by asking a college class of 25 students to write brief accounts of how they would obtain and pass a bad check if circumstances forced them to do so. The results showed that while the range of ingenuity was wide, nevertheless about the same

---

[7] See J. F. Brown and D. W. Orr, "The Field Theoretical Approach to Criminology," *Journal of Criminal Psychopathology* 3 (1941): 236–52; Cesar Castillo, "Una Teoría Gestalgica del Delito," *Archivo de Medicina Legal* (Buenos Aires) 18 (1948): 387–96.

class of techniques were described as those actually employed by the forgers in our sample. Only one female student was unable to devise a workable scheme. Sources of the ideas in a few cases were listed as radio programs and crime fiction, but most students simply put down "experience with checking account," "experience in retail stores," or "just imagination." Quizzing of the naive forgers in our interview group revealed few or none who could trace in retrospect the sources of their specific forgery behavior.

Another reason for the congeniality of the check forgery alternative lies in the previously mentioned facts that while it is formally treated as a serious crime, informally it is held to be a relatively minor offense and indeed in some forms not a legal offense at all. Thus when the situation or special variations in the subjective reactions of the person dissociate the more formal business and legal control symbols from the act it becomes a more attractive or acceptable choice for the crisis-bound individual. It is in this connection that the low social visibility of the crime excludes social clues which otherwise would weigh the forgery choice with unpleasant connotations for the self and person considering it.

Even more important than the low social visibility of check forgery in suspending the formal control symbols of this crime is the social isolation of the person. In general we believe from our data that this isolation brings about a real, albeit ephemeral, suspension, abeyance or distortion of the internal aspects of social communication. It led in our forgery cases to an attenuation of what Mead called the "inner forum of thought," and lowered sensitivity to the "generalized others" which might otherwise have produced a rejection or inhibition of the criminal alternative of forgery. The evidence for this came out in strong feelings of unpleasantness immediately following first forgeries, in the tendency for naive check forgers to give themselves up to the police, in great feelings of relief on being arrested, in desires to "pay their debts to society," in extreme puzzlement as to how they "ever could have done it," and in personality dissociations attributing the behavior to "another me," or to a "Dr. Jekyll-Mr. Hyde" complex.

A high degree of tension appeared in practically all of our cases, being manifested as a sense of urgency which also contributed greatly to the disturbance of the subjective aspects of the communication process.[8] In some cases this sense of urgency, as we have shown, arose from commitments to certain types of dialectical social behaviors. In other cases the sense of urgency seemed to arise from special definitions of the social situation. In

[8] It is to be noted that Lottier found a high degree of tension to be a significant factor in embezzlement, which bears many similarities to forgery. Stuart Lottier, "A Tension Theory of Criminal Behavior," *American Sociological Review* 7 (1942): 840–48.

such cases there appeared to be a heavy discharge of socially unshared or private meanings into the circumstances of the crime. The insurgency of these private meanings into the thought processes seemed clearly to be a function of the social isolation of the person.

Some of these private meanings proved to be specialized extensions of common cultural meanings. Thus, for some of the check forgers ordinary expenditure behavior in our society took on a desperate kind of meaning. Indulgence in clothes, automobiles, housing, and expensive leisure time pursuits seemed to fulfill intricate, specialized socio-psychological functions over and beyond the satisfactions people ordinarily or "modally" receive from buying such things. These people "get the bug," as one detective put it; they become fixated upon some object and spend most if not all of their waking moments scheming how to obtain it. Such fixating, in part a response to high pressure advertising and selling methods, is, we urge, more commonly the reaction of the socially isolated person.

In other cases the tension or sense of urgency felt by the person who resorted to check forgery emerged out of definitions of the situation which were more intimately personal perhaps interpersonal. In such instances checks or money came to have a special symbolic value apart from any which the culture assigns to them. Thus in a number of cases strong elements of aggression figured in the forgery act, often aggression against a particular person. In one such case a youthful epileptic man with a well-defined sense of isolation passed an illegal check immediately after quarreling with his father and preparing to leave for another city. While his need for money to travel was urgent, still it is significant that he wrote the check in such a way as to embarrass his father in the local community.

In many cases the impression is strong that forgery of checks becomes a way of punishing "others" or the "self," with banks, department stores, loan companies, and material objects taking on very private meanings for the check criminal. While it is not always clear just what these meanings are nevertheless they constrict the choices of behavior in the situation. In order to satisfy the immediate special subjective needs of the individual, such as aggression against a particular person or organization he must exploit the situation as it arises, or, in more familiar terminology, "strike while the iron is hot." The several or many legal alternatives which might serve the same function as a bogus check are "out of place" to him, or else the time required to use them causes them to lose their value to him.

The importance of the sense of urgency in narrowing the range of subjectively acceptable means of meeting the forger's crisis was supported in our data by the fact that as a group our forgers were not without resources. They possessed good clothes, jewelry, sporting equipment, and other things which could have been pawned or sold; some had families and relatives from whom they might have borrowed money. Some actually had money in the bank at the time the bad check was passed, and some had bonds which could have been cashed to obtain money. Indeed, one of our forgers was a wealthy landowner with large amounts of money on deposit in England and Australia.

8 THE BEHAVIOR OF THE SYSTEMATIC CHECK FORGER

The concept of behavior systems in crime was first approximated in this country in Hall's analysis of several types of larceny in terms of their historical, legal, and social contexts.[1] Later the concept was made explicit and formulated into a typology by Sutherland and by Sutherland and Cressey.[2] Although this has hitherto inspired only a few monographic studies, there seems to be a growing consensus that focusing attention on specific orders of crime or making behavior systems the unit of study holds considerable promise for criminological research.[3]

Reprinted with permission from Social Problems 6 *(Fall 1958): 141–48.*

[1] Jerome Hall, *Theft, Law and Society,* 2d ed. (Indianapolis: Bobbs-Merrill, 1952).

[2] Edwin H. Sutherland, "The Professional Thief," *Journal of Criminal Law and Criminology* 28 (1937): 161–63; Edwin H. Sutherland, *Principles of Criminology,* rev. ed. (New York: Lippincott, 1947); Edwin H. Sutherland and D. Cressey, *Principles of Criminology,* 5th ed. (New York: Lippincott, 1955); Alfred R. Lindesmith and H. W. Dunham, "Some Principles of Criminal Typology," *Social Forces* 19 (1941): 307–14; L. Puibaraud, *Les Malfaiteurs de Profession* (Paris: E. Flammarion, 1893); W. A. Bonger, *Criminality and Economic Conditions* (Boston: Little, Brown, 1916), pp. 579–89; H. W. Gruhle and L. Wetzel, eds., "Verbrechentype," cited in Bonger, ibid., p. 581.

[3] Walter C. Reckless, *The Crime Problem,* 2d. ed. (New York: Appleton-Century-Crofts, 1955), p. 134.

Because this paper proposes to assess the usefulness of Sutherland's formulation of the behavior system in analyzing or understanding the behavior of the systematic check forger, the typology outlined in his study of the professional thief will be employed. The five elements of the behavior system of the thief are as follows: (1) stealing is made a regular business; (2) every act is carefully planned, including the use of the "fix"; (3) technical skills are used, chiefly those of manipulating people; this differentiates the thief from other professional criminals; (4) the thief is migratory but uses a specific city as a headquarters; and (5) the thief has criminal associations involving acquaintances, congeniality, sympathy, understandings, rules, codes of behavior, and a special language.[4]

Altogether 72 persons currently serving sentences for check forgery and writing checks with insufficient funds were studied. Three additional check offenders were contacted and interviewed outside of prison. The sample included eight women and 67 men, all of whom served time in California correctional institutions.

Thirty of the 75 check criminals could be classified as systematic in the sense that they (1) thought of themselves as check men; (2) had worked out or regularly employed a special technique of passing checks; and (3) had more or less organized their lives around the exigencies or imperatives of living by means of fraudulent checks. The remaining 45 cases represented a wide variety of contexts in which bogus check passing was interspersed with periods of stable employment and family life, or was simply an aspect of alcoholism, gambling, or one of a series of criminal offenses having little or no consistency.

FINDINGS

Projected against the typology of professional theft, the behavior of the persons falling into the systematic check forgery category qualified only in a very general way as professional crime. In other words, although it is possible to describe these forgeries as *systematic*, it is questionable whether

[4] Edwin H. Sutherland, *The Professional Thief* (Chicago: University of Chicago Press, 1937); Sutherland, "The Professional Thief," *Journal of Criminal Law*; Marshall B. Clinard, *Sociology of Deviant Behavior* (New York: Holt, Rinehart & Winston, 1957), pp. 256–62; Reckless, *The Crime Problem*; R. S. Cavan, *Criminology* (New York: Thomas Y. Crowell, 1948), chap. V; Mabel Elliott, *Crime in Modern Society* (New York: Harper & Row, 1942), chap. IV; David W. Maurer, *Whiz Mob*, No. 24 (Gainesville, Fla.: American Dialect Society, 1955); Hans Von Hentig, "The Pickpocket: Psychology, Tactics and Technique," *Journal of Criminal Law and Criminology* 34 (1943): 11–16; H. A. Fregier, *Les Classes Dangereuses de la Population dans Les Grandes Villes* (Paris: Chex J. B. Ballière, 1840).

more than a small portion of them can be subsumed as *professional* under the more general classification of professional theft. A point-by-point comparison will serve to bring out the numerous significant differences between systematic forgery and professional theft.

1. Forgery as a "regular business."

It is questionable whether check men look upon their crimes as a "regular business" in the same way as do members of "other occupational groups" who "wish to make money in safety." [5] In virtually all cases the motivation proved to be exceedingly complex. This fact was self-consciously recognized and expressed in different ways but all informants revealed an essential perplexity or conflict about their criminal behavior. The following statement may be taken as illustrative:

> Nine out of ten check men are lone wolves. Those men who work in gangs are not real check men. They do it for money; we do it for something else. It gives us something we need. Maybe we're crazy. . . .

The conflicts expressed involved not merely the rightness or wrongness of behavior; they also disclosed a confusion and uncertainty as to the possibility of living successfully or safely by issuing false checks. All of the cases, even the few who had a history of professional thieving, admitted that arrest and imprisonment are inevitable. None knew of exceptions to this, although one case speculated that "it might be done by an otherwise respected business man who made one big spread and then quit and retired."

The case records of the systematic check forgers gave clear testimony of this. Generally they had but shortlived periods of freedom, ranging from a few months to a year or two at the most, followed by imprisonment. Many of the cases since beginning their forgery careers had spent less total time outside prisons than within, a fact corroborated by the various law-enforcement officers queried on the point.

Many of the check men depicted their periods of check writing as continuous sprees during which they lived "fast" and luxuriously. Many spoke of experiencing considerable tension during these periods, and two cases developed stomach ulcers which caused them to "lay off at resorts." A number gambled and drank heavily, assertedly to escape their internal stress and sense of inevitable arrest. A number spoke of gradual build-up of strain and a critical point just before their arrest at which they became demoralized and after which they "just didn't care any more" or "got tired

[5] Sutherland and Cressey, *Principles of Criminology*, p. 240.

of running." The arrests of several men having a very long experience with checks resulted from blunders in technique of which they were aware at the time they made them. Some of the men gave themselves up to detectives or FBI agents at this point.

In general the picture of the cool, calculating professional with prosaic, matter-of-fact attitudes toward his crimes as a trade or occupation supported by rationalizations of a subculture was not valid for the cases in question.

2. Planning as an aspect of forgery.

In regard to the second element of professional theft—planning—the behavior of check forgers is again divergent. Actually the present techniques of check passing either preclude precise planning or make it unnecessary. Although systematic check passers undeniably pay careful attention to such things as banking hours, the places at which checks are presented, and the kinds of "fronts" they employ, these considerations serve only as generalized guides for their crimes. Most informants held that situations have to be *exploited as they arise*, with variation and flexibility being the key to success. What stands out in the behavior of systematic check forgers is the rapid tempo—almost impulsiveness—with which they work.

The cases seemed to agree that check forgers seldom attempt to use the "fix" in order to escape the consequences of their crime. The reason for this is that although one or a small number of checks might be made good, the systematic forger has too many bad checks outstanding and too many victims to mollify by offering restitution. Although the forger may be prosecuted on the basis of only one or two checks, ordinarily the prosecuting attorney will have a choice of a large number of complaints upon which to act. About the best the check forger can hope for through fixing activities is a short sentence or a sentence to jail rather than to prison.

3. Technical skills.

Although the systematic check man relies upon technical skills—those of manipulating others—these are usually not of a high order, nor do they require a long learning period to master. From the standpoint of the appearance of the check or the behavior involved at the time of its passing, there need, of course, be no great difference between passing a bad check and passing a good check. This is particularly true of personal checks, which are at least as favored as payroll checks by check men.

When check men impersonate others or when they assume fictitious roles, acting ability is required. To the extent that elaborate impersonations are relied upon by the forger, his check passing takes on qualities of a confidence game. Most of the check men showed strong preference, however, for simple, fast-moving techniques. A number expressed definite dislike for staged arrangements, such as that of the "out of town real estate buyer" or for setting up a fictitious business in a community, then waiting several weeks or a month before making a "spread" of checks. As they put it, they "dislike the slow build-up involved."

4. Mobility.

Like the thief, the systematic forger is migratory. Only one check man interviewed spoke of identifying himself with one community, and even he was reluctant to call it a headquarters. Generally check men are migratory within regions.

5. Associations.

The sharpest and most categorical difference between professional theft and systematic forgery lies in the realm of associations. In contrast to pickpockets, shoplifters, and con men, whose criminal techniques are implicitly cooperative, most check men with highly developed systems work alone, carefully avoiding contacts and interaction with other criminals. Moreover, their preference for solitude and their secretiveness gives every appearance of a highly generalized reaction; they avoid not only cooperative crime but also any other kinds of association with criminals. They are equally selective and cautious in their contacts and associations with the noncriminal population, preferring not to become involved in any enduring personal relationships.

A descriptive breakdown of the 30 check forgers classified as systematic bears out this point. Only four of the 30 had worked in check passing gangs. Two of these had acted as "fences" who organized the operations. Both were close to 70 years old and had long prison records, one having been a receiver of stolen property, the other having worked as a forger. Both had turned to using gangs of passers because they were too well known to detectives either to pass checks themselves or to permit their handwriting to appear on the checks. The other two forgers who had worked in gangs were female drug addicts who had teamed up with other female addicts.[6]

Three other systematic check forgers did not work directly with other criminals but had criminal associations of a *contractual* nature. One old-

[6] One may question whether they were systematic check forgers in a true sense; other informants state that "such people are not real check men; they are just supporting a habit." Their self-definitions and the organization of their lives centers around drug addiction rather than forgery.

time forger familiar with the now little-used methods for forging signatures and raising checks usually sold checks to passers but never had uttered (passed) any of his forgeries. Two men were passers who purchased either payroll checks from a "hot printer" or stolen checks from burglars. Apart from the minimal contacts necessary to sell or obtain a supply of checks, all three men were lone operators and very seclusive in their behavior.

Six of the 30 systematic forgers worked exclusively with one other person, usually a girl or "broad." [7] The check men seemed to agree that working with a girl was equivalent to working alone. These pairs ordinarily consisted of the check man and some girl not ordinarily of criminal background with whom he had struck up a living arrangement and for whom he felt genuine affection. The girl was used either to make out the checks or to pass them. In some cases she was simply used as a front to distract attention. Some men picked up girls in bars or hotels and employed them as fronts without their knowledge.

The remaining 17 of the 30 systematic check forgers operated on a solitary basis. The majority of these argued that contact with others is unnecessary to obtain and pass a supply of checks. Most of them uttered personal checks. However, even where they made use of payroll or corporation checks they contrived to manufacture or obtain them without resorting to interaction with criminal associates or intermediaries. For example, one Nisei check man arranged with a printer to make up checks for a fraternal organization of which he represented himself as secretary-treasurer. Another man frequented business offices at noon time, and when the clerk left the office, helped himself to a supply of company checks, in one instance stealing a check-writing machine for his purposes.

It was difficult to find evidence of anything more than rudimentary congeniality, sympathy, understandings, and shared rules of behavior among the check forgers, including those who had worked in gangs. Rather the opposite seemed true, suspicion and distrust marking their relationships with one another. One organizer of a gang, for example, kept careful account of all the checks he issued to his passers and made them return torn off corners of checks in case they were in danger of arrest and had to get rid of them. Only two of the thirty forgers indicated that they had at times engaged in recreational activities with other criminals. Both of these men were lone wolves in their work. One other lone wolf stated that he had on occasion had dinner with another check man he happened to know well and that he had once or twice entered into a rivalry with him to see who could pass a check in the most difficult place.

The two men who had organized gangs of check passers worked with

[7] One of the "pair" workers consisted of two homosexual females. The other non-man-woman pair was made up of two brothers, both of whom had substantial prison records. They worked up and down the West Coast, alternating in making out checks and playing the part of passer.

a set of rules, but they were largely improvised and laid down by the fence rather than voluntarily recognized and obeyed by the passers. The other check men with varying degrees of explicitness recognized rules for passing checks—rules learned almost entirely on an individual trial-and-error basis. The informants insisted that "you learn as you go" and that one of the rules was "never use another man's stunt."

Such special morality as was recognized proved to be largely functional in derivation. Thus attitudes toward drinking and toward picking up women for sexual purposes were pretty much the result of individual perceptions of what was likely to facilitate or hamper the passing of checks or lead to arrest. Many of the men stated that since they were dealing primarily with business, professional, and clerical persons, their appearance and behavior had to be acceptable to these people. "Middle class" is probably the best term to describe their morality in most areas.

Careful inquiries were made to discover the extent to which the check men were familiar with and spoke an argot. Findings proved meager. Many of the men had a superficial acquaintance with general prison slang, but only four men could measurably identify and reproduce the argot of check forgery or that of thieves. Three more could be presumed to have some familiarity with it. Only one of these spoke the argot in the prison setting. Another said that he never used the argot either in prison or on the outside, except years previously when once in a great while he had "let down at a thieves' party." There were only two men who spoke of themselves as being "on the scratch." [8]

INTERPRETATION

How can these findings be reconciled with the specific statement of Sutherland's informant [9] that "laying paper" is a form of professional theft most often worked in mobs? The answer to this apparent contradiction requires

[8] The attitude of the lone-wolf check man toward the argot is illustrated by the following quotation: "It's just the older men in here (San Quentin) who use argot, or some of the young guys who think they are tough. I know the argot but when I hear it I tell them to talk English. Most people on the outside know it anyway. Why call a gun a heater? What is gained by it . . . ?" These findings coincide with Maurer's. He states that the argot of check forgery is relatively unspecialized and that forgers seldom have an opportunity to use it. David W. Maurer, "The Argot of Check Forgery," *American Speech* 16 (1941): 243–50.

[9] Sutherland, *The Professional Thief,* p. 77. Maurer refers to check forgery as a branch of the "grift," and also speaks of professional forgers without, however, defining the term. Yet he recognizes that check forgers are usually lone wolves. Maurer, "Argot."

that a distinction be made between forgery of *the nineteenth and early twentieth centuries and that of the present day*. In the past forgery was a much more complex procedure in which a variety of false instruments such as bank notes, drafts, bills of exchange, letters of credit, registered bonds, and post office money orders, as well as checks, were manufactured or altered and foisted off. A knowledge of chemicals, papers, inks, engraving, etching, lithography, and penmanship, as well as detailed knowledge of bank operations, were prime requisites for success. The amounts of money sought were comparatively large, and often they had to be obtained through complex monetary transactions.[10] The technological characteristics of this kind of forgery made planning, timing, specialization, differentiation of roles, morale, and organization imperative. Capital was necessary for living expenses during the period when preparations for the forgeries were being made.[11] Intermediates between the skilled forger and the passers were necessary so that the latter could swear that the handwriting on the false negotiable instruments was not theirs and so that the forger himself was not exposed to arrest. A "shadow" was often used for protection against the passer's temptation to abscond with the money and in order to alert the others of trouble at the bank.[12] "Fall" money was accumulated and supplied to assist the passer when arrested. Inasmuch as forgery gangs worked together for a considerable length of time, understandings, congeniality, and rules of behavior, especially with regard to the division of money, could and did develop. In short, professional forgery was based upon the technology of the period.

Although precise dating is difficult, the heyday of professional forgery in this country probably began after the Civil War and lasted through the 1920's.[13] It seems to have corresponded with the early phases of industrialization and commercial development before business and law-enforcement agencies developed methods and organization for preventing forgery and apprehending the offenders. Gradually technological developments in inks, papers, protectographs, and check-writing machines made the forging

[10] George Dilnot, *The Bank of England Forgery* (New York: Scribner's, 1929).

[11] William A. Pinkerton, "Forgery" (unpublished paper read before the Annual Convention of the International Association of Chiefs of Police, Washington, D. C., 1905); W. A. Pinkerton, *Thirty Years a Detective* (New York: G. W. Carleton, 1884), pp. 338–41; Dilnot, *The Bank of England Forgery*.

[12] Pinkerton enumerates the following roles of the forgery gang: (1) backer, (2) forger, (3) middleman, (4) presenter, (5) shadow in "Forgery"; Maurer, without specifying the historical period to which his description applies, distinguishes the following as check forger roles: (1) connection, (2) fence, (3) passer in "The Argot of Check Forgery."

[13] J. W. Speare, *Protecting the Nation's Money* (Rochester: Todd Protectograph Co., 1927).

of signatures and the manufacture of false negotiable instruments more difficult. According to one source, for example, raised drafts have been virtually nonexistent since 1905.[14] Similarly, at the present time raising of checks is quite rare. The establishment of a protective committee by the American Bankers Association in 1894, related merchants' protective agencies, and improvements in police methods have made the risks of organized professional forgery exceedingly great.[15]

Check gangs have always been vulnerable to arrest but this vulnerability has been multiplied many times by the large amounts of evidence left behind them in the form of countless payroll checks. Vulnerability is also heightened by the swiftness of communication today. If one person of a check-passing gang is arrested and identifies his associates, it becomes a relatively simple matter for police to secure their arrest. A sexually exploited and angered female companion may easily do the same to the check man. This goes far to explain the extreme seclusiveness of systematic check forgers and their almost abnormal fear of stool pigeons or of being "fingered." The type of persons who can be engaged as passers—unattached women, bar waitresses, drug addicts, alcoholics, petty thieves, and transient unemployed persons—also magnifies the probabilities that mistakes will be made and precludes the growth of a morale which might prevent informing to the police. These conditions also explain the fact that when the forger does work with someone it is likely to be one other person upon whom he feels he can rely with implicit confidence. Hence the man-woman teams in which the woman is in love with the man, or the case of two homosexual girls, or of two-brother check-passing teams.

Further evidence that organized forgery is a hazardous type of crime, difficult to professionalize under modern conditions, is indicated by the fact that the organizer or fence is apt to be an older criminal with a long record, whose handwriting methods are so well known that he has no choice other than to work through passers. Even then he does it with recognition that arrest is inevitable.

A factor of equal importance in explaining the decline of professional organized forgery has been the increasingly widespread use of business and payroll checks as well as personal checks. Whereas in the past the use of checks was confined to certain kinds of business transactions, mostly involving banks, today it is ubiquitous. Attitudes of business people and their clerical employees have undergone great change, and only the most perfunctory identification is necessary to cash many kinds of checks. Check men recognize this in frequent unsolicited comments that passing checks is "easy." Some argue that the form of the check is now relatively unim-

[14] Ibid.
[15] Pinkerton, "Forgery"; Maurer, "The Argot of Check Forgery."

portant to passing it, that "you can pass a candy bar wrapper nowadays with the right front and story." [16] It is for this reason that the systematic check man does not have to resort to criminal associates or employ the more complex professional procedures used in decades past.

These facts may also account for the presence among lone-wolf check forgers of occasional persons with the identification, orientation, skills, codes, and argot of the thief. Case histories as well as the observations of informants show that older professional criminals in recent decades have turned to check passing because they face long sentences for additional crimes or sentencing under habitual criminal legislation. They regard checks as an "easy racket" because in many states conviction makes them subject to jail sentences rather than imprisonment. Check passing may be a last resort for the older criminal.

The presence of the occasional older professional thief in the ranks of check forgers also may token a general decline and slow disappearance of professional thieving.[17] One professional thief turned check passer had this to say:

> I'm a thief—a burglar—but I turned to checks because it's getting too hard to operate. Police are a lot smarter now, and they have better methods. People are different nowadays too; they report things more. It's hard to trust anyone now. Once you could trust cab drivers; now you can't. We live in a different world today.

THE CHECK FORGER AS AN ISOLATE

The preference of many systematic check forgers for solitary lives and their avoidance of primary-group associations among criminals may also be explicable in terms of their educational characteristics and class origins. The history of forgery reveals that in medieval times it was considered to be the special crime of the clerical class, as indeed it had to be inasmuch as the members of this class monopolized writing skills.[18] It also seems to be

---

[16] Detectives in Santa Monica, California, showed the writer a collection of checks successfully passed with such signatures as, "I.A.M. Fool," "U. R. Stuck," and others not printable. For a discussion of the crudeness of bogus checks accepted by business people, see J. L. Sternitsky, *Forgery and Fictitious Checks* (Springfield, Ill.: Charles C Thomas, 1955).

[17] There is evidence that there has been a sharp absolute decline in the number of pickpockets in recent years and that most of the so-called "class cannons" (highly skilled) operating now are 50 years of age or over. Maurer, *Whiz Mob*.

[18] T. F. Tout, "Medieval Forgers and Forgeries," *Bulletin of the John Rylands Library* 5, 3, 4 (1919): 5–31.

true from the later history of the crime that it has held a special attraction for more highly educated persons, for those of higher socio-economic status and those of "refined" or artistic tastes.[19] The basic method of organized forgery is stated to have been invented and perfected in England, not by criminals but by a practicing barrister of established reputation in 1840.[20] An early gang of forgers organized by a practicing physician is described by Felstead.[21] A number of studies directed to the differentiating characteristics of check criminals point to an "above average" intelligence and formal education. This refers to the general population as well as to the criminal populations with which they have been compared.[22]

All of this is not to say that less-educated persons do not frequently pass bad checks but rather that the persons who persist in the behavior and develop behavior systems of forgery seem much more likely than other criminals to be drawn from a segment of the population distinguished by a higher socio-economic status. Generally this was true of the systematic forgers in this study. Eight of the 30 had completed two or more years of

[19] This is the thesis of Henry T. F. Rhodes in *The Craft of Forgery* (London: John Murray, 1934). Two of the four participants in the famous Bank of England forgery in 1873 were college educated, one being a Harvard graduate; see Dilnot, *The Bank of England Forgery*. Forgers coming from "good" families are described by Hargrave Lee Adam, *The Story of Crime* (London: T. Werner Laurie, 1908): fourteen of the nineteen persons tried for forgery at Newgate Prison in England during the late eighteenth and early nineteenth centuries were what can be termed "middle" and "upper" class, including three army or navy officers (one who commanded the royal yacht of Queen Caroline, consort of George IV), one banker, one physician (graduate of Cambridge), one prosecuting attorney, two engravers (one by appointment to George III), three "gentlemen" of good connections, and three bank clerks. Two of the three men who had "poor parents" had married women of "good means." Tegg and Bonger give data from France and Italy which support this idea: Thomas Tegg, *The Chronicles of Crime*, Vols. I, II (London: Camden Pelham, 1841); Bonger, *Criminality*, pp. 429, 430, 437. A number of writers have commented on the fact that forgery has been quite common among the educated classes of India, particularly the "wily Brahmins." Hargrave Lee Adam, *Oriental Crime* (London: T. Werner Laurie, 1908); S. M. Edwards, *Crime in India* (London: Oxford University Press, 1924), pp. 3–6; Hardless and Hardless, *Forgery in India* (Chunar: Sanctuary, 1920).

[20] Rhodes, *The Craft of Forgery*; George Dilnot, *The Trial of Jim the Penman* (London: Geoffrey Bles, 1930).

[21] Sidney T. Felstead, in *Famous Criminals and Their Trials* (New York: Doran, 1926).

[22] I. Berg, "A Comparative Study of Forgery," *Journal of Applied Psychology* 28 (1944): 232–38; Vernon Fox, "Intelligence, Race and Age as Selective Factors in Crime," *Journal of Criminal Law and Criminology* 37 (1946): 141–52; Ernest A. Hooton, *The American Criminal*, Vol. I. (Cambridge: Harvard University Press, 1939): 87; Lewis Lawes, *Life and Death in Sing Sing* (New York: Dial Press, 1938), p. 40.

college. Fourteen of the 30 had fathers who were or had been in the professions and business, including a juvenile court judge, a minister, a postmaster of a large city, and three very wealthy ranch owners. One woman came from a nationally famous family of farm implement manufacturers. Four others had siblings well established in business and the professions, one of whom was an attorney general in another state. Two of the men had been successful businessmen themselves before becoming check men.

The most important implication of these data is that systematic check forgers do not seem to have had criminal antecedents or early criminal associations.[23] For this reason, as well as for technical reasons, they are not likely to seek out or to be comfortable in informal associations with other criminals who have been products of early and lengthy socialization and learning in a criminal subculture. It also follows that their morality and values remain essentially "middle" or "upper" class and that they seldom integrate these with the morality of the professional criminal. This is reflected in self-attitudes in which many refer to themselves as "black sheep" or as a kind of Dr. Jekyll-Mr. Hyde person. Further support for this interpretation comes from their status in prison where, according to observations of themselves and others, they are marginal so far as participation in the primary groups of the prison is concerned.

CONCLUSION

The cases and data presented suggest that present-day check forgery exists in systematic form but does not appear to be a professional behavior system acquired or maintained through associations with other criminals. The technical demands of contemporary check forgery preclude efficient operation on an organized, cooperative basis. In addition to these factors the class characteristics and backgrounds of systematic forgers incline them to avoid intimate association with other criminals.

[23] Edwin M. Lemert, "An Isolation and Closure Theory of Naive Check Forgery," *Journal of Criminal Law and Criminology* 44 (1953): 296–307; Edwin M. Lemert, "Generality and Specificity in Criminal Behavior: Check Forgery Considered" (paper read before American Sociological Society, September 1956).

ROLE ENACTMENT, SELF, AND
9 IDENTITY IN THE SYSTEMATIC
CHECK FORGER

This paper [1] deals with certain consequences which commitment to living by means of passing forged checks have for social roles, self, and identity. Role is a term which summarizes the way or ways in which an individual acts in a structured situation. A situation is structured to the degree that others with whom the individual interacts expect him to respond in certain ways and to the extent that he anticipates their expectations and incorporates them into his behavior. The role reflects these expectations but also reflects claims of other roles and their evaluations by the individual, so that it is always a unique combination of common and diverse elements.

Identity is conceived here as the delimiting, boundary aspects of personality in time and space as perceived and symbolized (named)—the "who I am and who I am not." It has objective as well as subjective aspects,

---

[1] The original data on which this analysis is based consisted of 75 case studies of check forgers, most of whom were inmates of California penal institutions. Thirty of the 75 were classified as systematic check forgers. For more details on procedure and data see my earlier papers on "naive" and "systematic" check forgery. Edwin M. Lemert, "An Isolation and Closure Theory of Naive Check Forgery," *Journal of Criminal Law and Criminology* 44 (1953): 296–307; Edwin M. Lemert, "The Behavior of the Systematic Check Forger, *Social Problems* 6 (1958): 141–49.

and can exist in degree as well as differ in kind. Self is identity plus evaluation; it is a differentiating and evaluating awareness arising from social interaction, which has cultural content. Both identity and self can be thought of as cognitive structures or as aspects of a common cognitive structure.[2]

The problem addressed is to determine how prolonged enactment of a role or roles fashioned from actions grossly contrary to expectations of authenticity or "genuineness" produces changes in identity and self, and to relate these changes to the forms and limits of face-to-face interaction associated with systematic check forgery.

THE ACT OF FORGERY AND CHARACTERISTICS OF CHECK FORGERS

Check forgery, in contrast to crimes such as assault, robbery, or burglary, is distinguished by its low social visibility. At the time the bogus check is passed there is nothing in the act which reveals that it is deviant or criminal. No special tools or equipment are needed for the crime, as with burglary, nor is any special setting required for the action, as is true with the "store" or the front of a bank, where the confidence man activates his fraudulent enterprises. Furthermore, there are few or no cues in interaction which give feedback to the forger from the victim nor from his own overt responses to indicate that he is behaving contrary to expectations; only later does the act become so defined and then never in direct interaction between the forger and his victim. Here is deviant behavior whose manifest or "existential" qualities do not differentiate or identify the person as a deviant.

Studies of the characteristics of check forgers based upon samples of those in jails, prisons, or on probation show considerable heterogeneity. However, it can be said that in general they more nearly resemble the general middleclass population than they do the populations of jails and prisons. They tend to be native white in origin, male, and much older than other criminals when they commit their first crimes—somewhere in their late twenties or early thirties. Their intelligence averages much higher than that of other criminals and they equal or surpass the general population in years of education completed. Skilled, clerical, professional, and managerial occupations are at least as fully represented among forgers as in the general population, perhaps more so. An impressive small minority has come

---

[2] The distinction between identity and self, I will try to show, emerges from the data. For a discussion of several dimensions of the self considered cross-culturally see A. Irving Hallowell, "Self and Its Behavioral Environment," *Explorations Two* (1954), pp. 106–65.

from prestigeful, wealthy families, or those in which siblings have achieved social eminence, although considerable discounting of forgers' claims on this point is necessary. A high percentage of forgers have been long-time residents in the communities in which they committed their first offenses, but relatively few have lived in so-called delinquency areas. Forgers are less likely than other criminals to have had a record of delinquency in their youth.

Prior socialization as delinquents or criminals is insufficient to explain the crimes of a large percent, or even the majority, of persons who pass bad checks. Many have acquired and lived a considerable part of their early adult lives according to conventional middle-class morality. Typically they tend to express aversion to the idea of using violence in interpersonal dealings for whatever purpose. At the same time it must be said that an occasional person comes into forgery via the criminal route—the "short" con man turned forger, or the "old pro" burglar fallen on hard times, who has turned to passing bad checks for a livelihood.

Little effort has been made at systematic personality assessment of check forgers. Yet detectives have for a long time looked upon them as a distinctive criminal type, particularly those designated as professionals.[3]

> The professional forger is a man of great ability, and naturally a cunning and suspicious sort of individual. Cautious in extreme, he likes to work in secret, and probably never more than two of his most intimate companions know what he is about until counterfeits he has produced are ready to be put into circulation. He never permits anyone to watch him at work.

Probation officers, prison workers, and parole officers often describe check forgers with such adjectives as "impulsive," "dependent," "lacking ego strength," "unstable," and "immature." In most instances these are reifications of the criminal act itself, more in the nature of invidious labels than separately defined variables demonstrable in case histories of the forgers.

Check forgers with long records who end in prison or those who pass through diagnostic centers are sometimes termed "compulsive"; some observers speak of their having a "disease," underscoring a common belief, "once a check forger always a check forger." Such statements also tend to be circular deductions and serve little useful purpose for analysis or research in the absence of definitions which separate them from the fact of recidivism. Nevertheless, these adjectives indicate that law enforcement people and prison staff members do in some way differentiate check forgers from other convicted criminals, especially in regard to a kind of cyclical pattern and inevitability in their actions.

[3] Thomas Byrnes, *Professional Criminals of America* (New York: Cassell, 1886), p. 12.

Check forgers themselves also provide cues and verbalizations which can be inferentially useful for the analysis of their behavior. In jail and prison they often are apathetic toward their predicaments and they seem less inclined than other prisoners to rationalize their behavior. First offenders frequently express continuing deep perplexity about their motivations; some speak of the "other me" as responsible for the check passing; some refer to themselves as "Dr. Jekyll and Mr. Hyde"; and some say that they "must be crazy." Such statements may also come from those with long criminal histories, from those who are "check artists," as well as first offenders. Systematic check forgers seldom have the "businessman" ideology which was attributed to professional thieves by Sutherland.[4]

Check forgery is associated with a wide variety of personal and social contingencies, the nature of which has been dealt with elsewhere in a theory of naive, i.e., criminally unsophisticated, check forgery.[5] Some forgers pass worthless checks only once and quit; others, casual offenders, intersperse periods of stable employment with check writing sorties quickly followed by arrest. Some people imprisoned for bad checks are alcoholics who have unwisely passed worthless checks during a drinking spree, drug addicts "supporting a habit," or gamblers desperately trying to cover losses. The comments which follow are directed not to check forgers in general but to those who have a commitment to check forgery, who develop a system of passing bad checks, and who live according to the dictates of this system as they progressively perceive them. The characteristics of this system have been described in some detail in a previous article.[6] It is only necessary to recapitulate that committed check forgers typically work alone and while they develop a criminal behavior system, it is an individual system. It is neither the same nor the equivalent of professional crime, for it lacks social organization, occupational orientation, careful planning, common rules, a code of behavior, and a special language. In the present context the concern is with the exigencies from which the systems develop and the sociopsychological consequences of the adaptations making up the systems. These revolve around pseudonymity, mobility, and seclusiveness.

PSEUDONYMITY

Once a check forger passes a series of worthless checks, the central fact of his existence becomes the threat of arrest. The business community through the police is strongly organized against the check forger, and when

---

[4] Edwin H. Sutherland, *The Professional Thief* (Chicago: University of Chicago Press, 1947), chap. VI.

[5] Lemert, "An Isolation and Closure Theory of Naive Check Forgery."

[6] Lemert, "The Behavior of the Systematic Check Forger."

his checks appear, a number of procedures are activated. The more checks he has outstanding the more intensified and widespread are the efforts to apprehend him. Nearly all of these procedures have to do with identification, for once the check forger is identified as working in an area, apprehension and arrest quickly follow. Consequently if he is to survive as a forger he must develop and use techniques which prevent his identification.

Other criminals anticipate and adapt to the threat of arrest through anonymity, e.g., the burglar who works at night, or the bank robbers who work swiftly, sometimes wearing masks, which will confuse witnesses and make subsequent identification difficult or impossible. The confidence man manipulates his victims so that they often remain unaware they have been duped, or so that they fear to go to the police. The check forger cannot use these alternatives as a defense against arrest because he must work during daylight hours and face large numbers of victims who require identification before they will cash his checks. While the forger might "cool out" a few victims in the manner of the con man, he can't psychologically disarm them all, nor can he employ the "fix" with any great degree of success. The district attorney usually has stacks of checks in evidence and numerous complainants ready to testify against him when he is arrested. The check forger by necessity relies upon pseudonyms as the preferred solution to his technical problem.

In a very literal sense the check forger becomes a real life actor, deliberately assuming a variety of roles and identities which both facilitate the cashing of checks and conceal his former or, if preferred, his "real" identity. Thus he may become a spurious customer in a supermarket, a guilty husband purportedly buying his wife a gift, an out-of-town real estate buyer, a corporation executive seeking to set up a branch office, an army officer on leave, or even an investigator for the Department of Internal Revenue.

The systematic forger's problem is the selection or fabrication of roles rather than the learning of new roles. His role models are occupational or leisure time roles of conventional society. Their distinctive quality is their high degree of superficiality.[7] While they require some acting ability, it is of a low order and easily learned. Such roles, as Goffman [8] suggests, are easily put together in response to situational cues from "bits and pieces of performances" which are already in the repertoire of most people.

Some negative learning is done by forgers in jail or prison, in the sense of things not to do, through listening to the stories of other check

---

[7] One forger reported using 285 names during his career. He also argued that the less documentary identification used the less suspicion aroused in the victim. Leonard Hart, "You're a Sucker If You Cash My Check," *Colliers*, February 7, 1953.

[8] Erving Goffman, *The Presentation of the Self in Everyday Life* (New York: Doubleday Anchor, 1959), pp. 72 ff.

criminals. This is reflected in an adage followed by some, of "never try another man's stunt." While check forgers are responding to what they expect of others and what others expect of them, they do so in order to maintain deception and avoid arrest. Their behavior is fundamentally more in the nature of strategy or a swiftly moving game than it is a formal or constituted pattern. In this sense it is generically similar to that of the confidence man, representing, however, a lower order of creativity and strategy.

MOBILITY

While the check man employs pseudonyms to avoid exposure when passing his worthless checks, he cannot simply don a different or innocuous identity afterward; he must move on, out of the vicinity of his crime or crimes. This, of course, can be said for other kinds of crimes, but mobility is more or less "built in" the check forger's situation largely because he preys upon resident businessmen, rather than on transients, as do pickpockets or con men.[9] His mobility is shaped by continual awareness of the time required to deposit checks, clear them, and communicate notification of non-payment to law enforcement and business protective agencies. In large part his daily activities are geared to the tempo and rhythms of banking and business, which demarcate the length of time he can pass checks and remain in a given area, ending in a critical intreval during which danger of arrest is ubiquitous.[10] Experienced check forgers develop an almost intuitive sense of these points in time which punctuate their periodic movements.

The movements of the systematic check passer take on a circularity of action and motivation in the sense that their mobility begets more mobility. When queried as to why they stay on the move, check forgers usually explain that it is expensive to travel, and also that if they are to impress their businessmen-victims they must appear to have a bank account appropriate to the checks they cash.[11]

[9] Sheldon Messinger thoughtfully suggests that this factor prevents the forger from setting up accommodative relationships with police which are the basis of the fix, by which professional thieves protect themselves—personal communication.

[10] In one case, a forger traced his itinerary for the author. It covered a nine-month period, during which he worked in 25 cities between Oakland, California, and Atlanta, Georgia, never remaining longer than two weeks in each.

[11] This is only partially revealing of the motivation of the forger; it will become apparent that he also needs large amounts of money to underwrite the kinds of recreation or activities he pursues to relieve his tensions and sense of loneliness.

When you're moving around like that you've got to put up a front and look the part. You can't cash checks if you look seedy. How can I impress a clerk that I'm a businessman with a fat bank account if I don't have good quality clothes and stay in better hotels and drive an expensive make of car (rented).

The result of their high levels of expenditure is that forgers usually cash numerous checks in order to defray costs of constant travel and to maintan their prosperous style of life. The local "spreads" of checks stir strong indignation in the business community and quickly mobilize law enforcement people; sensing this becomes the forger's motivation to move frequently. This suggests one of the main reasons why some check forgers speak of being caught up in something they can't stop.

SECLUSIVENESS

The vulnerability of the forger to recognition and identification impels him away from unnecessary contacts with other persons. Furthermore he must, if he is to remain free from arrest, keep himself from progressive involvement in social relationships, for with intimate interchange of experiences there comes the danger of inadvertent as well as deliberate exposure by others. Free and unguarded interaction, even with persons whom he likes and trusts, becomes an indulgence.

The forger's seclusiveness, in large part a learned response of wariness, is reinforced by his high mobility, which necessarily makes his contacts and interactions of short-lived variety; he simply does not have the time to build up close relationships with the people he meets. His relationships or social activities tend to be those which he can enter and leave quickly, with a minimum of commitment; the roles he enacts apart from the passing of his checks are for the most part casual in nature. In addition to this role selectivity he learns to avoid specific forms of behavior likely to lead beyond casual interaction.

The forger often meets people in settings where drinking is expected behavior, yet he must take care not to drink to the point of intoxication for fear of letting slip revealing or inconsistent facts about himself. If he gets drunk he is likely to do it alone, but this is risky, too, for he might be picked up on a drunk charge and be exposed by a routine fingerprint check. If the forger gambles it is likely to be at a crowded race track or casino, not at a friendly poker game.

The preference for seclusiveness puts its stamp upon the sexual participation of the forger. He is more limited than other criminals in seeking erotic pleasures; for he seldom has a common law wife or a regular traveling companion. Prostitutes are not in keeping with his pseudonyms of respectability, and association with them may lead to unwanted brushes with the police. When he picks up a girl he is apt to be discriminating in his choice, and typically he will treat her lavishly, but seldom will he give her his true name. In this role, as in others, he remains an actor, although at times the temptation to be otherwise is great.

THE EXTRINSIC NATURE OF CHECK FORGERS' REWARDS

Systematic check forgers are properly described by themselves and by others familiar with their ways as people who like to live fast and well. The money which flows into their hands is spent freely, often with refined taste, on clothes, food, drink, travel, and entertainment. Their satisfactions are limited to those which can be had from conspicuous expenditure and display, or those which stem from the honorific qualities of assumed names, titles, or identities which a generous supply of money makes possible in our society. The attendant rewards are the result of automatic or unreflective deference cued by external or immediately recognizable symbols of high economic status. Even the sexual rewards of forgers have much of this quality.

The status pleasures of forgers are further tempered by the fact that they cannot and dare not, for any length of time, assume specific identities of those who are in high positions in a particular local community. They can be rich cattlemen from Texas, but not a particular, known, rich cattleman from Texas. They may use specific identities or impersonations of this sort to pass checks (known as "high powered") but if they are wise they will not register as such persons later at a local hotel.

Some of the rewards which forgers seek arise out of a context of private meanings which can be understood only in terms of idiosyncratic life history factors. Thus for some reason they may have disliked bankers or credit managers, and they derive a particular zest or satisfaction from foisting bad checks on these people or on those who work for them. Unfortunately, the rigorous exactions of their criminal technology leave few opportunities for the indulgence in these more subtle gratifications. Furthermore, they have no way of making public these private psychic triumphs, for they have no audience. At best they can only laugh silently later over their beer or pre-dinner cocktail.

THE GROWTH OF ANXIETY

An unavoidable conclusion seems to be that the more successfully the forger plays his roles the greater becomes his anxiety. The more checks he has outstanding the greater is his perception of the danger of arrest, and hence the greater his necessity to move on and devise new identities which conceal his previous behavior. The mounting sense of strain is made real to the forger by occasional "close calls" in which he barely escapes identification and arrest. As the anxiety magnifies it is reflected in jumpiness, stomach upsets, and other physical disturbances. A few check forgers develop acute symptoms, such as stomach ulcers.

> My routine ran like this: I usually picked my city, then after I arrived I opened a savings account with cash. That's on Monday. On Tuesday I deposited some checks to my account, no good, of course. Wednesday I deposited another check and then drew out part of the account in cash. Then I left town. I worked this all over California, depositing maybe $50,000 altogether in I don't know how many banks I suppose I got about $10,000 in cash. By this time the ulcers kicked up and I laid off in a resort.

Anxiety serves to amplify the suspiciousness of the forger; in some instances it is aggravated into a paranoid-like state, called the "bull horrors" by professional criminals. This is what it implies—abnormal fear of the police. In this state any unusual behavior of a victim, or a chance knock on a hotel room door, may be taken by the forger to mean that he has been discovered or that detectives have arrived to arrest him. At this point it is clear that the symbolic process has been affected; anxiety has begun to distort or interfere with the forger's ability to take over or realistically appraise the responses of others to his actions.

Cooler or highly experienced forgers may be able to objectify the sources of their anxiety and symbolize it in the jargon of the professional criminal as "heat." As one forger put it, "The checks get hot, not me." As a solution to their psychic problems some forgers take a vacation, or "lay off at a resort." In this setting they continue to use a pseudonym but refrain from passing checks during the interim. This has the merit of reducing anxiety attributable to the fear of being recognized by victims or police, but it does not solve what by now has usually become an identity problem. In any event, contingencies or the need for more money are apt to cut short these palliative respites.

PERSONAL CRISIS

Detectives, police, and the check forgers themselves all agree that arrest is inevitable for the person who persists in passing bad checks for any length of time. A few check men manage to evade detection for several years, and one is known to have foiled the FBI for ten years, but these are the rare exceptions which prove the rule. Efficiently organized police work and fortuitous events undeniably have much to do with the forger's ultimate downfall, but from the point of view adopted here, these are constant factors with which he contends. That with which he is unable to cope is a kind of massive personal crisis which inheres in the prolonged enactment of his spurious roles.

That the forger reaches a dead end in his motivation can be inferred from the circumstances and attendant behavior at the time of the arrest. While a number of systematic forgers are apprehended entirely by chance or by police efforts, an impressive number of others engineer their own downfalls. For example, some phone the police or a parole officer and tell them where they can be found. Closely akin are those who foreclose their current criminal careers rather simply by remaining where they are, knowing full well that police or detectives will soon catch up with them, to find them in a resigned mood awaiting their arrival.[12] Still other forgers, like fabled animals wending back to their mythical graveyard to die, return to their home community, there either to court arrest or to arrange for the inevitable in familiar surroundings. In more complex cases an otherwise accomplished check man makes a mistake, knowing at the time that it is a mistake which probably will land him in jail or prison.

> After a weekend of drinking and sleeping with this girl I had known before, I woke up in my room at the Mark Hopkins with a hangover and no money left. I had one check left from those I had been passing in the city. It was over two weeks since I had started passing this series and knew I shouldn't try to cash this one. But I did anyway— and now here I am at Folsom.

When queried as to reasons for their sometimes open, sometimes oblique surrenders to detectives or other law enforcement agents, check forgers frequently refer to a cumulative state of apathy or sense of psychic exhaustion,[13] expressed in such statements as the following:

[12] One check man, who spent much of his free time in bars, sensed that bartenders had been alerted to his presence in the area. He brought about his arrest in a bar simply by talking a little louder than was his custom. The owner overheard him and phoned the police.

[13] An appropriate descriptive term for this state is not easily found. It resembles the indifference to the threat of death which appeared among some inmates of Nazi concentration camps, as a response to "provisional detention without a time limit." See Bruno Bettelheim, "Individual and Mass Behavior in Extreme Situations," *Journal of Abnormal and Social Psychology* 38 (1948): 434; Elie Cohen, *Human Behavior in the Concentration Camp* (New York: W. W. Norton, 1953), p. 129. The reaction also suggests the idea of a "breaking point" or limits of effective response under stress. See Eli Ginzberg, et al.,

After that I began to appreciate what a heck of a job it is to pass checks.

In Seattle I got just plain tired of cashing checks.

The thrill I got from passing checks was gone.

I reached a point where I didn't care whether I stayed in Balboa or went to jail.

It's the same thing over and over again; you get tired of running.

It gets to be more and more of an effort.

You have a sense of being caught in something you can't stop.

One meaning that can be readily assigned to such statements is that, assuming satisfactions or rewards of the forger's activities remain unchanged or constant, their costs of acquisition in terms of effort and expenditure of psychic energy (anxiety) increase to a prohibitive point. What started out as "easy" check passing becomes more and more work or sheer labor, until that game is no longer worth the effort.

A second, less apparent implication of the sense of apathy which finally overwhelms the highly mobile check forger was suggested by a thoughtful older inmate of San Quentin prison, who had in his lifetime been both con man and a notorious utterer of very large checks. His interpretation was simply that during the course of a check passing spree, "You come to realize that kind of life has a false structure to it." This in sociological terms speaks of the inherent difficulty of establishing and maintaining identity by reference to purely extrinsic rewards. To admit this is for the forger in effect to admit that the roles he plays, or his way of life, make impossible a stable identity or the validation of a self-ideal. An excerpt from an older published autobiography of a forger states the problem clearly.[14]

> I could not rid myself of the crying need for the sense of security which social recognition and contact with one's fellows, and their approval furnishes. I was lonely and frightened and wanted to be where there was someone who knew me as I had been before.

At best the forger can seek to use his affluence to buy from others the approval and recognition important to a sense of personal worth. But

---

The Ineffective Soldier (New York: Columbia University Press, 1959). Something of "acute depersonalization" also seems involved. See Paul Schilder, The Image and Appearance of the Human Body (London: Kegan Paul, Trench, Trubner, 1935).

[14] Roger Benton, Where Do I Go From Here (New York: L. Furman, 1936), p. 80.

persons endowed with the intelligence and insight of a systematic check criminal quickly perceive the spurious qualities of such esteem, founded as it is only upon his generosity.

> Sure, you get big money. But it's easy come, easy go. You start out on Monday morning with a stack of checks. Maybe it's hard to get started, but after the first check it's easier. You work all week and by Thursday or Friday you have a pocketful of money. Then you pick up a girl and hit the bars and night spots. You have plenty of quick pals to pat you on the back and help you spend that money. Pretty soon it's Monday morning and you wake up with a hangover and empty pockets. You need more money so you start again.

While conspicuous expenditures on goods and services are important means of locating a person with reference to others, close observation of interaction reveals that these are necessary rather than sufficient factors for the purpose. They become most significant when they establish position in a *particular* group within a stratum or social category. The forger, by choice, enacts the form but not the substance of social roles. He lacks, avoids, or rejects contact with reference groups which could validate these roles or fix an underlying identity. He cannot particularize his social interaction, hence has no way of getting appreciation as a separate person. Appreciations must remain superficial imputations to the persons whose real or hypothetical identities he assumes.[15] Apart from the lack of opportunity to do so, the forger dares not put too much of what he regards as his "true self" into these identities; he cannot readily convert them and make them his own either in part or whole. To particularize his interaction to such an end would disclose his essential difference from others, i.e., his commitment to living by passing bogus checks and deceiving others. This disclosure, of course, would destroy the identities or assign him the criminal identity which he does not desire.

When put into a time perspective, the forger's interplay of role and identity has a dialectical quality. The forger sets out on his check writing and passing journey with an initial sense of fulfillment which is exciting or even exhilarating. This is related to the ease of passing checks and the sense of enjoyment of things he has always wanted but could not afford, or to the enactment of roles which on the surface at least are perceived as in keeping with the self-ideal he holds. There is also an

[15] Mills' concept of "status cycles" may be enlightening here. Like the white-collar worker on vacation, the forger seeks to create a "holiday image of self." The difference, of course, is that there is cultural sanction for the former but not for the forger's holiday image, financed as it is by fraudulent means. C. Wright Mills, *White Collar* (New York: Oxford University Press, 1951), p. 258.

awareness of fulfilling or satisfying some of the more highly subjective values previously alluded to. The sense of fulfillment undoubtedly varies from forger to forger in degree and content, depending upon whether he has been in jail, on probation, in prison, or on parole. However, it is present in any case.[16]

The passage of time brings no lasting respite to the fast moving check passer and the tendency is for his anxiety to mount to higher and higher levels. His attempts to cope with this anxiety at most are palliative and may lead to secondary anxieties which are added to his basic anxiety. Reference has already been made to "laying off in a resort" and to the ephemeral nature of the surcease it provides. In addition this may become risky if he is tempted to overstay or to depart from his system.

Some forgers who acutely sense the organized hue and cry against them or who realize that "they are hot" may try to reduce their tensions by "dropping down" to less hazardous methods. Instead of passing payroll checks, checks on accounts of actual persons, or large personal checks, they may cash small checks in supermarkets or drugstores. This is safer, but it is infinitely more labor and less productive. It may mean a jail rather than a prison sentence if the forger is caught, but this merely offers a choice between the lesser of two evils.

> In Minneapolis things began to get real rough. I had trouble getting name cards of businessmen to make my system work and I had this feeling that the FBI was around. Anyway, I had to cash $25 checks in supermarkets and it was damned hard work nearly all day just to get enough to live on, let alone play the horses.

> I'm a thief—a paperhanger. I go for high-powered cashiers checks of $85 to $100. But you won't find any of that high-powered stuff on my record. When I feel the heat is on I drop down to personal checks. Then if I get arrested it is on a less serious charge.

There are, of course, status degradation implications in having to descend to "small time" personal checks. In extreme cases a check man may be driven to engage in forms of petty crime or activities even more compromising to his sense of self-respect. This is apparent in the apologetic tone of the following tersely expressed account of a passage in the life of a long-time check man in jail awaiting the outcome of his trial.

> You have to understand that I'm an old man and I'm so well known that if my checks appear most detectives in the state can tie them to me. I've got to be smart and I have to lay off when things get hot.

[16] One female forger described feelings analogous to sexual orgasm which followed cashing checks in stores.

Once I was living with a pimp and his broad who were both on drugs. It was costing them $40 a day just for the stuff. I went out with the girl at night to help her hustle. Actually I was just doing them a good turn for letting me live with them. Naturally the police didn't come looking for me in places where she hustled, but I kept out of sight as much as possible just the same.

A not uncommon means chosen by check forgers for relief from tension is to increase their alcohol intake, a tendency which has led to some confusion in crime literature between alcoholics who pass checks to get liquor and the bona fide check man. The association between intoxication and felt anxiety and the instrumental quality of liquor for the latter is made vividly clear in the following:

> You ask me if my drinking pattern changed and I can say yes—definitely. I even remember where—in Cincinnati. It was there that my system really began to pay off and I cashed several $400 and $500 checks in the banks. Ordinarily I had one, or at most, two, highballs or a couple of beers before dinner. That night I remember it went up to four drinks, plus a bottle of wine with dinner and liqueur afterwards. I went around in a fog that evening and most nights thereafter.

The urgent need of some forgers to find relief for their troubled inner selves is shown in the willingness to drink liquor despite long established or culturally ingrained attitudes favoring sobriety. Such was the case of a Jewish check forger:

> In reality I am not a drinking man; I dislike any kind of beer or whiskeys, and the only time I actually drink is when I'm in trouble, meaning exactly when I write bad checks. I become very troubled, even though I haven't as yet been apprehended, but I am troubled because I know deep down in my heart that my life of freedom will be short-lived, so to forget my trouble I start drinking. I might add that the first drink tastes like castor oil, and after the first I can tolerate it. When I sober up again I become troubled because of the bogus checks I wrote . . . and, as a fool would figure, I just say to myself I might as well go write checks till I get caught.

While intoxication provides some temporary relief for the troubled forger, he knows that it is risky. Furthermore, passing bad checks the next morning with a hangover can be a harrowing experience, which, some forgers say, they have never quite forgotten.

The other significant change which comes with passing time in the criminal cycle of the check forger lies in the meaning or function of the rewards of his labors. The zest and satisfaction originally gained from his large affluence declines. The same is true for such idiosyncratic "thrills," whatever their psychic derivation, he may have originally felt in passing the checks themselves. Whatever reference value they may have had at one time, they are now diminished in their function for delimiting identity and validating self. If the interpretation advanced here is correct, the decline persists until a critical "turning point" is reached, and arrest occurs.

A schematic representation of the three variables involved in the personal crisis is suggested in Figure 1. The point at which the anxiety gradient and the gradient representing identity and self-validation cross indicates the hypothetical point in time at which personality crisis occurs. While lines with constant and equal gradients are shown in the figure, their application to specific cases might show different slopes, or they might be curvilinear. For maximum clarity objective rewards are shown as constant. In actual cases they might fluctuate or decline somewhat and thus impart a sharper gradient in the decline in self-validation.

THE FORGER'S AVERSION TO CRIMINAL ASSOCIATIONS

It may be protested that the experiences and feelings of the systematic check forger are but similar to those of any person who lives outside the law and plagues society with a long series of crimes. While there is some surface truth in this, it also has to be noted that professional thieves follow hazardous criminal lives yet still manage their occupationally in-

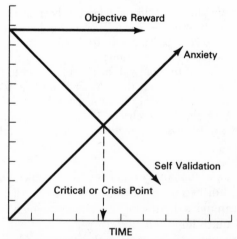

FIGURE 1. *Schematic representation of the relationship of anxiety, rewards, and the self-validating function of rewards for the systematic check forger.*

duced anxieties and solve their identity problems. The comparison becomes even more pointed when it is limited to con men, who closely resemble check forgers in their necessary assumption of fictitious identities and in their vulnerability to exposure by victims. Furthermore, con men experience high anxiety levels, fed by the additional probability of exploitation or "shakedowns" by police and detectives if they are recognized.[17]

A significant difference between the check forger and the con man is that the latter retains a locus of the self by means of intimate interaction with other con men.[18] Identity is further maintained by interaction with lesser criminals, and, paradoxically, through accommodative relationships with police.[19] Gambling, drinking, and sexual byplay for the con man tend to take place in the context of primary groups. As such they appear to be more efficient means for relaxing tensions and are less likely than with the forger to generate secondary anxieties. In some cases con men have been able to integrate their criminal forays with a relatively stable family life.

The comparison adumbrated here is intended less to apotheosize the con man than to point up the query as to why check men do not follow his bent and enter into associations with other check criminals or with other types of criminals in their leisure-time pursuits thereby acquiring a criminal identity. In part the answer to this already has been given; such intimacies are contrary to the perceived dictates of the forger's criminal behavior system. The spectre of the stool pigeon who can ruin him with one phone call is never far from the check man's mind, but a loose-tongued male companion in crime, or an angry erstwhile girlfriend can be equally dangerous to him.

It may be that the learned aversions of the check man to close human associations rests upon some kind of pre-criminal personality attributes or selective factors which operate in the recruitment to careers of check passing. This is suggested by the forger's frequent designation of himself as a "lone wolf," which in a number of cases is consistent with a history of family alienation or with a history of marginal participation in social groups. From this perspective, recruits to systematic

[17] See David Maurer, *The Big Con* (New York: Bobbs-Merrill, 1940). The comparison is best regarded as a historical one, for it is doubtful whether big con games, and con men of the sort described by Maurer, have existed for several decades.

[18] While late nineteenth-century check forgers worked in groups, they usually split up after passing a large check on a bank. See Lemert, "Behavior of the Systematic Check Forger."

[19] The best evidence of this is the distinctive names, used by con men in the past, e.g., The Yellow Kid Weil, The Boone Kid Whitney, and The High Ass Kid. Maurer, *The Big Con.*

check forgery of necessity would have to be isolate types in order to survive long enough to perfect a system or become anything more than amateurs or casual offenders. Unfortunately, separating learned aversion from predisposition requires kinds of data difficult or impossible to obtain.

Much firmer and less speculative ground for explanation of the check forger's disinclination for criminal colleagues or playfellows is at hand in the middle-class backgrounds of many forgers and their lack of acquaintance with criminal ways until they come to late adulthood. From such facts it can be inferred, as well as demonstrated by verbalizations of the forgers, that their values or orientation remain conventional, "middle class." Put into more specific context, they retain an image of themselves as "nice" persons, of "good" antecedents, or even of refinement, who, as they sometimes phrase it, "wouldn't have the guts to commit any other kind of crime." Associations with other criminals thus become distasteful for them, or even threatening in that they would validate a contradictory, rejected version of the self.

This interpretation is quite consistent with the seclusiveness which carries over into the forger's jail or prison behavior, and his tendency, whenever he can manage it, to occupy intermediary roles on the peripheries of the formal and informal groups in the prison. Examples are the role of a prison runner or that of a bookie in a contraband betting pool.

Such analysis strongly suggests that the problem of the systematic check forger is a special case of self-role conflict, or, more simply, a constantly aggravating moral dilemma. This requires the assumption of something like Sarbin's [20] "constancy principle," i.e., a cognitive structure (the self) tends to maintain its organization despite forces directed toward changing it. From this vantage, the forger's crisis results from the retention of a cognitive picture of himself as essentially a "good" person, but playing social roles in a way which violates the expectation of honesty in money matters. The disjunctive relation between the two structures, self and role, gives rise to the perturbations within the organism which are experienced as anxiety.

While this straightforward explanation is attractive, nevertheless, it is difficult to reconcile it with the fact that although some forgers experience guilt and remorse, many do not—at least not in any form which can be demonstrated through interview or case history materials. Furthermore, the small minority of systematic forgers with a history of delinquency or of crime beginning in their late teens display the same suspiciousness and avoidance of contacts with other criminals as is found

[20] Theodore Sarbin, "Role Theory," in *Handbook of Social Psychology*, ed. G. Lindzey (Cambridge: Cambridge University Press, 1954), chap. 6.

among those who have been categorized as "middle class." Nor is the personal crisis any less exacerbated in the former when it occurs.

For the class of systematic forgers with prior criminal sophistication the roots of dilemma are quite different, revolving about the low or dubious status which check passers hold in the eyes of other criminals. In many ways they are like the nouveau riche, or the "lower-upper" class in a New England town, envied because of their ready possession of money but suspect because of the source of their money.

Check passing is not viewed as a highly skilled criminal vocation [21] and the frequent prison sojourns of forgers implies the lack of any effective solution to the problem of ultimate arrest. The demeanor of forgers can be irritating to less well-educated criminals; in prison they are sometimes disliked because, as one burglar inmate acidly commented, "They like to pretend to be someone they ain't." Back of such attitudes is a vague distrust of the forger, a disapproval of his tendency to try to "con" others inside of the prison as he does on the outside.

It may be that there is a more generalized moral problem for all systematic forgers; the threat of exposure or designation as a "phony" may be the common dilemma which cuts across the psyche of the middle-class forger as well as one who is the product of early criminal socialization. Being a "phony," i.e., defining one's self in terms of a status while lacking the qualifications for the status, may be, as Goffman [22] claims, the "great cardinal sin." Nevertheless, there is good reason to believe that systematic forgers successfully protect themselves from the degradational implications of "phoniness." This they do less through rationalization or other psychodynamic mechanisms than they do by means of selective social participation and managed presentation of the self, which limits organismic involvement in role enactment.

That guilt is seldom more than of marginal importance for the forger so long as he doesn't become "too involved" and so long as he avoids victimizing those with whom he more closely identifies seems clear from the following.

> The only times I felt bad was with the "nice people." Usually when I was with people who liked me and I them, I stopped passing checks, or if I did, I was careful to see that nothing I did could harm them in any way. In Alabama when I went to church with my "friends" I put a check in

[21] ". . . they all (thieves and professional criminals) assume an air of superiority in the presence of the lowly 'short story writer,' as the bum check artist is known in the underworld." Sutherland, *The Professional Thief*, pp. 76–78.

[22] Erving Goffman, "On Cooling Out the Mark," *Psychiatry* 15 (1952): 451–63.

the collection, but I made sure that it was good, so that they would not be publicly embarrassed later.

Many of the so-called nice people who come into the forger's life never learn that he is a "phony" person, or if they do, it is after he has left town. Consequently there is seldom any direct or immediate validation of the stigma. Guilt remains largely retrospective and remote for the forger, without social reinforcement. He "leaves the field" before it can be generated in social interaction.

IDENTITY CRISES AND NEGATIVE IDENTITY

The foregoing argues strongly that the personal crisis of the systematic forger stems less from a moral dilemma than it does from the erosion of identity. So conceived, his problem resides in a neutral component or dimension of the self, namely the sense of separateness and relationship to others, which is assumed to have its own consequences for behavior apart from substantive social value, "good or bad," assigned to it.[23] In a sense the forger fails because he succeeds; he is able to fend off or evade self-degradative consequences of his actions but in so doing he rejects forms of interaction necessary to convert his rewards in positive, status-specific self-evaluations. In time he reaches a point at which he can no longer define himself in relation to others on any basis. The self becomes amorphous, without boundaries; the identity substructure is lost. Apathy replaces motivation, and in phenomenological terms, "life" or "this way of life" is no longer worth living. This is the common prelude to the forger's arrest.

There is, of course, an adaptive aspect to the psychic surrender which precedes or attends the forger's almost casual entry into legal custody, which can be seen quite clearly in the sense of relief which is experienced at the time and also later in jail. From a moral perspective, the forger is "being brought to justice"; he "pays his debt to society." However, from the perspective of this chapter, his apathy or carelessness and subsequent arrest function to end his anxiety which is the subjective aspect of the organized "hue and cry" of modern crime detection. More importantly, they solve his identity problem; arrest immediately assigns the forger an identity, undesirable though it may be, as a jail or prison

---

[23] A conception approximating this distinction can be found in D. L. Burnham, "Identity Definition and Role Demand in Hospital Careers of Schizophrenic Patients," *Psychiatry* 24 (1961): 96–122.

inmate. In effect, he receives or chooses a *negative identity*,[24] which despite its invidious qualities, is nearest and most real to him. At this juncture he is much like the actor who prefers bad publicity to none at all, or the youth who is willing to be a scapegoat for the group rather than not be part of the group at all.

CONCLUSION

Systematic check forgery comes closest to being a way of life which contains the seeds of its own destruction, or one which generates its own "phychopathology." This pathology, if the term is allowable, is less the product of the structural characteristics of specific roles and their interrelationships than it is of the gamelike manner in which they are chosen, fabricated, and enacted. For this reason, not too much of current "role theory" is germane to the forger's adjustment problems.

Neither role-role conflict nor role-self conflict, nor the availability or nonavailability of institutional ordering of roles (hierarchization, segregation), emphasized by Toby,[25] seem directly relevant to the psychic troubles of the systematic forger. Similarly, the degree of clarity of the roles enacted, stressed by Cottrell,[26] does not seem to have much bearing on his adjustment. Instead, it is the self-perceived or intuited ground rules of the forgery game—pseudonymity, mobility, and seclusiveness—which condition both his success and failure in role playing and adjustment. They do so by placing clear limits on his role involvements.

In this connection Sarbin's [27] concept of the "degree of organismic involvement" obviously becomes centrally important in the behavior of the check man. In fact, his role playing fits rather neatly into the upper two of Sarbin's seven-level classification of roles; the forger, for the most part, is limited to casual roles and dramatic roles (mechanical acting), with the occasional need, perhaps, for "heated acting" (class III).

Skill in "taking-the-role-of-the-other," as conceived by Cottrell, Sarbin, and others, does not seem to be especially important in explaining the forger's ultimate failure in role adjustment, except insofar as it may

[24] Erik H. Erikson, "The Problem of Ego Identity," in *Identity and Anxiety*, ed. M. R. Stein, et al. (New York: Free Press, 1960), pp. 60–62.

[25] Jackson Toby, "Some Variables in Role-Conflicting Analysis," *Social Forces* 30 (1950): 324–27.

[26] Leonard Cottrell, "The Adjustment of the Individual to his Age and Sex Roles," *American Sociological Review* 12 (1942): 618–25.

[27] Sarbin, "Role Theory."

be temporarily reduced or distorted by isolation and anxiety from extraneous sources. Generally it would have to be conceded that check forgers are "good role takers"; consequently, although their difficulties possibly qualify as "psychopathological," they can scarcely be held to be psychopaths either in Gough's [28] sense of lacking ability to see the self as an object or in Sarbin's sense of being deficient in "tension binding" capacity.

It seems impressively clear that the forger's adjustment difficulties lie primarily in the attenuation of motivation to enact his social roles rather than in their attributes or in the constant aspects of his character. The final bankruptcy of motivation tends to be a dialectical product of prolonged enactment of pseudonymous and casual roles which preclude the establishment of identity. "Establishment" is the term most appropriate to the issue because, as Foote [29] convincingly argues, identity is always problematic. Failing to establish identity, the systematic forger reaches an impasse at which he no longer sees value in everyday existence. Yet valuation, which is at the core of motivation, is problematic, too. Without identity there cannot be valuation.

[28] H. G. Gough, "A Sociological Theory of Psychopathology," *American Journal of Sociology* 53 (1948): 359–66.

[29] Nelson N. Foote, "Identification as a Basis for a Theory of Motivation," *American Sociological Review* 16 (1951): 14–21.

10 STUTTERING AMONG THE NORTH PACIFIC COASTAL INDIANS

The following is a report and tentative interpretation of research findings of a field investigation into the incidence and cultural aspects of stuttering among a number of Indian tribes in the North Pacific coastal area of British Columbia.[1] The project was part of a larger enterprise to gather comparative materials on deviant behavior but more specifically followed certain lines of inquiry initiated by clinical psychologists working on the problem of speech disorders in American Indian societies, who were unable to find evidence of stuttering in these groups.[2]

Reprinted with permission from Southwestern Journal of Anthropology, 8 (Winter 1952): 429–41.

[1] The writer is indebted to Professor Abraham M. Halpern for several very helpful suggestions and for assistance in the transcriptions in this paper.

[2] Wendell Johnson, "The Indians Have No Word For It: Stuttering in Children," *Quarterly Journal of Speech* 30 (1944): 330–37; also, Wendell Johnson, *People in Quandries* (New York: Harper & Row, Publishers, 1946), chapter 17; John Snidecor, "Why the Indian Does Not Stutter," *Quarterly Journal of Speech* 33 (1947): 493–95. Inquiries by an investigator of stuttering among the Navaho brought to light altogether five cases, some obviously complicated by acculturation problems. She concluded that while cases do occur in this tribe, nevertheless it was quite rare. Adelaide K. Bullen, "A Cross Cultural Approach to the Problem of Stuttering," *Child Development* 16 (1945): 3–7.

Our field contacts covered five reserves of Salish Indians, two Kwa-kiutl and one Nootka or west coast tribe, all located on Vancouver Island and the mainland of British Columbia. In addition to these con-tacts with the cultures *in situ* we had two Haida informants, one Tsim-shian, and one Nootka who were not living in their respective areas. All informants except two spoke English and interviews were necessarily conducted in this language. In addition, our body of interview data was supplemented by information from school officials and some written materials from Indian children at the Port Alberni and Alert Bay resi-dential schools.

In general our findings emerged as exceptional or at considerable variance from those indicating an absence of speech disorders among the American Indians. Thus we encountered: (1) both stuttering speech and persons regarded as stutterers among the contemporary coastal In-dians; (2) evidence of pre-acculturational existence of this class of speech disorders; (3) well-defined concepts of stuttering and stutterers in the language and culture of all the bands of which we came to have knowl-edge.

Since our investigation was in no sense a systematic survey, it was impossible to arrive at any measure such as a percentage or a rate of stutterers in the Indian population. However, the following facts indis-putably establish the existence, if not the frequency, of the speech defect in the area. In the residential school at Alert Bay two stutterers (both female) were identified out of a total enrollment of 220. Also two were reported and described for us at the residential school at Port Alberni where the enrollment reaches 240. At the Cowichan day school, with a student group of 110, no stutterers were known to the teachers but "quite a few" had trouble with "g" sounds, which caused them con-siderable shame and embarrassment.

All of our Indian informants (ten) with the exception of one[3] whom we queried on the subject were acquainted with at least one or two cases of stuttering, and several gave clear statements that the dis-order was commonplace among their people, especially the two Nootka informants. Information from the Homalthko Salish band testified to the presence of the disorder in several families. In one of these there are two brothers who stuttered as children and who do so currently, although one of them experiences his broken speech only when drunk. There is another adult stutterer in a second family, and in still a third family there is an adult who stuttered as a child but was later "cured." This man's deceased grandfather also stuttered, both as a child and when

---

[3] Other informants stated that there were quite a few stutterers from his reserve.

grown to maturity. The population of this band fluctuates around 150. In a closely related band, the Tlahoose, we talked directly with a man and his sister who had been very bad stutterers as children.

Apart from these we were able to interview two Indians who were currently stutterers, one a Tsimshian youth of 20 years, the other a young Salish boy. A brief case history of the latter discloses the nature of the stuttering.

> Stanley Jones was born 14 years ago at Sliammon, a reserve located a few miles outside of Powell River, British Columbia. He is an illegitimate child, having three younger siblings and one older sister. The mother apparently was sexually promiscuous when younger and at the present time is one of those on the reserve who make and get drunk on home brew. At times Stanley has been left in the care of his older, married sister when his father and mother move away to live at logging camps. This sister is drunken and sexually promiscuous, and regards Stanley as incorrigible. Stanley has had tubercuolsis and bears a scar from an operation on his neck. He has stuttered "as long as he can remember" and encounters the difficulty in both Salish and English, although more so in the latter language. His speech is most noticeably broken by a disruption of his breathing in the form of gasps before words and extremely long hesitations between words and phrases, with some syllable repetitions. As he blocks on words he blinks and draws his head down toward his chest, all of which is associated with marked spasmodic contractions of the diaphragm. The blocks are exeprienced at home but more at school, where he has become increasingly sensitive. He says that the other children laugh at him, and it makes him feel bad.

This case in our estimate exemplifies stuttering as it appears in white persons in our own society in several important particulars, namely in the presence of word blocks, anxiety, and awareness of social disapproval. We note especially the so-called "secondary" manifestations of stuttering in the blinking of the eyes, drawing the head down, and the disturbed breathing. These symptoms, which are commonly interpreted as a function of the person's anxiety or anticipation of probable social penalties of the defect, also come out in several other cases. In the one other individual we interviewed they assumed the form of covering the mouth with his hand, breaking eyecontact, and fiddling with his necktie. In another reported case the man "danced up and down to get the words out," and in still another the man "squeezed his eyes shut," often giving up the struggle to speak by announcing that he could not say the word.

Evidence for the aboriginal existence of stuttering among the coastal Indians in the Northwest is somewhat attenuated but still impressive. First of all, the individual we interviewed, who had stuttered as a child, was 70 years old. Allowing 60 years for the period since he stuttered we are removed to 1890, at which time the degree of direct interaction with Whites by the Indians of this man's band was almost negligible. The first priest, for example, did not visit his band until 1880. Prior to that contacts with Whites were largely trade contacts. Even today this band remains quite isolated geographically and socially. Another informant at Nanaimo, who was 80 years of age, spoke of a stutterer who was a grown man when he (the informant) was a boy. Here the first mission and mission school were not established until some time after 1865, so that the childhood of this stutterer dated back to a period when White religious and educational influence must have been at a minimum.[4] Sapir's informants, who described the speech disorders of the Nootka, were young adults at the time of his field work in 1910. This means that the data pertain to the historical period from 1875 to 1890 on, the earlier dates barely coinciding with the establishment of missions and schools on the west coast of Vancouver Island.[5]

A somewhat different type of data pointing to the early, pre-White contact occurrence of stuttering among the coastal Indians came from descriptions given us to several native methods of "curing" stuttering. For example, the Nootka had a practice of striking the stutterer on the arm to help him get the words out. According to the Comox, stuttering "could be cured" by having the afflicted person take a bite of food and pass it from one hand to another under one knee before placing it in the mouth. This had to be done four times. The Tlahoose and the Homalthko treated stuttering even more uniquely; the stutterer was instructed to find a board with a knothole in it, and every morning on arising recite to it *ha'ak'ok chen*, "I give stuttering to you," and then spit or blow through the hole in order to get the stuttering out of his throat. Also in these bands a shaman could be hired to cure stuttering, using special native medicine in the process.

The likelihood that well-defined methods of treatment for stuttering such as we have described arose after culture contact and interaction with White populations seems improbable. We are inclined to believe that a considerable length of time would be necessary for the evolution of such folk techniques, or that if they were nonaboriginal inventions they would reveal signs of White influences.

Perhaps even more telling proof of the very early, pre-acculturative presence of stuttering in the North Pacific Indian areas lies in the widespread linguistic recognition of the disorder. Every tribal language

[4] Thomas Crosby, *Among the An-ko-me-nums* (Toronto: Briggs, 1907), chapter 1.

[5] Edward Sapir, *Abnormal Types of Speech in Nootka* (Ottawa: Canada Department of Mines, Geological Survey Memoir 62, Anthropological Series, 1915), p. 3.

of which we inquired contained words for stuttering as well as for certain other speech disorders. As far as we could tell there were no borrowed English words nor any inter-tribal borrowings of words to designate stuttering. The various tribal terms for the disorder are as follows:

Salish
  Homalthko, Sliammon,
    Tlahoose   *ha'ak'ok*
    Comox   *hahk'ok*
    Nanaimo   *skeykulskwels*
    Cowichan, Seschelt,
      Squamish   *o'tsa'tsa*
  Tsimshian
    Nass River   *ah'al*
    Kitimat   *amkwa*
  Haida
    Skidegate   *kilekwigu'ung*
  Kwakiutl
    Nimpkish, Kingcome
      Inlet   *kaketsakwa'*

The Nootka of the west coast of Vancouver Island merit special comment with respect not only to the cultural recognition given stuttering, but also for the way in which their language has been modified and adapted to reckon with a relatively wide variety of speech defects. Our two Nootka informants described three and four different speech defects respectively in their accounts, both including stuttering. The older of the two, from Nootka Sound, spoke of the following: *hahuchin*, stuttering; *tlatlachkin*, blocking or "pinching off" words; *ninichin*, straining to get words out. The other man, from the reserve at Port Alberni, gave a somewhat different set of four categories: *hachucha*, stuttering; *hahuting*, lisping; *tlatlaching*, "collapsed speech"; *ninichin*, talking through the nose (probably cleft palate speech).[6]

In Sapir's earlier research on the Nootka he described, in all, five speech abnormalities, although two of them probably can be reduced to variants of lisping. The other three are nasalization, stuttering, and cleft palate speech. He gives no native term [7] for stuttering, which frees us to

[6] In transcribing the native words here we have employed the method suggested by Sapir and Swadesh for using native terms in English context. Edward Sapir and Morris Swadesh, *Nootka Texts* (Philadelphia: Linguistic Society of America, 1939), p. 13.

[7] We have not attempted to reproduce Sapir's phonetic transcriptions of the native terms used in this older research. Later he adopted a different system. Readers who are interested may consult his *Abnormal Types of Speech in Nootka*, pp. 20 f.

believe that the term we obtained (*hahuchin*) may well be the proper one or its close approximation.

ATTITUDES TOWARD STUTTERERS

The attitudes of the coastal Indians in the North Pacific toward stutterers range from mild to serious disapproval, through humorous tolerance, to pity and condescension. Members of the three mainland tribes, the Homalthko, Sliammon, and Tlahoose were easily moved to laughter by mention or discussion of the subject. Their reaction is best summed up by the statement of one man who said: "Oh, we laugh at such people at first but then we get used to them." Another man interviewed on the Nanaimo reserve expressed essentially the same attitude, adding the observation that "outsiders" continued to laugh at stutterers even though their immediate associates came in time to accept them without comment. Several of the undirected, freely associated stories which we had children of the Port Alberni residential school write on the subject of "A Person Who Couldn't Talk Right or Who Stuttered" conveyed ideas that in the Bella Bella and Tsimshian areas parents tended to be shamed by their children if they stuttered. This is not unexpected in the light of the high standards of decorum for children, especially of high-ranking parents, held in the old Tsimshian culture, in which, among other stringencies, children were forbidden to run in their play lest they accidentally fall and thus shame their parents.[8]

A more specific demonstration of negative attitudes toward stutterers came from our case history of a Tsimshian stutterer. His father severely criticized him as a child for his faulty speech, invoking the native term for "acting crazy" (in contradistinction to insanity) to express his strong disapproval of his son's verbal failures. This concept was generally applied to anyone deviating in disapproved ways from the norms of the culture. This man's father also had told him disapprovingly that in former days boys with speech defects had to take a back seat in the potlatch ceremonies and could not actively participate in them. A Haida woman confirmed that this was also the case in her tribe in former times. A Kwakiutl spokesman said he had known of stutterers but had never known of one who took part in a potlatch. However, all of this does not mean that anyone in these tribes was free to insult a person because of his

[8] Viola Garfield, *Tsimshian Clan and Society*, Vol. 7 (Seattle: University of Washington Publications in Anthropology, 1939), 193; if our information is correct, this also held for the old Nootka culture. The Kwakiutl likewise were shamed by injuries to their children. See Helen Cordere, "Fighting with Property," *American Ethnological Society Monograph* 18 (1950): 80.

speech difficulties, for there was always the threat that the family of the offended man or woman would give a potlatch to shame the person or clan responsible for the insult.

It is from the Nootka that we get the most abundant evidence of social penalization of persons with physical and speech defects. In this culture fat persons, very small persons, sore-eyed, squinting, cock-eyed, hunchbacked, lame, circumcised, left-handed people, and those with different speech disorders became the object of pity, mockery, satirization, humor, and patronage of the sort shown small children. This is most apparent in the myths of the Nookta, but emerges with equal clarity in associations of animals, mythological characters, and defective persons with various linguistic and stylistic processes involving the symbolic use of sounds. Thus when a person who had a speech defect was addressed or talked about, his defect was imitated or mocked, with changes in word forms—such as suffix changes—which carried implications of smallness, childishness, animal quality, or of some physical defect.[9]

The analysis of myths occurring throughout the broader culture area of the Northwest reveals much the same social rejection and social isolation of such child deviants as orphans, crippled, blind, stupid, dirty, lazy, weak, and those with scabs or skin diseases. Most of these myths are analogues of the success stories of our own culture and have been specifically analyzed as variants of the Cinderella theme in Grimms' fairy tales.[10] It is perhaps significant that the Swaixwe mask, whose mythological origin concerns a boy who gets cured of a bad skin disease and is enabled to invent and use a new dance ceremony, has the widest distribution of any mask in the Northwest.[11] While stutterers are not mentioned in any of these myths, we found in several of the stories written for us by the residential school children there were equivalents of Horatio Alger-like stutterers who overcome their defect to go on and become famous. Since the analysis of the myths was a content analysis and not a stylistic or linguistic one, we do not know whether abnormal speech forms were used in telling the myths as was found by Sapir in Nootka.

With the Nootka these abnormal speech forms could have varying meanings of mere smallness, contempt, or even pitying affection, depending upon the nature of the relationship between the speaker and the person addressed or discussed. Imitation of the defects of one person

[9] Sapir, Abnormal Types of Speech, pp. 3–15.

[10] Betty Randall, "The Cinderella Theme in Northwest Coast Folklore," in Indians of the Urban Northwest, ed. Marian Smith (New York: Columbia University Press, 1949), pp. 243–85.

[11] Helen Cordere, "The Swaixwe Myth of the Middle Fraser River," Journal of American Folklore 61 (1948): 1–18.

might be done in a friendly spirit, whereas the same mimicry of another would be an insult. Furthermore, it seems that some restraint was exercised in mocking adults when they were present, although this was not the case for children. An expression of this qualified attitude toward persons with speech disorders is seen in the application of special names by the Nootka. Our informant recalled, for example, one lame man who was known as "rotten foot," another known as "the man whose wound healed with skunk cabbage in it," and lastly, of more direct interest, one called the "stuttering man." He said that such names could be given the person either by himself or by close relatives. However, it would be insulting for unrelated persons to impose the name, and only such a man's close friends were free to address him in this fashion.

Insofar as our data permit us to say, the Nootka differed from the Tsimshian in respect to the more formal discrimination against persons with speech disorders. Being a stutterer did not bar one from giving a potlatch if he were otherwise able and entitled to do so. A stutterer who formerly lived at Barclay Sound was the head man of one of the four clans there and took part in and gave numerous potlatches. It might be added that this man was exceptionally well-liked for his personal characteristics. It should be borne in mind that while a high-ranking Nootka might make his own speeches at potlatch ceremonies, still it was culturally permissible to hire professional speakers for this purpose. However, doing this to show a person's wealth would be quite different from doing it because the person was an ineffective speaker.

THE RELATION OF STUTTERING TO CULTURAL FACTORS

With the time and resources available our research could not result in the collection of data which would permit testing of any considerable number of the current theories of stuttering. Some isolated facts may be taken as bearing upon one or two of these theories. For example, there seems to have been very little mental disorder among the Nootka,[12] which may be interpreted to mean that speech disorders there were unlikely to have been the function of neurotic or personality disorders. The theory that stuttering is related to dysphemia and changed-handedness gets some oblique support from the recorded aversion of the Nootka to left-handedness and their rather painful method used to discourage children

---

[12] Robert Brown, ed., *The Adventures of John Jewitt* (London: C. Wilson, 1896), p. 175.

from using their left hands.[13] However, the limited nature of our knowledge of these things can permit little beyond speculation.

The particular data we secured and those available in ethnographies of the Northwest coastal culture areas lend themselves far more readily to testing sociopsychological theories of stuttering which make room for the interplay of cultural factors. Here we have in mind the explicit recognition of the importance of such factors in Johnson's "evaluational" theory of stuttering and their implicit emphasis in Van Riper's formulation of the growth of stuttering as a process.[14] Both theories, which have been widely influential in the study and treatment of stuttering, lay stress upon (1) the penalizing reactions of others, especially those of anxious parents, critical siblings, and ridiculing playmates, toward the speech of the young child; (2) the internalization of these reactions or negative evaluations by the child; (3) the growth of anxiety in the child about his own speech; and (4) the pathological disruption of the child's speech rhythms by this anxiety.

The main difference in the two views regarding the development of stuttering concerns the appearance of the initial symptoms of stuttering, with Van Riper holding that disorganization of the child's immediate social environment can produce generalized conflict or anxiety, of which the stuttering is an expression. At this stage of the "primary symptoms," the reactions of others enter by the above indicated process to create the exaggerated blocks we commonly recognize as stuttering. Johnson apparently believes that early as well as late stuttering is entirely due to the way in which others *define* (evaluate) the normally variable speech of children.

Our data can best be cited to test the more general socio-psychological proposition upon which there seems to be agreement in the theories of the two writers to whom we have referred. Insofar as it is possible we will examine data which bear upon the second, perhaps less important, point on which there is divergence of viewpoints. The most significant socio-cultural factors, of course, are those which affect parent-child in-

[13] Phillip Drucker, "The Northern and Central Nootkan Tribes," *Bureau of American Ethnology Bulletin*, 144 (1951): 130. We found one Homalthko woman whose parents had attempted to change her from left- to right-handed, but there was no stuttering in her family.

[14] Johnson, *People in Quandaries*, chap. 17; also Wendell Johnson, "The Role of Evaluation in Stuttering," *Journal of Speech Disorders* 3 (1938): 85–89; Charles Van Riper, "The Growth of the Stuttering Spasm," *Quarterly Journal of Speech* 23 (1937): 70–73; also Charles Van Riper, *Speech Correction* (Englewood Cliffs, N.J.: Prentice-Hall, 1947), pp. 280–90; Charles Van Riper and Wendell Johnson, *Stuttering* (Chicago: National Society for Crippled Children and Adults, 1948), pp. 24–33.

teraction, for there seems to be a consensus that practically all stuttering begins in childhood. Consequently a consideration of child-rearing practices in relation to stuttering among the Northwest coastal Indians is directly relevant.

No trait of primitive society, particularly in North America, has been more widely commented upon than that of parental indulgence of children.[15] The primitive cultures of the North Pacific prove to be no exception with respect to this characteristic. In general the reconstructed picture of primitive practice in this area is one in which corporal punishment plays a minor part or is absent entirely in the discipline of children. One exception we discovered, in recounts of the old culture of the mainland Homalthko, Tlahoose, and Sliammon, serves to emphasize the generalization. Here a child, if extremely recalcitrant, might be spanked with a beaver tail in front of other children of the band. However, this was always done by two persons especially designated for the job, never by the parents. The socialization of the child generally seems to have been brought about through teaching by example, long moral lectures and morality stories—often repeated—given by the grandparents, and private scoldings heavily laced with the shame motif. Threats seldom if ever entered into these.[16]

Granting what seem to be obvious similarities between the child-rearing methods of the northern Pacific Indian cultures and those in the rest of North America, it does not follow that the standards of childhood decorum, aspiration, and expectations of the child's ultimate participation in the formal rituals of the culture which served as goals of the educational process were comparable. Indeed it is precisely here, in the rich ceremonial solo drama and theatricality of feasts and potlatches captioning the life crises of the individual, that we perceive the differentiation of the Northwest coastal Indian cultures from those broadly conceived as North American. The importance of the ceremonial vindication of the individual's position in society was impressed quite early, with the indoctrination of adult values and goals beginning almost at birth. Parents in the Nootka tribes often began their discourses on mores while the infant was still cradle-bound, with high ranking fathers seriously lecturing sons at this time on the merits of giving feasts and potlatches. Most Nootka children while still quite young were expected to learn their privileged dances and sacred songs, and adults worked continuously with them to achieve the necessary competence in their performances. At very tender ages they were required to perform alone before assemblies of

[15] George Pettit, *Primitive Education in North America*, Vol. 43 (Berkeley: University of California Publications in Archaeology and Ethnology, 1946): 6.

[16] Drucker, "Northern and Central Nootka Tribes," p. 131.

their own and other tribesmen. The Nootka ordinarily initiated children into the Shaman's dance at the age of seven or eight years; a chief might have his one-year old son inducted as a novice, or even have his pregnant wife treated as a "novice" as a means of initiating his unborn child into the adult ceremonial life.[17]

This ritual, more or less central to the whole ceremonial complex of the Nootka, by its rough nature was undoubtedly a traumatic experience to many of the small children who were necessarily spectators and participants. On this point Drucker says:

> Small children were usually frightened during the performance . . . the hullabaloo and running about, the rough practical jokes (carried to the point of throwing people bodily into the sea), kidnapping and purported slaying of siblings and playmates all combined to make small children the least entertained and most perturbed of the spectators.[18]

By the time children were old enough to become active participants in the Shaman's dance it is true that their fears inspired by it tended to disappear, but in their place came anxieties as to whether they would "remember their instructions" and whether they would perform adequately.[19] This anxiety, when it occurred, clearly seems to have been a

---

[17] Drucker, "Northern and Central Nootka Tribes," pp. 386 ff. The same early initiation of children into special societies occurred among the Tsimshian. See Garfield, *Tsimshian Clan and Society*, p. 299. The desire to make the child into a "little adult" appears to some extent in Salish culture even today. See Joanne Schriver and Eleanor Leacock, "Harrison Indian Childhood" in *Indians of the Urban Northwest*, p. 199. Apparently from early times the Kwakiutl expected adult type behavior in children. C. S. Ford, *Smoke from Their Fires* (New Haven, Conn.: Yale University Press, 1941), p. 56, chap. 3.

[18] Drucker, "Northern and Central Nootka Tribes," p. 130. There are a number of other characteristics of the Northwestern Pacific primitive cultures which might be thought of as anxiety-inducing for the child. The large households apparently continually underwent change with comings and goings of relatives and others. Marriage was generally associated with considerable conflict of the spouses and divorce was fairly common, followed by shifts in residence of mother and child. Warfare presented the constant threat of death or enslavement of children. The ideal warrior was one who was utterly bloodthirsty and terrible in aspect. Several of our Salish informants recalled the great dread they held as children toward warriors of their own tribes, a dread which remained very real to them as adults today. Whether such cultural phenomena gave rise to abnormal anxieties or whether cultural techniques were adequate to permit the child to handle such anxieties is a large subject which we cannot undertake to discuss here.

[19] Ibid., p. 138. A Kwakiutl man to whom we talked said that his going through the *hamatsa* ritual when he was 12 years old caused him much anxiety and that his grandfather practically forced him to do it. A Comox man told of

reciprocal of socially invidious distinctions and the praise-rewards reactions of adults in terms of competency in performing rituals. In this connection it is informative to read of an Ehetisaht Shaman's dance in which the "wolves" going through the village announced that they wanted only those novices who could sing their songs and sing them well.[20] An observer as far back as 1868 tells how Nootka boys in their evening play on the beach frequently mimicked famous orators of the tribes and recited parts of legendary speeches before an audience of old men who pointed out this boy or that boy as destined to do great things.[21] That parents of the Nootkan tribes had anxieties concerning the future verbal facility of their children seems demonstrated by the custom of putting a finger far down in the infant's throat to insure his becoming a good singer.[22]

It is to be noted that Nootka culture admitted of little or no deviation from ordinary rules of inheritance of songs or rituals, private or public, simply because the proper heir could not learn them. But along with this a person did not automatically gain acceptance in his rank purely by inheritance; it was necessary to show his right to social position by his personal traits, proper conduct, and ritualistic versatility. From the standpoint of the child the standards of the culture were not only rigorous and exacting but also inexorable, and their early imposition indubitably played a significant part in creating a very shame-conscious person, highly sensitive to his own behavior deviations and to those of other persons, including members of his own family. That this sensitivity extended to speech behavior is emphasized by Sproat's early remarks on the "standard of correct speech" held by the Nootka and the extreme care with which they pronounced names and words they heard for the first time.[23]

---

similar feelings at his first potlatch. Potlatching among the Kwakiutl called for careful memory of numerous ancestors' names, their histories and social positions, as well as the social positions of all living ranking tribe members. In addition, entry into potlatching meant one could not be "foolish" in spending his money. It is not unusual that many children were more or less compelled even to enter into "play potlatches." See Ford, chapters 3, 5, p. 86.

[20] Drucker, *Smoke from Their Fires*, p. 159.

[21] Gilbert Sproat, *Scenes and Studies of Savage Life* (London: Smith, Elder, 1868), p. 63. The Kwakiutl did not attend "play" potlatches of their children but nevertheless kept informed about them and criticized their conduct later. Ford, *Smoke from Their Fires*, pp. 85 ff.

[22] This was also related to the desire to make the child physically attractive. Drucker, "Nootka Tribes," p. 123.

[23] Sproat, *Scenes and Studies*, p. 266. In aboriginal times death was sometimes the penalty for mentioning tabooed names or words associated with them. Drucker, "Nootka Tribes," p. 149.

The competitive, rank-conscious stress of the culture undoubtedly made the deviant person especially vulnerable to mimicry, humorous anecdotes, and gossip, and, although the cultural ideal specified that the deviant accept all of this in good grace, it seems unlikely that he was able to do so. Thus, in speaking of persons who are *o'ucshaid* (bunglers, clumsy ones), the Nootka say they are teased without malice and that they tell stories on themselves, but also insightfully add that the teasing "seems to make them worse; they do more and more funny things." [24] In the case of the stutterers it seems clear that they would be at the additional disadvantage of not being able to tell stories on themselves or to use effectively verbal aggressions when goaded beyond endurance.

While the general adult population of these Northwestern Indian tribes may have been partly restrained in criticizing the stuttering child, in all likelihood this was not true for his immediate family. It is also probable that in play groups the stutterer aboriginally encountered much open ridicule from other children—especially away from the presence of adults. The only deterrent here seems to have been cautions from parents to their children to be careful what they said to sons of chiefs. We guess that such cautions were ignored as frequently by, say, Nootka children in early times as comparable injunctions are by children in our society today.

The potlatch, of course, was the main defense of the deviant against insult, but it is questionable whether the speech deviant was free to avail himself of the device, for by its very nature it would lead to a public display of the behavior occasioning the insult. Even if relatives or a friendly chief gave the potlatch for the insulted person, his defect would still be publicized. Indeed potlatches of this order seem to have been used more for wiping out shame related to incidental deviations from norms and accepted practices rather than that associated with a permanent or continuing social inadequacy.

CONCLUSION

There is fair to good evidence that stuttering is present among the people of the northwest coastal Indian tribes and for the probabilities of its aboriginal incidence. The cultural setting in these Indian societies in the past as well as in the present seems favorable to the development of stuttering. The facts indicate that aboriginally stuttering was culturally defined, that stutterers were and still are socially penalized, that parents tended to be specifically concerned or anxious about the speech development of children, that children were anxious about ritual performances

[24] Ibid., p. 328.

involving solo verbal behavior, and that Indian stutterers showed and still show "secondary" symptoms of the defect, which are ordinarily interpreted as distortions of the speech induced by internalizations of anxiety about the speech.

We have no particular reason for questioning the authenticity of Johnson's and Snidecor's reports of an absence of stuttering and concomitant cultural definitions of the defect among the Bannock and Shoshone, inasmuch as their sample was large and as specialists in their field they presumably know what they were looking for.[25] Consequently we are left with the possibility that a real differentiation exists between these cultures and Northwest Coast Indian cultures in these respects. However, such differences are not incompatible with the general nature of the theory which we have been interested in testing. Indeed one study of child development among the Wind River Shoshone gives much evidence that the culture differs sharply from the cultures we have described with respect both to degree of pressure on children and treatment of defective persons.[26]

[25] Supra.

[26] Dmitri B. Shimkin, "Childhood and Development among the Wind River Shoshone," *Anthropological Records* 5 (University of California, 1947): 289–325.

11

STUTTERING AND SOCIAL
STRUCTURE IN TWO
PACIFIC ISLAND SOCIETIES

One of the chief concepts in the intellectual stock in trade of sociologists and anthropologists is that of culture. Unfortunately the term is often abused and frequently it is reified or converted into an explanatory concept; it is treated as if it were a causative entity much like older usages of instinct or heredity. Carefully considered, the concept can be used most appropriately as an orientation to a body of data. It is a way of symbolizing in the large those aspects of human behavior which are patterned and which are cumulative through time, i.e., with an ongoing existence independent of the biological individuals who participate in them. It includes directly observable behavior and also such items as values, norms, themes, meanings, and sentiments which are inferences of higher level abstractions from sense observable data of human behavior.

It should be said here that the present trend in sociology is away from emphasis upon the culture concept in favor of more attention to groups, collective behavior, social stratification, and social structure. The reason for this is that traditionally patterned behavior is less and less significant as an influence in urban industrial societies of the West. This is increasingly true even in preliterate and so-called underdeveloped societies of the

Reprinted with permission from the Journal of Speech and Hearing Disorders 27 *(February 1962): 3–10.*

present-day world, which are fast being absorbed into world regional industrial systems.

Such things as values are somewhat more durable aspects of culture which appear to survive the attrition or destruction of overt cultural forms through which they are expressed. Hence the current interest of anthropologists in values or value systems in non-industrial societies and likewise a revival of sociological concern with values in American society.

However, the inquiries of American anthropologists in the form of "culture-personality" studies or studies of basic personality structure are incomplete instruments for understanding behavior because they fail to show how intervening social relationships and structures limit, preclude, and shape the expression of value systems in individuals. For this reason sociologists insist on the importance of social structure and social interaction in research leading to predictions and understanding of human behavior. It is also true that they have turned to special ways of conceptualizing the class of behavior under consideration here.

Stuttering may be regarded sociologically as a form of deviant behavior. Because musculature is apparently involved, it suggests the possibility of a biological basis for its etiology. Testing this hypothesis presumably can be done with comparative studies of societies. Thus, if societies can be found in which there is no current incidence of stuttering and no historical evidence of stuttering, then the notion of a genetic constitutional basis for stuttering can be summarily set aside. The alternative would be to conclude that whole populations or races differ in their potentialities for stuttering, which in the scope of present knowledge concerning race does not seem tenable.

Thus far it has to be said that data on the distribution of stuttering in world societies are thin, in some cases little more than "reports." Fortunately, interest has been aroused in the problem, and a start has been made in accumulating sociological data on stuttering by trained investigators. Kluckhohn,[1] after assessing extant studies, concluded that "as yet no single unequivocal case of the absence of stuttering among a people has been found." From this he goes on to say that "biological or idiosyncratic life history factors can be productive of stuttering in all cultures." There will probably be those who disagree with this conclusion or question the speculative reasoning on which it rests, namely, that because such cases haven't been found they won't be found. Yet I must admit a leaning in this direction after my recent research survey in Hawaii and other island societies of the South Pacific.

Probably the eventual usefulness of comparative sociological studies

---

[1] Clyde Kluckhohn, "Culture and Behavior," in *Handbook of Social Psychology*, Vol. II, ed. G. Lindzey (Reading, Mass.: Addison-Wesley, 1954).

will be to establish the differential incidences of stuttering and to relate these to selected variables of culture and social structure in the societies under examination. At the present time we can safely say that the incidence of stuttering does indeed vary from society to society, but the magnitude of these differences remains to be determined. The significant variables which will be most useful in studying the etiology of stuttering in high- and low-incidence societies also remain a research problem.

As a start in this kind of analysis, I propose to compare two societies. One of these, on basis of admittedly limited data, I regard as a low-incidence society, and one I can more confidently designate as a high-incidence society. The first is Polynesian society, the second is Japanese.

The data are based upon interviews with informants. They were collected incidental to a study of a somewhat different area of deviant behavior, during nine months spent on the large island of Hawaii and four months spent in Samoa, the Society Islands, and the Cook Islands.

STUTTERING AMONG POLYNESIANS

Speaking very generally, my inquiries in the Polynesian area indicated that while stuttering existed, was recognized, and was symbolized in the language, nevertheless, it was not very common. As one educated and informed Hawaiian woman put it, "There are *some* among us who stutter." Hawaiian stutterers are called *uu uus*, because "they can't get the words out before they speak." Several other Hawaiian informants confirmed this woman's statements. They spoke of one case of an 80-year-old woman who had died one year previously in the Lunalilo Home in Honolulu, whom they unequivocally identified as a stutterer. She had spasms of the mouth, got red in the face, and showed difficulty in her breathing when she tried to speak. She spoke only Hawaiian, for the most part to her close friends, very little to others, and never to strangers.

My study on the island of Hawaii of 30 case histories of public welfare families in which a drinking problem existed disclosed one Hawaiian family having a child with a "speech defect" who was at the same time "retarded." In another family with a child who stuttered, the mother was Korean and the father part Hawaiian. Finally, there came to light a Hawaiian family of five children, one of whom stuttered and also was delinquent. While this incidence for the aggregate of families may seem high, it must be remembered that they were largely disorganized families. Furthermore, the mixing of Hawaiians with other races and the fragmentary nature of any surviving Hawaiian culture make statements about rates of stuttering difficult for this group.

As far as I could determine from older informants, not much attention was paid to stutterers in early Hawaiian society. Stutterers were "thought to be born that way." No cure for the condition was known, and Kahunas, the Hawaiian medicine men, made no effort to administer remedies or otherwise treat stutterers. Stutterers were not socially rejected, and, as the informants put it, "could be good hand workers, at fishing or in taro patches."

In American Samoa as in Hawaii, informants agreed that stuttering did exist and they gave the word *nu nu* to describe it. This is also the word applied by Samoans to mutes. However, informants had difficulty in recalling specific cases of the disorder. One *matai*, or chief, knew of but one case, a man in another village. This man had great difficulty in his speech, which was accompanied by visible spasms in his mouth and throat. Another *matai* knew of two cases, one a man living in a distant village and another an old woman who lived in Pago Pago.

Samoans, again like the Hawaiians, believe that stutterers are born that way. No treatment is known or attempted, although a medicine is employed to treat mutes. Samoan children make fun of stutterers, but they are corrected by their parents when they do so. There is no rejection of stutterers in regard to occupation and stutterers do not withdraw socially. One stutterer, who was somewhat better known by one of the informants, ran a store in American Samoa. He was depicted as a "smart man who knew his business." His customers readily adjusted to him, and he "used gestures for communication when necessary."

Responses to my inquiries in the Cook Islands were consistent with findings for Hawaii and Samoa. On Rarotonga several informants knew "there are people like that" (stutterers) but had never known any personally. They also said that there is a word for stuttering. However, due to the confused linguistic situation, I could not reliably ascertain what the term was.

Data were more specific for the island of Mangaia, about 110 miles from Rarotonga. Here there are a number of stutterers, personally known by my informant, all coming from one family. The Mangaian word used to describe stuttering is *teté teté*. In common with Hawaiians and Samoans, Mangaians neither laugh at nor ridicule the stutterers. The individuals who stutter are not socially rejected and are under no handicap as to marriage or occupation.

No attempt is made by Mangaians to treat or correct stuttering, since it is accepted as an inborn characteristic of the family in question. However, the interesting comment was made that a native priest in former times could make a person stutter. Relative to this, is a story or legend that an ancestor of the Mangaian family of stutterers resisted belief in the God of the missionaries and one of the missionaries put a curse on the family, saying its people "would not talk right."

STUTTERING AMONG JAPANESE

I will now turn to the Japanese, first in Hawaii, then in Japan. By chance on my first visit to Honolulu I encountered a Nisei stutterer in front of a Shinto shrine. I noted spasms of the mouth and jaw as he talked and frequent breaking of eye contact during the spasms. Several times he put his hand over his mouth; his nose was reddened, possibly from the continual hand contact. Some jerkiness was noted in his whole body when spasms occurred. He confided that he stuttered in both English and Japanese, but more in English. His speech was worse at some times than at others, his main blocks appeared on [s] sounds and on the first word of sentences.

This man's history sounds fairly typical of American stutterers; it included difficulty in grammar school with oral work, special handling by a series of Japanese, Chinese, and Haole (Caucasian) teachers, and a final decision not to go to high school because his stuttering would be too much of a handicap. He got by as a sergeant in the army except when he had to give oral reports. Subsequently he became a carpenter and has done well with a Japanese contractor's firm, although he turned down a chance for advancement. He said that his boss and also the assistant superintendent of the firm stutter worse than he, but both of them "talk right through their blocks." He further claimed to know many Japanese stutterers.

My informants from Japan were about evenly split as to whether stuttering (do'mo'ru) was common in their country, although all of them had known stutterers (do'mu'ri) personally. Three informants knew one male stutterer each; another informant knew three female and one male stutterer; and one informant had known "10 or 15," mostly boys in school. Another informant, educated in a Buddhist school, was adamant that more girls than boys stuttered in Japan. In talking with these Japanese it seemed that their perception of stuttering as a problem was considerably affected by differing conceptions of the defect itself and also by their sex and amount of education.

Most of the informants described redness of the face as a concomitant of stuttering but were vague about other manifestations. However, the most widely informed of the Japanese said he had seen grimaces and bodily contortions among Japanese stutterers. He also held that stutterers most frequently met with difficulty on the following series of sounds: *ta, chi, tsu, te, to*. Whether Japanese stutterers employ subterfuges to reduce the social visibility of their blocks could not be answered, but the comment was made that it is very difficult to substitute words and expressions in speaking Japanese.

Stuttering appears in pre-school children but more frequently comes to the attention of others among children in primary schools. Stuttering is believed to be a sickness but one which can be "cured" or, perhaps better, something that can be "corrected." In doing this mothers generally rely on verbal injunctions, urging the child to slow down and not get excited. The underlying theme is that the stuttering is incorrect or improper and will leave a bad impression on other people. Parents, especially the mother, are not free to disregard stuttering because relatives or neighbors will criticize them for not correcting the habit in their children. However, the strongest motive to correct the stuttering is the mother's self-criticism. In moments of exasperation she may conceivably blame the child, but this seems contrary to the socially defined maternal role.[2]

Punishment is never used on the Japanese child although something like scolding may be. In the background of child rearing is the threat of okyu, burning of the back with punk, which is widely feared by Japanese children. A mother who believes strongly in the curing efficacy of okyu, or of moxabustion "might" use it on her child to correct stuttering. Parenthetically we note that left-handedness is considered to be very awkward in Japan and according to my informants there are no Japanese who use their left hands for writing or eating. Parents very firmly manage children to insure the use of the right hand, even rapping the offending appendage to convey their attitudes to the child. In extreme cases moxabustion may be applied to the back of the left hand. The rationale for this is that a left-handed person looks awkward and that chopsticks must be held in the right hand to avoid interfering with others when eating. It is especially unsightly in a girl, interfering with the proper procedure for pouring sake or with the tea ceremony. It is doubtful whether Japanese, save those familiar with western psychology, see any connection between the social control of handedness and the genesis of stuttering.

Less well-educated mothers may take a stuttering child to a Shinto priest to have evil spirits exorcised. There is nothing traumatic in this for the child. The Shinto rituals are used mainly to discover wherein the parents have erred or offended the spirits. Mothers with more sophistication may consult a relative, a teacher, or a medical doctor in their effort to help stuttering offspring.

Children in primary schools are known to imitate and tease stutterers, but they are warned by their parents that this can become a habit. There is a firm conviction that imitation is the cause of stuttering in Japan. Adults never ridicule stutterers. Teachers give stutterers informal "correction" after school, stressing exercises in talking slowly. There is a commercial school in Tokyo, called Domori Kyosei Gakuin, "stuttering correcting school," which has branches in many larger cities of Japan. Magazines

[2] As in T. Gondaira, "Case Study of a Boy with Stuttering and Physical Malformation: Some Remarks on Counselling with Mothers," *Japanese Journal of Child Psychiatry* 1 (1960): 340–50.

carry advertisements of booklets for correcting stuttering, mailed at a price to hopeful stutterers or their parents.

Stuttering apparently is also treated by ear, nose, and throat specialists, some of whom have published papers on the subject. According to one source, there are only ten persons studying speech correction in Japan; one recently has come to the United States on a Fulbright exchange for this purpose.

Shyness has been noted in some Japanese stutterers and possibly social withdrawal; the latter is based upon reports of an unusual number of stutterers living in isolated villages and rural areas of Japan. Stuttering is a disadvantage for persons entering and seeking advancement in certain occupations. Because of the use of matchmakers, girls from middle- and upper-class families who stutter may suffer a disadvantage in obtaining a husband. To a lesser degree this can be a handicap for the man in getting acceptance from a much-desired girl or possibly from her family.

It should be noted that pressures arising out of the Japanese mother-child relationship are directed to achievement as well as toward social conformity. Achievement pressures in the Japanese family reflect and are reinforced by the extreme importance placed upon education as a means of upward mobility in urban Japan—particularly education in the "right school." This is shown by the fact that in Tokyo entrance examinations are given to determine which children will be admitted to junior high schools, elementary schools, and even to some nursery schools. Vogel [3] described an interesting case of a Japanese mother who brought her three-year-old son to a psychiatric clinic in Tokyo specifically with the idea of correcting his stuttering so that he might have a better chance of being accepted in a particular nursery school. The distinctive Japanese attitude is illustrated by the action of the mother, who stopped bringing him to the clinic once he was enrolled in the school.

INTERPRETATION

In general, my findings have been those which I would more or less expect, building upon my earlier investigation of stuttering among Northwest Coast Indians.[4] My estimate that Polynesian society has a low incidence of stuttering seems consistent with Polynesian culture values and social organization. The belief of Polynesians that stutterers are born that way

[3] Ezra F. Vogel, "Japanese Family Dynamics and Achievement Pressure" (paper read at the Tenth Pacific Science Congress in Honolulu, August, 1961).

[4] Edwin M. Lemert, "Some Indians Who Stutter," *Journal of Speech and Hearing Disorders* 18 (1953): 168–74.

and nothing can be done about it contrasts sharply with the conviction of Japanese that it can and should be corrected, and with the well-developed methods for eliminating stuttering found among the Kwakiutl Indians of the Northwest.

Narrowing our focus to a better known Polynesian area, Samoa, we see a society integrated around ceremonial recognition of authority and hereditary status differentials, identification of family with land, generosity in sharing food, admiration of beauty and physical prowess, arts of love, and the dance. The Samoan social system demands strict compliance with its norms and has strong elements of competition in it. However, its structuring is such that these do not impinge directly on the education of the child. Moreover, Samoans, like most Polynesian peoples, have a generalized rather than a specialized love for children; mutual nursing of babies, adoption, and other exchanges are often used to gratify adult needs for the affection of children. It is typically Polynesian to be very unhappy if there isn't "a baby around the house."

The norms inculcated in Samoan child training are largely physical avoidance having to do with tabooed areas of the Fale and objects therein, bodily position in the presence of an adult, exposure to the sun, covering parts of the body, crying, and making noise. These are usually enforced by cuffings, exasperated shouting, and almost automatically repeated injunctions. Note, however, that the weight of punishment usually falls not on the young child but upon the next oldest child who is saddled with responsibility of his control. One uppermost desire of adults is to see that small children "keep quiet," "sit still," or "stop that noise." This emphasis leads me to suggest that further investigation may show retarded speech and mutism to be more frequent problems among Polynesians than is stuttering.

Older children carry a heavy burden of baby tending and baby appeasing in Samoan society as well as a heavy load of household and other chores. Yet there are two outlets for the child who is placed under excessive pressure. One is to run away under the guise of a "visit" and to live with other relatives, who gladly welcome the child. The other outlet for the child's unintegrated impulses and feelings is the dance, in which all sexes and ages participate on a basis of equality. In the dance gracefulness, originality, and pantomime humor are the means of gaining prestige and favorable response. Defective persons are not discriminated against in the spontaneity of the dance and they often capitalize on their defects. A hunchback, an albino, a psychotic man, a deaf-mute, a feeble-minded boy, and a blind girl, all may exploit their handicaps in the individualized expression of the dance.[5]

[5] Margaret Mead, *From the South Seas* (New York: William Morrow, 1939), pp. 120 ff.

It is true that political ability and skill in oratory are prerequisites for upward mobility in Samoan society, i.e., achieving a chief's title. Yet equally important are economic ability and skill in crafts, deportment, and general leadership qualities. Furthermore, a man is not expected to aspire seriously to the role of *matai*, or chief, until he is 30 or 40 years old. Meantime he remains a *taulalea*, a person who works under the direction of the *matai* but enjoys himself in his free time.

The fact that about 50 percent of male Samoans become *matai* sometimes during their lives [6] reveals the relative ease of upward mobility. Furthermore, even if elected, a man is free to decline the role of *matai*. No *particular* children are singled out at an early age and subjected to exacting training for demanding adult roles, as is done in Northwest Coast Indian societies. Pressures are greater on higher ranking persons to become chiefs, but it is interesting that such a person, if he is inarticulate, can lean heavily upon his talking chief to make his speeches.

Recent attention given to the presence of reduplicative baby talk in certain American Indian languages as a possible explanation for the reported absence of stuttering in certain tribes [7] makes it of some interest to note an older study by Churchill [8] reporting the complete lack of baby talk by Samoans. On the surface this seems contrary to expectation for a low-stuttering-incidence society. Churchill described the Samoan language as monosyllabic, with duplicative expressions making up 60 per cent of its word forms. Among other duplicatives, diminutive iteration was conspicuously used with adults as well as with children. This observation led him to conclude: "It may well be that a speech of monosyllables needs no reduction, and therefore each such underlying monosyllabic unit is as easy for the child's brain to grasp and hold as it is for the adult intelligence to employ."

While Churchill's ideas are outdated, there may be a residual grain of truth in his conclusion, inasmuch as it can be safely said that Polynesian languages differ from others, such as our own, in having no consonant clusters; consequently they may be easier for children to learn. At the same time it is necessary to reconcile other data, namely, that baby talk is commonly used by Japanese mothers in teaching their children to talk. If I am correct in designating the Japanese as a people with much stuttering, then the presence or absence of "little language" for use with infants may not be germane to the problem. More likely it is the characteristic use of

[6] Felix Keesing and M. Keesing, *Elite Communication in Samoa: a Study of Leadership* (Palo Alto, Calif.: Stanford University Press, 1956), chap. 3.

[7] Joseph L. Stewart, "Studies of North American Indians of the Plains, Great Basin and Southwest" (paper read at the 1960 American Speech and Hearing Association Convention in Los Angeles).

[8] W. Churchill, "Duplicative Mechanisms in Samoan and their Functional Value," *American Journal of Philology* 29 (1905): 35–54.

language forms to convey associated attitudes which is the significant cultural factor in the genesis of stuttering.

In conclusion, it would seem that stuttering in Samoan society is most likely a product of adventitious social interaction rather than a consequence of some kind of recurrent or reinforcing patterns of interaction. On the other hand, from our available facts, Japanese society seems to create a regime of fixed manual and verbal coordinations for the young child for which there is no escape or adequate psychological compensation. Because of the special nature of speech coordinations and emphasis on "correcting" behavior, deviation becomes a reinforcing context for stuttering when it appears.

SUMMARY

Current theoretical developments in sociology stress the importance of the study of structural factors in order to complement cultural analysis, which alone is insufficient for understanding deviant behavior. Research based upon data from informants indicates that the incidence of stuttering is low in Polynesian society, high in Japanese. While cultural and adventitious factors produce stuttering in both societies, differences in social structures reinforce and maintain stuttering behavior in Japanese, not in Polynesian. These differences center around the nature of the compliances demanded of the child, the mediating of its discipline, and culturally provided opportunities for escape from excessive pressures for conformity. The use or non-use of baby talk does not seem directly relevant to the development of stuttering in the two societies.

12

SOCIOCULTURAL RESEARCH
ON DRINKING

I wish to offer here a generalized overview and critical assessment of more recent sociological and anthropological research on drinking. These will reflect two conceptual orientations: that of culture in the case of anthropology and that of groups and social structure in the case of sociology. Discussion will be focused on methods, data, hypotheses and theories, hopefully reserving some time for concluding comments on implications of the "sociology of deviance" for alcohol studies.

The antecedents of sociocultural research on drinking lie in early speculations about the distinctive sobriety of Jews, amplified somewhat later by attempts to explain the contrasting high rates of insobriety among Irish-American drinkers. This initial preoccupation with abnormal drinking has persisted, despite Bacon's lucid plea in an early issue of the *Quarterly Journal of Studies on Alcohol* for social scientists to broaden their interests and to accentuate the study of normal drinking.[1] This in itself may be a datum, suggesting the inherently problematic nature of drinking alcoholic beverages.

From Proceedings of the 28th Congress on Alcohol and Alcoholism 2 (1969): 56–64, edited by Mark Keller and Timothy Coffey; reprinted by permission of Hillhouse Press, Highland Park, New Jersey.

[1] S. D. Bacon, "Sociology and the Problem of Alcohol; Foundations for a Sociological Study of Drinking Behavior," *Quarterly Journal of Studies on Alcohol* 4 (1943): 402–45.

While the body of sociocultural research on drinking has grown in substance and in sensitivity to theoretical and methodological issues,[2] as yet it is uneven with regard to the breadth and depth of the accumulated data and also with regard to their reliability. Extant research is marred by inconsistency and lack of clarity in many of its key concepts, and skepticism about the validity of instruments used in surveys of drinking is endemic. In some ways, sociocultural research on drinking stands almost where it begins, painfully stymied by problems of definition. These are notable strictures generally hampering sociocultural studies on drinking; others are more specific or germane to the kinds of methods which have been employed.

METHODS

If certain kinds of quasijournalistic impressionistic reports are excluded, methods utilized in sociocultural research on drinking fall into a threefold classification: (1) case analysis—usually single-culture studies or studies of selected groups; (2) comparative analysis of drinking in two or more societies or of different groups or strata within the same society; (3) statistical analysis, making use of cross-cultural data.

Case studies of drinking in different cultural settings have been primarily descriptive, with secondary or residual attention given to theoretical issues. Typically in such studies, patterns of drinking are described, either with words or survey data, internal differences are noted and assertions are made about relationships between the patterns of drinking and selected sociocultural factors. The method is one of assertion supported by illustration. Some of the more formalized case studies seek to test hypotheses, while others are written in a pointed way to disprove or to take exception to prevalent assertions about drinking. The salient need to support assertions or to challenge hypotheses selectively influences the kinds of descriptive facts presented, and accounts for some of the unevenness in such studies. However, some of the better drinking studies must be counted in the case-study class, including Snyder's work on alcohol and the Jews;[3] Barnett's investigation of alcoholism[4] among the New York Cantonese, Simmons's studies of Peruvian drinking;[5] Heath's

[2] D. G. Mandelbaum, "Alcohol and Culture," *Current Anthropology* 6 (1965): 281–93.

[3] C. R. Snyder, *Alcohol and the Jews; A Cultural Study of Drinking and Sobriety*, Rutgers Center of Alcohol Studies, Monograph No. 1 (New Brunswick, N. J., 1958).

[4] M. L. Barnett, "Alcoholism in the Cantonese of New York City; An Anthropological Study," in *Etiology of chronic alcoholism*, ed. O. Diethelm, (Springfield, Ill.: Charles C Thomas, 1955).

of drinking among the Bolivian Camba;[6] Lolli's works on Italian and French drinking;[7] and a recent study by Hamer of drinking and personality among the Forest Potawatomi of Upper Michigan.[8]

Single-culture case studies of drinking are limited in the scientific sense because they lack control data to test or validate hypotheses. However, they can challenge assertions or expose their limitations. Their chief value is to generate new hypotheses and to enlarge the body of data available for comparative or statistical studies.

COMPARATIVE ANALYSIS

True comparative studies of drinking are rare. An older classic in this category, unexcelled in many ways, is Ruth Bunzel's treatment of the role of alcoholism in two Central American cultures.[9] Glad's comparison of drinking among Jewish and Irish youths and adults qualifies here,[10] as well as the investigation into alcoholism, sorcery and homicide in two Mexican communities by Viquiera and Palerm.[11] Comparative analysis, which seeks to relate drinking differences to factors present or absent in several or a series of cases in its most ambitious form becomes typological analysis. Bales pioneered along this line with his distinction between the

---

[5] O. G. Simmons, "Ambivalence and the Learning of Drinking Behavior in a Peruvian Community," *American Anthropologist* 62 (1960): 1018–27; O. G. Simmons, "Drinking Patterns and Interpersonal Performance in a Peruvian Mestizo Community," *Quarterly Journal of Studies on Alcohol* 20 (1959): 103–11.

[6] D. B. Heath, "Drinking Patterns of the Bolivian Camba," *Quarterly Journal of Studies on Alcohol* 19 (1958): 491–508.

[7] G. Lolli, E. Serianni, G. M. Golder, and P. Luzzatto-Fegiz, *Alcohol in Italian Culture; Food and Wine in Relation to Sobriety among Italians and Italian Americans*, Rutgers Center of Alcohol Studies, Monograph No. 3 (New Brunswick, N. J., 1958); R. Sadoun, G. Lolli, and M. Silverman, *Drinking in French Culture*, Rutgers Center of Alcohol Studies, Monograph No. 5. (New Brunswick, N. J., 1965).

[8] J. H. Hamer, "Acculturation Stress and the Functions of Alcohol among Forest Potawatomi," *Quarterly Journal of Studies on Alcohol* 26 (1965): 285–302.

[9] R. Bunzel, "The Role of Alcoholism in Two Central American Cultures," *Psychiatry* 3 (1940): 361–87.

[10] D. D. Glad, "Attitudes and Experiences of American-Jewish and American-Irish Male Youth as Related to Differences in Adult Rates of Inebriety," *Quarterly Journal of Studies on Alcohol* 8 (1947): 406–72.

[11] C. Viquiera and A. Palerm, "Alcoholismo, Brujeria y Homicidio en dos Communidades Rurales de Mexico," *América Indígena* 14, no. 1 (1954): 7–30.

ritual—sacred drinking of Jews and the convivial—affective drinking of the Irish, plus recognition of a degenerative subtype of the latter he called utilitarian drinking.[12] More recently I proposed a threefold typology of festive drinking, ritual-disciplined drinking, and secular drinking to depict differences between Tahitian, Cook Islander, and Samoan drinking practices.[13]

In part, Jellinek's classification of alpha, beta, gamma, delta, and epsilon alcoholisms grew out of observed cultural differences in the manifestations of pathological drinking in France and the United States.[14] Finally, although it has been the product of almost pure ratiocination rather than empirical research, it is worth mentioning Fallding's typology of drinking as it relates to what he calls the "burden of civilization": ornamental–community–symbolic drinking, facilitation drinking, assuagement drinking and retaliation drinking.[15] The last three types are deemed "unsafe" or pathological.

Comparative analysis is a broad step beyond single-culture case studies of drinking practices in the direction of scientific validation; it has been termed the halfway house between the heuristic value of assertive illustration and the objective analysis made possible by designed testing procedures of statistics. However, comparative analysis lacks control data; also, it is imprecise and nonobjective when data on drinking must be fitted to specified types.[16] Nevertheless, it forces the researcher to isolate the variables with which he works, it sharpens descriptions, and may provide explanations useful for delimited purposes.

STATISTICAL ANALYSIS

Genuine testing and verification of hypotheses require the use of control data and, ideally, precise quantification. It marshalls the full apparatus of science for sociocultural research on drinking, and has been carried out by persons imbued with confidence and optimism less apparent among

[12] R. F. Bales, "Cultural Differences in Rates of Alcoholism," *Quarterly Journal of Studies on Alcohol* 6 (1946): 480–99.

[13] E. M. Lemert, "Forms of Pathology of Drinking in Three Polynesian Societies," *American Anthropologist* 66 (1964): 361–74.

[14] E. M. Jellinek, *The Disease Concept of Alcoholism* (Highland Park, N. J.: Hillhouse Press, 1960).

[15] H. Fallding, "The Source and Burden of Civilization, Illustrated in the Use of Alcohol," *Quarterly Journal of Studies on Alcohol* 25 (1964): 714–24.

[16] W. J. McEwen, "Forms and Problems of Validation in Social Anthropology," *Current Anthropology* 4 (1963): 155–83.

researchers identified with case studies and comparative analysis. Horton's study of drinking in 59 primitive societies,[17] which was inspired by Murdock's revival of cross-cultural anthropology at Yale, still stands as a monument to this type of research. After a long interval this was followed by Field's publication, in 1962, of his new cross-cultural study of drunkenness.[18] The most recent cross-cultural study of drinking, by Child, Bacon, Barry, Buchwald, and Snyder, draws ethnographic data from 139 societies and seeks to overcome some of the methodological problems posed by Horton's research.[19]

A number of general criticisms leveled at cross-cultural studies in anthropology are equally applicable, perhaps more so, to cross-cultural investigations of drinking. These have to do with the availability of data, choice of units for comparison, representativeness of cultures sampled, meanings imputed to classified data, and an oversanguine faith in tests of statistical significance.[20] Only a few of these can be discussed here.

First, cross-cultural workers have to use what data on drinking are at hand; the data on drinking are reported unevenly, present concerning some items, absent or uncertain on others. Tabulations on particular items often fall below the total sample in number and the composition of the sample changes with the tabulations. When experts have checked data used in cross-cultural studies they have been highly critical of the reports in some cases.[21]

Sampling remains a problem in these studies. Data must be taken from reported societies as an unbiased sample, a presumption made questionable by the influence of contiguous societies on each other. This issue is crucial in drinking studies, because many primitive peoples have learned to drink as a result of culture contacts; their drinking has flowered or become patterned when their cultures were breaking down, becoming attenuated, and their peoples mingling or fusing with others.

A final caveat concerns the meaning imputed to cross-cultural data

[17] D. Horton, "The Functions of Alcohol in Primitive Societies; A Cross-Cultural Study," *Quarterly Journal of Studies on Alcohol* 4 (1943): 199–320.

[18] P. B. Field, "A New Cross-Cultural Study of Drunkenness," in *Society, Culture, and Drinking Patterns,* eds. D. J. Pittman and C. R. Snyder (New York: John Wiley, 1962).

[19] I. L. Child, M. K. Bacon, H. Barry III, C. Buchwald and C. R. Snyder, "A Cross-Culutral Study of Drinking," *Quarterly Journal of Studies on Alcohol,* supplement no. 3 (1965).

[20] A. J. Köbben, "New Ways of Presenting an Old Idea; The Statistical Method in Anthropology," *Journal of the Royal Anthropological Institute* 82 (1952): 129–46; McEwen, "Forms and Problems."

[21] McEwen, ibid.

or to the classifications of variables whose associations with drinking are being measured. Köbben in 1952 examined Horton's criteria of anxiety about sexuality which he assumed to be shown by the presence of cultural restrictions on premarital sex indulgence.[22] As a result, Köbben concluded that three and possibly four tribes belonged in an adjoining cell. The change obliterates Horton's test of significance, i.e., the differences he found become nonsignificant.

An inescapable conclusion is that cross-cultural studies of drinking can only be as good as the data on which they rest and the validity of the criteria they employ. At present, drinking data on cultures of the world are uneven in coverage and in quality; the salient research problem remains the accumulation of reliable data and the use of more uniform field work procedures than have been followed in the past. Meantime, while hologeistic studies are not to be discouraged, it would appear that more immediate promise lies in comparative studies in which the same individual or group of investigators collect as well as analyze first-hand data from several or a series of societies.

This counsel is easier to follow in small homogeneous societies than in large complex ones. It is obvious that data on drinking in the latter necessarily must be gathered by survey methods, implemented by questionnaires and schedules. Yet such methods have well-known shortcomings, among them the difficulty of ascertaining what meanings respondents give to questionnaire items and what effect interview interaction has upon replies to scheduled questions. In some questionnaires tested by the Bay Area (San Francisco, Calif.) drinking studies group, it was found that changing the position of a box on the page significantly changed the number of drinks which respondents checked as their average.[23] Similarly, Mulford discovered significant differences in replies to interview questions on drinking depending on the attitudes of the interviewer toward drinking.[24]

Whether such anomalous findings simply indicate the necessity to develop more refined survey tools or whether they speak softly but insistently of the need for qualitatively different perspectives on drinking are questions which must be raised, but for which there are no ready answers. But it would not be wrong to say that two nagging questions about drinking have not been answered, i.e., what are we studying, and why?

[22] Köbben, "New Ways."

[23] W. Lipscomb, personal communication.

[24] H. A. Mulford and D. E. Miller, "The Prevalence and Extent of Drinking in Iowa, 1961; A Replication and an Evaluation of Methods," *Quarterly Journal of Studies on Alcohol* 24 (1963): 39–53.

THEORIES OF DRINKING

Substantive theories and hypotheses which have been generated in socio-cultural research on drinking cover a broad gamut of ideas, ranging from Immanuel Kant's group-protection theory of Jewish sobriety to Jellinek's global vulnerability–tolerance theory of all alcoholism.[25] A complete cata-loguing of these theories together with respective critiques and evalua-tions is beyond the scope of this paper. It must suffice to group them roughly according to the emphasis given to the following factors: anomie, status deprivation, anxiety reduction, attitudinal ambivalence, and social control. Partisans of theories subsumable under these several factors can take comfort that data can be cited which give each and all some de-gree of support. At the same time negative evidence for most or all theories makes it difficult or impossible to defend the preeminence of any one at this juncture. Hence it may be more profitable to confront the question as to what kinds of perspectives are represented by these classes of theory and to what extent they are germane to sociocultural research on drinking.

Drinking as Symptomatic.

The first four classes of drinking theories outlined above share a common view of drinking, excessive drinking in particular, as sympto-matic of perturbations or maladjustments in individuals. These in turn are seen as functions of defective social organization, disordering of culture, or discontinuity in socialization as affected by culture. Anomie, for example, specifies a condition of society in which culturally indoctrinated mass achievement goals are conjoined with structured inequalities of access to these goals. Status deprivation theory has stressed the breakdown of cul-ture, attenuation and disappearance of ceremonials and intrinsically satisfy-ing roles and primary group participation, with drinking behavior portrayed as the spurious substitute for missing cultural elements. Ambivalence theory has accentuated conflicts, contradictions, and confusions in drinking practices, plus their lack of integration within the larger culture. Anxiety-reduction theories trace sources of drinking-producing anxieties to maladap-tation and disorganization of culture as a whole, but also find the locus of anxiety in family constellations.

One of the salient deficiencies of the symptomatic view of drink-

---

[25] E. M. Jellinek, "Immanuel Kant on Drinking," *Quarterly Journal of Studies on Alcohol* 1 (1941): 777–78; E. M. Jellinek, *The Disease Concept of Alcoholism* (Highland Park, N. J.: Hillhouse Press, 1960).

ing is that it is psychocultural rather than sociocultural. Without denying that inebriety in individuals may arise from anxiety, it is apparent
that when this conception is applied to whole societies it becomes reductionistic, i.e., it attributes some common psychic state to entire groups
and ignores the fact that people engage in common action, drunkenness
no less, for a diversity of reasons and motivations. Field research has
made it abundantly clear that inebriety or drinking to get drunk can be
and frequently are institutionalized parts of culture; they may be learned
as patterns, be reinforced by normal expectations and serve social as well
as individual needs. Intoxication and drunkenness may satisfy positive
sought-after values; they are not necessarily nor exclusively ways of ridding
individuals of psychic distress.[26]

The Importance of Meaning.

Another serious oversight in the symptomatic view of drinking more
or less inheres in the term itself. To perceive drinking as a symptom
downgrades its analytical importance, for it makes drinking a mere reflection or a measure of trouble in the individual. Lurking here is the
medical idea that it is pointless to try to deal with symptoms; the underlying disease must be treated. Put somewhat differently, a symptomatic
perspective on drinking tends to ignore or give only secondary importance
to the meaning of acts of drinking. I hasten to add that this is something
of a distortion, because researchers such as Horton, Bales, McCord and
McCord, Child et al., Snyder, and the more anthropologically oriented
workers most certainly have been concerned with variable meanings of
drinking.[27] But the bulk of the concern has been with abstract coded
meanings (e.g., Horton's sex and aggression counteranxieties) or with
more or less inert values which cluster around the individual drinking
act. Missing or minimal is a concern with the dynamic flow and interchange of culturally specific meanings which accompany drinking in
social interaction or, more simply, a concern with drinking as a symbolic
social process.

Research seeking to establish a sequence of symptoms in the growth
of alcoholism in individuals or in family settings erred largely because
the search was for constant identifiable behaviors rather than meanings.

[26] E. M. Lemert, *Alcohol and the Northwest Coast Indians*, Publications
in Culture and Society, vol. 2, no. 6 (Berkeley: University of California Press,
1954).

[27] Horton, "The Functions of Alcohol"; Bales, "Cultural Differences";
W. McCord and J. McCord, *Origins of Alcoholism*, (Stanford, Calif.: Stan-
ford University Press, 1960); Child et al., "A Cross-Cultural Study"; Snyder,
Alcohol and the Jews.

Jellinek himself was to discover that symptoms of alcoholism relevant to American culture did not necessarily apply to French alcoholism. His subsequent formulation of the vulnerability–tolerance hypothesis was a grand swing toward meaningful sociocultural analysis of drinking. Popham has shown that this hypothesis is consistent with a large number of known sociocultural facts about rates and forms of alcoholism.[28] However, closer inspection reveals it to be more a perspective or designation of factors for study than a true theory. Furthermore, Jellinek followed an older perspective when as concomitants of his theory he sought to distinguish types of alcoholism in behavioristic terms.

If the substance of terms like "psychological vulnerabilities" or "cultural tolerance" resides in a processual flow of meanings, then we are left with a pressing need to build a conceptual bridge between society and culture on one hand and the individual on the other, a conception which will combine dual aspects of drinking "from within" and drinking defined "from without" by others selectively expressing culture through social organization. It is herein that the questions as to what we are studying and why may have their answers, particularly if the reactions of society to drinking and drinkers as well as private worlds of drinkers can be shown to be primary data for sociocultural research. It is portentous that Mulford should arrive at a similar conclusion after extensive experience with survey research on American drinking practices.[29] He states: "Drinking behavior, including extreme deviant drinking that renders the actor a likely candidate for the label 'alcoholic,' will probably be understood eventually in terms of public definitions—definition of alcohol, of drinkers, of what we call alcoholics, not to mention definition of self."

Drinking as Deviance.

This discussion, in a rough dialectical way, has now reached a position from which drinking can be conceived as deviance. The underlying perspective is one of symbolic interaction; the more explicit theory is one of social control, emphasizing study of the processes by which drinking gets defined, the kinds of societal reactions and controls which confront drinkers, the problems these create for drinkers, the ways in which the problems are met, and the consequences of all of these for symbolic feedback to the self of the drinker.

There is, of course, substantial empirical support for a social-control

[28] R. E. Popham, "Some Social and Cultural Aspects of Alcoholism," *Canadian Psychiatric Association Journal* 4 (1959): 222–29.

[29] H. A. Mulford, "Drinking and Deviant Drinking: U.S.A., 1963," *Quarterly Journal of Studies on Alcohol* 25 (1964); 634–50.

conception of drinking: in Horton's early study, in Barnett's, in Snyder's work on Jewish drinking, in my studies of Northwest Coast Indian drinking and that of Polynesians, in Field's cross-cultural study of drinking, and finally, in Honigmann and Honigmann's demonstration of how control measures reshaped drinking among Baffin Eskimo.[30] Moreover, a social-control theory fits easily with the known physiological facts about alcohol, particularly the depression and attenuation of inhibitory processes in the nervous system, resulting in actions often unpredictable for self and society. In culturally relevant terms, drinking is precarious behavior that can easily lead to improprieties;[31] awareness of this makes for caution in drinkers and wariness in others—lest they become victims of the drinker's incompetence or transgressions.

Viewing drinking as inherently problematic frees researchers from the need to define drinking and alcoholism in positivistic universalistic terms. It also diminishes the necessity to explain why populations drink or why they indulge in drunkenness, for it logically follows that in the absence of social controls, drinking readily leads to intoxication as well as creating individual and social difficulties. Last among its merits, social-control theory makes room for human volition, so conspicuously absent in the symptomatic view of drinking. It does not exclude rational choice in the process by which people learn to drink, nor the possibility that collectively they may thoughtfully perceive unwanted consequences of drinking and search for workable ways to contain them.

Problems of drinking which result from deliberate, self-conscious, or organized social control must be distinguished from normal problems of drinking. Here it must be noted that a vast number of the problems or troubles associated with drinking in societies of the world are normalized, i.e., discounted, written off, forgotten, or simply treated as everyday problems of living, part of the inevitable diversity and perversity of the human condition. In widest cultural perspective it may be more important to explain why some people develop and use the concept of alcoholism than why they do not.

Where drinking problems are recognized as part of culture, they present the task of accounting for the seemingly anomalous differences in their content from society to society, e.g., why do the French see their nation's drinking problems as primarily economic; why do Americans

---

[30] Horton, "The Functions of Alcohol"; Barnett, "Alcoholism in the Cantonese"; Snyder, *Alcohol and the Jews*; Lemert, *Alcohol and the Northwest Coast Indians*; Lemert, "Forms and Pathology of Drinking in Three Polynesian Societies," *American Anthropologist* 66 (1964): 361–74; Field, "A New Cross-Cultural Study"; J. J. Honigmann and I. Honigmann, "How Baffin Island Eskimo Have Learned to Use Alcohol," *Social Forces* 44 (1965): 73–83.

[31] S. Cavan, *Liquor License* (Chicago: Aldine, 1966).

see theirs mainly as characterological or moral problems; why do Finns see their alcohol problems chiefly in a context of crime causation. Within societies there is need to account for other anomalous facts, such as the variation between rural and urban physicians in France in their judgments of the amount of daily wine consumption compatible with health or the fact that in American hospitals social-class attributes and stereotypes of the "derelict" have been found to affect significantly the assignment of an "alcoholic" diagnosis to patients.[32]

CONCLUSION

As a kind of concluding exercise I would like to propose an alternative "deviance" interpretation of the cultural facts to which Jellinek's tolerance–vulnerability hypothesis was directed. Briefly it is this: In societies with high tolerance for heavy frequent drinking, alcoholism or serious "problem drinking" will be socially perceived, defined or diagnosed late in the careers of drinkers and will be more likely to be conceived as medical pathology. France, Japan, and primitive societies may well furnish substantiating or test data here.

In contrast, in societies with low tolerance for heavy repeated drinking, problems growing out of drinking will be socially defined early in drinking careers, before organic pathology appears. In these societies, problems and others will be more difficult to normalize, hence will generate sociopsychological problems with drinkers and their families. In low-drinking-tolerance cultures sociopsychological problems are more likely to be a result of drinking than its cause.

How the problems concomitant to drinking in such cases get symbolized in terms of drinking itself or become motives for further drinking in all probability cannot be sufficiently explained by cultural facts. But the existence of psychiatric categories and concepts of alcoholism, their tendency to be reified and invoked to justify social control are sociocultural phenomena. Their presence or currency may be a necessary if not a sufficient factor in explaining more complex forms of drinking problems emerging in low-drinking-tolerance cultures.

[32] Sadoun et al., *Drinking in French Culture*; H. T. Blane, W. F. Overton, Jr., and M. E. Chafetz, "Social Factors in the Diagnosis of Alcoholism: I. Characteristics of the Patient," *Quarterly Journal of Studies on Alcohol* 24 (1963): 640–63.

13

FORMS AND PATHOLOGY OF DRINKING IN THREE POLYNESIAN SOCIETIES

Studies of drinking by primitive peoples have ranged from descriptive treatment in single societies to large scale uses of statistical data exemplified in the cross-cultural method employed by Horton,[1] and more recently by Field.[2] For those who prefer to move beyond a descriptive emphasis yet seek to keep generalizations about drinking within a societal context, the modern comparative method offers a possible alternative meeting ground. In any event it seems well adapted to inquiries as to how or to what degree drinking practices get integrated into whole cultures.

Bunzel[3] initiated anthropological interest in the problem with her detailed comparison of "alcoholism" in two Central American cultures,

Reprinted with permission from the American Anthropologist 66 (1964): 361–74.

[1] Donald Horton, "The Functions of Alcohol in Primitive Societies: a Crosscultural Study," *Quarterly Journal of Studies on Alcohol* 4 (1943): 199–320.

[2] Peter B. Field, "A New Crosscultural Study of Drunkenness," in *Society, Culture and Drinking Patterns*, eds. David J. Pittman and Charles R. Snyder (New York: John Wiley, 1962).

[3] Ruth Bunzel, "The Role of Alcoholism in Two Central American Cultures," *Psychiatry* 3 (1940): 361–87.

concluding that drinking was a pivotal mechanism of social integration for one, the Chamula (Mexico), but for the other, the Chichecastenengo (Guatemala), largely a symptomatic response to conflict-producing situations of extraneous origins. A number of single culture studies, including those of Honigmann and Honigmann, Mangin, Lemert, Heath, Sangree, and Field,[4] have stressed the integrative function of drinking in primitive societies along with considerable recognition of its importance in primary group formation and continuity. On the other hand, Berreman [5] from his observations of drinking among Aleuts concluded that drinking can be integrative or disintegrative, tending to be a by-product or symptomatic of the same factors which make for social disorganizations.

Ullman [6] proposed that rates of alcoholism, in the sense of addictive drinking, will vary indirectly with the degree to which drinking customs are well established and consistent with the rest of culture. The reciprocal of dissensus on drinking customs and values among different segments of society is ambivalence on the part of the individual toward his own drinking, which becomes the immediate causative agent in alcoholism. Simmons,[7] from his investigation of drinking among Peruvian villagers, found support for the first part of this hypothesis but not for the second. In other words, there may be a high degree of integration of drinking in a culture, a low rate of alcoholism, yet substantial ambivalence of attitudes toward the use of alcohol.

One of the difficulties complicating the study of integration of drinking practices in cultures is the lack of an explicit meaning for the term integration. Thus Bunzel [8] stated that the Chamula did not regard their drunkenness as a problem, but she herself did so regard it. Apparently she was impressed by the costs of their drunkenness in a different way

[4] John J. Honigmann and Irma Honigmann, "Drinking in an Indian-White Community," *Quarterly Journal of Studies on Alcohol* 5 (1945): 575–619; William Mangin, "Drinking Among Andean Indians," *Quarterly Journal of Studies on Alcohol* 18 (1957): 55–66; Edwin M. Lemert, "The Use of Alcohol in Three Salish Tribes," *Quarterly Journal of Studies on Alcohol* 19 (1958): 90–107; Dwight B. Heath, "Drinking Patterns of the Bolivian Camba," *Quarterly Journal of Studies on Alcohol* 19 (1958): 501–8; Walter H. Sangree, "The Social Functions of Beer Drinking in Bantu Tiriki," in *Society, Culture and Drinking Patterns*; Field, *A New Crosscultural Study*.

[5] Gerald D. Berreman, "Drinking Patterns of the Aleuts," *Quarterly Journal of Studies on Alcohol* 17 (1956): 503–14.

[6] Albert D. Ullman, "Sociocultural Backgrounds of Alcoholism," *Annals of the American Academy of Political and Social Science* 315 (1958): 48–54.

[7] Ozzie G. Simmons, "Ambivalence and the Learning of Drinking Behavior in a Peruvian Community," *American Anthropologist* 62 (1960): 1018–27.

[8] Bunzel, "The Role of Alcoholism."

than were the Indian drinkers, for she notes that they recognized and to some extent deplored the costs of their indulgence. This together with the fact that ambivalence may coexist with culturally integrated drunkenness, suggests two significant perspectives from which drinking can be described: (1) the form and behavioral consequences of drinking as seen by the detached observer; and (2) the situational valuations placed upon these by drinking participants and by those affected in the society, resulting in a kind of cost assessment.

Lemert[9] argues that all that we know about alcohol use indicates that while it is socially integrative in the sense of bringing people together in ritual and convivial groups and useful to individuals for anaesthetizing psychic ills, nevertheless, certain costs are created thereby not only in economic terms but also in terms of threatening or destruction of societal and individual values. These costs, theoretically estimable in time, energy, and psychic stress, can serve as a measure to which drinking is culturally integrated or, conversely, non-integrated or pathological.

It is a reasonable assumption that human beings at whatever cultural level become aware of costs of satisfying their values but that the action they take to minimize such costs is variable. Thus social control, not only to lessen insobriety, as Horton[10] saw it, but to change the form of drinking or drunkenness, must be reckoned with as a factor in accounting for the integration or non-integration of drinking in culture. The conditions under which social control of alcohol use emerges, the availability of means of control to those whose values are threatened, and the motivations and ability of individuals to utilize controls, are all important aspects of the complete analysis of cultural integration and drinking.

In this paper I will present some descriptive and interpretive materials on forms and pathology of drinking in three Polynesian societies which represent a historical continuum of contact and experience with alcohol and which, in my estimation, approximate a "series" in regard to its cultural integration. These are Tahiti and Bora Bora in the Society Islands; Aitutaki, Rarotonga, and Atiu in the Cook Islands; and Upolu and Savaii in Western Samoa. With these data I hope to illuminate some of the possible relationships between forms of drinking, cultural values, costs, and social control, together with certain tentative conclusions in regard to addictive drinking.

[9] Edwin M. Lemert, "Alcohol, Values and Social Control," in *Society, Culture and Drinking Patterns*, pp. 553–71.

[10] Horton, *The Functions of Alcohol*.

THE HISTORICAL SETTING

Historical sources are unequivocal that Polynesians, like most of the Indians of America north of Mexico, were without alcoholic beverages in their pristine state. Liquor was first brought to Polynesians by European voyagers in the middle and late eighteenth century. While the original reaction to liquor was one of distaste, this soon changed to avid liking, and a lively trade grew up in many areas. Around 1800, escaped convicts from Botany Bay in Australia taught Hawaiians how to distill a highly potable liquor, *okole hao*, from the fructose sugars of the *ti* root. Hawaiians in turn carried their skills to the Society Islands, where the consumption of locally distilled liquor from ti root and breadfruit underwent a period of efflorescence and then decline. It was replaced by *ava anani*, a crude wine made from the juice of oranges, perfected by enological [11] experiments conducted with a kind of early technical assistance program of whaling crews. In 1848 traveling Tahitians carried the techniques of brewing and drinking "orange beer," as it came to be called, to the Cook Islands, where much to the discomfiture of the missionaries, it quickly became established in a distinctive pattern of drinking known since 1910 as "bush beer schools."

While alcohol consumption quite early spread throughout most of Polynesia, Samoa in Western Polynesia remained as a kind of brooding citadel of sobriety until quite recent times. Samoa, even more than the Pueblo Indians of our southwest, stands as a classic case of cultural conservatism in relation to the readily diffusable and utilizable cultural item of alcohol.

PROTOTYPE DRINKING

The prototype for patterns of alcohol consumption in all areas of Polynesia except New Zealand is found in the kava circle. Kava, an astringent infusion made from the root of the plant *piper methysticum*, was everywhere drunk in sacred, ceremonial, and secular contexts. Drinkers customarily sat cross-legged in a circle and were served in a common cup from a fixed point by one or two persons charged with responsibility for its preparation. Drinking was pretty well confined to men, and it tended to be monopolized by chiefs and priests. In Western Polynesia, especially Samoa and Tonga, kava drinking became a sacred ceremonial distinguishing titled from untitled persons and symbolically validating status differences between chiefs.

[11] Enology or Aenology: the science of wine-making.

The linguistic continuity between Polynesian kava terms and those used for alcoholic drinks is unmistakable. At the same time, a common overlay of European influence is apparent from the use of such terms as *tuati* and *barmit* to designate the man given control over the drinking group, these being Polynesian conversions of steward and barmaid. In part, the older tendency to reserve distilled liquor for use by the ruling class has been perpetuated by "permit" systems which were set up by colonial administrators to control the distribution of imported liquors, to which chiefs and high ranking natives as well as white persons are allowed access.

FORMS OF DRINKING—FESTIVE

For purposes of description I have used a threefold classification to differentiate drinking in the three areas under consideration: festive, ritual-disciplined, and secular. These do not exhaust all of the forms of drinking in the areas but rather call attention to what I regard as the dominant patterns.

The earliest drinking in Tahiti and Bora Bora, on which there are data, was essentially festive in form. Fermented orange juice was added to food as an item around which feasts were organized, or by itself became the basis for festive indulgence. Festive drinking in Tahiti and Bora Bora took place during the orange harvest season, spring, and early summer. While brew was made and drunk by families, the more spectacular fetes were collective enterprises of the village under the direction of one of several brewmasters called *aito* (champions). The work was done by ten to 25 helpers called *rima tauturu* (hand helpers) who peeled and cut the oranges with a split bamboo knife and squeezed them through a cloth into a large barrel, which was then covered with a spray of leaves and buried for three to five days, depending upon the presence or absence of active dregs from previous brewings. When the brewmasters found by testing that two glasses produced intoxication, they pronounced it ready. The barrel was then hoisted by a sling and brought to the village for drinking.

Drinking was on a come-one–come-all basis but confined to married adults. Youths under 20 years were roughly driven away from the area and single women discouraged from attending. Drinkers sat in a circle around the barrel, with women in the front rows, to "show respect," and were served or helped themselves with a common coconut cup. Choral singing and dancing to the accompaniment of nose flutes and drums took place either in the vicinity of the barrel or in nearby houses. Festivities continued as long as ava anani remained in supply, which could mean several days. There was also an effort to program the brewing so that drinkers could move from one village to another on a rotation basis, and prolong the fete into one or several weeks.

On certain occasions, twice during the orange season according to one informant, drinkers from one or several villages retreated to an upland grove for night-long drinking and dancing. At a critical point, drinkers were served small amounts of *namu*, distilled coconut toddy made for the occasion (possibly learned from Marquesans), which became a signal for the beginning of nude dancing and promiscuous sexual pairings. Such fetes were ended by passing out, exhaustion, or both. In some cases they were ended by the appearance of *mutois*, village police, for increasingly toward the end of the nineteenth century the French authorities actively sought to repress these drinking rites.

Although beverages, time, and place of drinking have changed, Tahitian drinking remains essentially festive in form. A blight on the orange groves and the dying off of foremost native brewmasters in the influenza epidemics of 1918 pretty well put an end to orange brew making. In 1920, wine and beer were made available to Polynesians who were French citizens, and penalties against brewing were severely applied. Along with this, native drinking was structured by administrative manipulation of dispensing outlets and encouraging festive celebrations during July and at Christmas time.

The workweek and increasing dependence on a money economy have further shaped drinking in the Society Islands, weekend drinking becoming commonplace, together with periodic small-scale recurrences of village type festive drinking when money becomes available to families from vanilla and copra crops. Society Islanders have a decided preference for beverages of low alcoholic content, especially beer at the present time, which undoubtedly is meaningful in terms of achieving desired physical and psychic states associated with their singing and dancing. Plateau drinking, or the "long slow drunk," in my opinion, aptly describes the ideal pattern of alcohol consumption for these people. Many Tahitians have indicated their dislike for strong liquor on grounds that it makes them "*très fatigués*," or makes them go to sleep. As one cogently put it, "Two drinks of whiskey and you are no good."

RITUAL-DISCIPLINED DRINKING

While festive drinking similar to that in Tahiti and Bora Bora appeared in the Cook Islands, the latter are noted for the growth of highly ritualized drinking. Indeed, the most distinctive patterns of drinking in all Polynesia are found in the so-called "bush beer schools" on the island of Atiu and, to a lesser extent, on Rarotonga and Aitutaki.

On Atiu, during the orange season, drinking was a daily occurrence and brewing a highly organized activity, tokened by the sound of the conch shell summoning the drinkers. One steward, a cook, and three helpers are delegated on a rotation basis to prepare and squeeze oranges while the rest of the group carries on its libations. Drinkers are ranged around the beer barrel, which until recent times was a hollowed-out base of a coconut tree called a *tumunui*. The drinkers numbered from 6 to 20 men, although jumbo groups of 40 or 60 are not unknown on Sundays. The rule against female participation varies but it is very strict on Atiu, on the grounds that a drunken female is a highly disruptive and unesthetic element. Single men above 20 years are the core of the group, with older men and married men being the marginal participants. Drinking groups tend to get organized along kinship lines.

A drinking session on Atiu ordinarily begins with a single round of drinks, which is followed by a prayer and a church hymn. Then the *tuati* delivers a speech urging those present not to fight and to be careful on going home not to cause trouble. He then announces that the time has come for a good time and starts the coconut cup on its periodic rounds. There is considerable pressure on the individual to drink, although he may pass up a round. He may not, however, sip the drink, and if he tarries too long, the steward makes a quick stamping movement which scatters sand over the reluctant drinker.

Informal conversation covering sex, politics, fishing, and crops accompanies the drinking. Genealogies may be recited, and, even more distinctive, choral singing and the chanting of *utes* takes place. These utes deal with historic events, often those of drinking itself. If the beer barrel is a new one, it is dedicated by a specially composed ute, which heralds its great size or importance, in some cases by comparing it to cargo boats which have visited the islands.

Drinking is disciplined in a very real sense, for the tuati, who remains sober, has complete control over the session and may determine when a person has had too much to drink. When thirsty strays or roamers from other groups approach, he alone determines if they may join the drinkers. Troublemakers are evicted from the group and by common understanding are blacklisted by other groups. They remain on probation for a month or year, after which they are eligible for readmission to a school. The system works well, particularly on Atiu and the outer islands.

THE SECULAR DRINKING OF SAMOA

For purposes of describing and discussing drinking in Samoa I have employed the term "secular." This classification is residual because

Samoan drinking lacks all but the basic elements of patterning, is without ritual, and seldom if ever has it been the basis of village or district wide festive behavior. While it indirectly expresses some of the values of Samoan culture, it is much more conspicuously a mechanism or device through which individuals in group settings find release for a variety of unintegrated feelings and impulses. It has evolved under conditions of continuous prohibition.

Some surreptitious drinking was indulged in by Western Samoans under German rule, but the great mass of Samoans learned their brewing and drinking from New Zealand troops and government workers who took control of the island after 1914. American soldiers stationed on the islands during the last war also gave a big impetus to brewing through their willingness to pay extremely high prices for almost any kind of alcoholic drink. There has been very little use of native sugar bearing fruits or plants for brewing. Imported ingredients, malt, hops, sugar, and yeast have been relied upon almost from the first to concoct brew. This, known in Samoan as *fa'amafu*, has a quite high alcoholic content, ranging from 12 to 18 of even 20 percent, suggesting its frequent fortification by the addition of spirits. Besides fa'amafu, Samoans consume considerable amounts of methylated spirits, which are "purified" by boiling in various ways.

Fa'amafu is manufactured in Samoan houses, *fales*, or in the bush, depending on the current degree of risk. It is made by women as well as men and there is an extensive illegal trade at a going price of two shillings per bottle. Some notion of the scale of brewing is gained from the situation in a village near Salailua, on Savaii, where there are at least 20 brewmakers for an adult male population of 250. At least one of these brewers averages an output of 200 twenty-six ounce bottles per week. The brewer usually sells his surplus to finance his own drinking; women brewers supply their drinking spouses and sell the rest to meet family expenses.

Drinking takes place either in the bush or in unused fales in the back part of the villages. Drinkers sit in a circle, and the host who has made or bought the beer serves, sometimes using one glass, sometimes several. While some etiquette is observed, it is quite generalized. Guitar playing and singing occur but drinking interaction more commonly is in the form of discussion and gossip. Large groups, such as are sometimes found in the Cook Islands, are absent because of the risk of arrest. Participants generally are young, untitled, single men, and one of the impressive facts about Samoan drinkers is the extremely young age at which they have begun. In one village on Savaii, a sample poll showed that 66 percent of the *taulelea* had begun to drink before the age of 15. Beyond a few exceptions in the Apia area, Samoan women do not drink—not because of any rule to the effect, but because they find liquor distasteful or un-appealing.

In both the Cook Islands and Samoa, liquor is an indispensable means of recruiting labor for certain kinds of work. In Samoa it has been found that money will not induce workers to carry out tasks of clearing and planting on small plantations. Workers for this are usually rounded up by a foreman with the promise of "mea miti," "something to sip." This takes the form of several bottles of brew for a four o'clock drinking session after the day's work has been done.

DRINKING PATHOLOGY

In keeping with my introductory statements, drinking pathology here refers to drinking which is costly to society and costly to the individual, costs taken to be the extent to which other values are sacrificed in order to satisfy those associated with drinking. In this broad sense drinking pathology does exist in Polynesia, although care must be taken to specify whose value hierarchies are being invoked when the costs of drinking are assessed.

French authorities in Papeete are convinced that drinking is a very serious problem among their Polynesian peoples, primarily because they see earnings of the native population going for heavy weekend drinking and periodic, fete-type indulgence instead of into housing and other forms of material self-improvement. They are also distressed by the growing number of traffic accidents and injuries in the Papeete area which are traceable to intoxication. Yet it is doubtful that Tahitians see their expenditures for liquor as sacrifices in the same sense as do the French, largely because as yet their commitment to material values is quite tenuous. In fact, it can be argued that many Tahitians work or grow crops to obtain money for the indulgent pleasures it makes possible. Thus when one informant was asked why his fellows use their money for liquor instead of better housing and furniture, he laughed and said the Tahitian is likely to say: "If I spend money for those things I won't have any for beer and wine." Even when Tahitians are motivated to spend money for material improvement, they are compelled to put first the hospitality claims which relatives and others have on the products of their land or earnings, which often means that it goes for a communal drinkfest.

Intoxication does lead to quarreling and fighting among Tahitians, which run contrary to their values, but the overt aggression involved is mild, being mostly verbal, or random pushing and slapping. Stones or weapons are never used. Fights between drunken Tahitian women are far more spectator-inspiring than those between men, and women are not reluctant to tackle a male they find offensive. This reveals some of the essential personality characteristics of males who, when sober, are quiet, shy, and almost timid. It also suggests one of the main motivations for male drinking—to overcome shyness sufficiently to make sexual approaches to their women. This, in turn, is probably related to residual sacred values which sexual communion has for Society Islanders under certain circumstances.

As in other societies, drunken quarrels between spouses are common, but the wife can usually give a good account of herself in these. Both the husbands and the wives are to vent their hostilities toward one another by seeking out another sexual partner rather than through physical combat. This is capriciously interactional, but eventually the two are reunited usually through the offices of a pastor. In the background of this are older cultural values disapproving of sexual jealousy.

Intoxication or its effects does run directly contrary to health values and to important native values of excelling in sports and physical prowess, and this may be one of the more important psychic stresses created by drinking. It is significant that fairly successful organized programs of sports have been instrumental in decreasing drinking in certain areas, particularly where there is a strong authority figure, such as a church pastor. This usually operates through an older movement of nineteenth-century European origins, the Blue Cross, which prescribes a self-imposed taboo on drinking for given periods of time. The agreement is ordinarily written out on a piece of paper in the presence of a priest, pastor, judge, or a doctor. This strongly resembles an individual variant of the old technique by which chiefs tabooed scarce food items to allow for a period of retrenchment.

I conclude that drinking and intoxication have been and still are reasonably well integrated with the basic values of Society Island peoples. Liquor undoubtedly is instrumental in the periodic satisfaction of esoteric values which natives can only vaguely phrase as *la vie tahitienne*. Central to these is the value of psychic rapport overtly symbolized by collective eating, singing, dancing, and sexual communion. The preference of Tahitians for low or moderate alcohol beverages and slow drinking suggests an adaptation of the pattern of drinking to achieve or preserve physiological states compatible with these values. While the results of intoxication contravene certain of their values, these people seem to have a technique for bringing them under control which, at least in certain contexts, appears to be effective. Their drinking, of course, is contrary to the demands of a wage-work economy, and, as they are more drawn into such an economy, the form of their drinking can be expected to change, presumably in a more secular direction.

DRINKING PATHOLOGY IN THE COOK ISLANDS

Drinking by natives of the Cook Islands is now and has been illegal for many decades. Quite early it was condemned by dominant Protestant mission or church of the islands. In earlier years drinking and drunkenness were the main expression of anticlericalism and cultural reaction, clearly indicated by missionary references to their native opposition as the "drunken party" in their writings. At one time youthful bush drinkers, influenced by Tahitian migrants, conducted military drill, which hinted at more than symbolic resistance to the new religion. This led to a historic compromise between the recalcitrant drinkers and a perceptive missionary, James Chalmers, who was an early advocate of cooptative philosophy not unlike the American idea: "If you can't lick 'em, join 'em." In effect, an organizational syncretism grew up in which, according to a Rarotongan proverb, "The church was taken as a lap child on one knee." The missionary church was transformed into a native institution, and, while formally repudiating the use of liquor, at the same time allowed for the evolution of a patterned evasion of Christian temperance ideology.[12]

Cook Islands society, in my estimation, represents an equilibrium or a contrapuntal balance between Christian, Western values, and many of the older values and organization of native society. Patterned evasion of the law has been facilitated by a continuity of experience in the life history of the male adult, which permits a conventionalized inconsistency between creed and action. Thus, many church members—even deacons and occasionally pastors—have youthful histories of participation in beer schools. Today it is not unusual for a married man to attend church on Sunday morning, then change his clothes and join a beer school for the rest of the day. Respected church members are known to cooperate in supplying *kava ainga*, beer for work gangs on their plantations.

Most of the police in Rarotonga and elsewhere in the islands are church deacons and they have an espionage system which keeps them well apprised of brewing and drinking activities. Until 1900 fines for brewing were divided three ways: one part for the government, one for the church, and one for the arresting officer, who sometimes split this with informants. This suggests that law enforcement in relation to liquor offenses was in reality a taxation system, in which the church had a stake. It is also known that brewing and drinking by persons with high status seldom has resulted in arrest or fines. This is consistent with older feudalistic exploitive patterns and notions of monopoly of liquor for chiefs. Status is protected in other ways; thus the wife or relative of a man

[12] Richard Lovett, *James Chalmers, His Autobiography and Letters*, 6th ed. (London: Religious Tract Society, 1903).

caught brewing often pleads guilty in his place. Arguments in court usually concern who is guilty rather than whether the illegal act occurred.

A somewhat idyllic illustration of the spirit of compromise between drinkers and law agents occurred in Atiu during the orange season about ten years ago. Getting sufficient oranges to fill the cargo vessel was imperative if it was to be induced to call again. Yet orange beer drinkers threatened to consume the oranges as fast as they ripened. Consequently the resident commissioner asked all the beer school stewards to bring their tumunui to police headquarters, with the promise that they would be returned after the cargo was made. The arrangement was dutifully observed on both sides and drinking resumed after the ship had sailed.

Unquestionably, Cook Island drinkers are much more aggressive than those in the Society Islands. Disputes often arise in drinking sessions over women, land, and genealogies, and they not infrequently end in fights with fists or with sticks. Men become hungry when they drink and mistreat their wives when they wander home late and food is not immediately made available to them. Sometimes, wives retaliate by informing on their husbands, which aggravates the quarrels.

The men of Atiu are even more hostile and aggressive when intoxicated than are those from the other islands, reflecting something of the history of their reputation as invincible and ruthless warriors. A fair number of brutal assaults and murders have followed drinking sessions on their island. At the same time, it is to be noted that their drinking discipline is stronger and their rule against female drinking stricter than elsewhere. One gets the impression that male Atiuans enjoy their warlike image from the past and may see the assaults and murders as its contemporary validation.

DRINKING PATHOLOGY IN SAMOA

Western Samoa most clearly exemplifies a Polynesian society in which the consequences of intoxication directly threaten or destroy cherished values which are central to the *fa'a Samoa*, the "Samoan way." This was frequently captioned in statements made by paramount chiefs and the minister of police during my last visit, who stated in several ways and on different occasions that "Drinking is the most serious problem we have."

Samoan society differs from that of the Society and Cook Islands in that it successfully absorbed Christianity, resisted foreign domination, and maintained its village-based social organization relatively intact. Its conservative emphasis is revealed by the values placed on conformity, acceptance of group decisions, ceremonial compliance, and politeness in interpersonal interaction. The dominance of these values is guaranteed by a prompt and rough system of social control, administered by the matai (chiefs). Respect for the matai who make and carry out decisions is crucial to its continued functioning.

It can be expected that this kind of system, particularly inasmuch as it makes no place for direct contradiction and openly symbolized hostility, will develop a deep substratum of aggression in its members which readily comes to the surface with intoxication. The focus of drunkenness and aggression appears among the *taulelea*, the young, untitled men, upon whom fall the greatest demands for silent conformity and respect. It is also true that their aggressiveness is in part culturally inculcated, that it is encouraged in certain kinds of structured situations.

A fairly common occurrence is for a drunken taulelea to stand at one end of a village and shout drunken defiance and challenge to any and all who wish to test him in combat. This, even when not motivated by hostility toward the matai, is nevertheless a desecration of Samoan custom, an insult to the whole village, and particularly to the matai. In other instances drunken young men parade in front of the chief's house, which is sacred ground, shouting insults and threats. In some cases matai have been attacked physically.

Samoan aggression differs from that met with in Tahitians and Cook Islanders in being cumulative, slow burning, and explosive. In some forms it comes very close to the psychiatric concept of "free floating" aggression, subject to hair trigger release. A Samoan may brood for weeks over what he regards as an injustice and then with an apparently trivial provocation burst into a murderous rage. Moreover Samoans often fight with rocks in their hands or with bush knives, which cause serious injuries and deaths. Such offenses cannot be handled easily through village justice; they bring the offenders to the attention of central authorities, thus adding a further dimension of stress to the system. The problem has been sufficiently distinctive that a local jurist has proposed legal recognition of criteria of provocation differing from those applicable to Anglo-Saxon societies.[13]

Rapes, in which drunken Samoans beat up a man and take away his girl, are not unknown. Rough beatings of wives by drunken husbands also occur, and children may be harmed. Another form of drunken aggression against wives is the destruction of all the furniture in the fale, and I encountered cases in which a man's drunken rage had led him to burn down the fale. Wives are far from acquiescent in the face of such treatment and the economic deprivation drinking causes. A sub-

[13] C. C. Marsack, "Provocation in Trials for Murder," *Criminal Law Review* (1959), pp. 681–744.

stantial number have left their heavily drinking spouses and sought divorces.

While there are Samoan villages in which brewing and drunkenness are effectively controlled, there still are periodic outbreaks of disorder. This usually happens when a split or a cleavage appears among members of the village council. Most villages have their "drinking matai," who sit solemnly in council, pass rules against drinking, and fine liquor offenders. These same matai at times may be found drinking with taulelea or be driven to buy brew from them. This gives a further impetus to the slow erosion of their authority already at work from other intrusive forces.

CONCLUSION

It seems clear that cultural conservatism has importantly shaped the forms of drinking in the three Polynesian societies under consideration, although it has asserted itself in quite variable ways. Undoubtedly the perspectives and decisions of administrators from the wine-drinking culture of France has helped give form to drinking in the Society Islands, especially in the light of their willingness or conscious efforts to preserve native cultural practices through organized fetes. The replacement of Protestant Anglo-Saxon missionaries by Catholics beginning in 1840 likewise tempered the climate of drinking. Beyond these factors, a variety of others, ecological, those of physical isolation, and perhaps sex ratio of the population, have had a bearing on the permutations of drinking in these islands. While the persistence of Tahitian values requires a more complete explanation, there is little question that intoxication has had a significant function in their recurrent expression and validation.

The drinking group in the Cook Islands, originally a collective reaction to institutional stresses, evolved into a form which also serves to maintain continuity with older cultural values and to preserve certain types of organization. Some of my data suggest that kinship patterns are articulated and probably strengthened through drinking experiences. Despite extensive study by legislative committees in recent years, no significant changes have been made in the church-government system of control of drinking in these islands.

In both the Society Islands and in the Cook Islands, the more intimate drinking situations serve to promote in-group solidarity by releasing symbolic aggression against governing elites, although in true Polynesian tradition it is linguistically subtle and well concealed. I do not regard it as a central element in the drinking in either area.

In Western Samoa the determination by traditional native elites to maintain the old way of life in the face of increasing contact and inter-action with the outside world had made it difficult for the government to entertain alternatives to the makeshift permit system of liquor dis-tribution which denies it to all save a few native Samoans. The situation has been complicated by hostility toward Europeans and the halfcaste population who have strongly advocated liberalizing the law. When pushed too hard on the issue, Samoan leaders have spoken ominously of prohibition for all, a threat which today has pretty well silenced the voices of thirsty Europeans in Apia.

Everywhere the form of drinking shows evidence of the close as-sociation which exists between drinking and cycles of work and play in Polynesian society. The heaviest burden of work rests upon young, un-married males, and even from aboriginal times it may have had qualities of exploitation and anomie. Entrance into the money economy and wage-work have imposed daily and weekly routines and goals which are alien and tension-creating for Polynesians. As this increases, heavy week-end drinking and periodic indulgence, coupled with absenteeism, can be expected to figure large in the labor problems of these people.

Numerous data reveal that control of drinking can be and has been successfully organized in the three societies under consideration. However, status rivalry, which is endemic in Polynesia, complicates control by producing cleavages in authority. This does much to explain the so-called outbreaks of drunkenness commented on in historical accounts of these societies and currently observable in Samoa.

Alcoholism in the sense of addictive drinking, with complex per-sonality changes and serious organic pathology, such as cirrhosis of the liver, is nowhere found among full-blooded Polynesians. The only such case I was able to locate, despite persistent and careful inquiries, was that of a noble in Tonga, and his was clearly that of a deviant. At the same time cases do occur in all areas, but especially in Samoa, of persons who have drunk very heavily—to the detriment of their family life—and have be-ginning physical complications such as gastritis. In addition, I met a few on Savaii who told me they got sick if they didn't drink, by which they meant that their hands would shake. Yet equally impressive is the large number of heavy drinkers who have successfully stopped their drinking.

One fact which may be important to note in understanding the absence of organic pathology among heavy drinkers in Polynesia is that, in contradistinction to patterns of drinking found in our urban society, indulgence stimulates appetite. It is not unusual for a late-carousing Samoan to disturb the whole household rummaging around for food before he goes to sleep. Food and the well-rounded belly stand high in the order of Polynesian values, with at least as much anxiety surrounding eating as drinking. This may help explain why the development of gastritis and interference with food assimilation by drinking become a motive for giving up liquor in some cases.

Another relevant paramount value for Polynesians is that of psychic rapport with one's fellows. Destructive drinking ultimately thwarts the desire for this state by isolating the drinker from relatives and friends; it may cause him to lose his wife, and above all, his children, through divorce. Yet Polynesian ideology and institutions provide no support for "living alone and liking it." The pleasures of solitary drinking, which is almost a contradiction in Polynesia, are poor recompense for the isolated drinker's losses.

A final consideration is that guilt over drinking or drunkenness does not seem to develop in Polynesian society. A person is in no way disadvantaged by a history of drunkenness, particularly after renouncing drinking. Samoans, when they think on the problem, objectify liquor; typically they ask the question as to whether "this liquor is good for *me*?" or "for Samoans?" They seldom think in terms of whether it is morally right or wrong to drink or get drunk. Such attitudes, I believe, leave Polynesians relatively free to utilize what we would regard as naive methods to stop drinking. They are, however, consistent with the system of overt avoidances and compliances which seem to be characteristic of Polynesian education methods and social control.

The Samoan case clearly is a negative one insofar as Ullman's hypothesis is concerned, for here is a society in which drinking practices are unintegrated culturally and disruptive in extreme, yet addictive drinking has not developed. At most it can be said that individual Samoans develop relatively serious drinking problems; however, they do not eventuate in organic pathology and psychic deterioration of the sort characterizing much alcoholism in Western societies. I am inclined to explain this on the basis of the kinds of values contravened by intoxication, the possible physiological effects of values on the form of drinking (eating), and the ways in which a particular kind of social organization confronts the individual with the costs of his intoxicated behavior.

In general, my survey indicates that values are a crucial factor in understanding the forms, cultural integration, and pathology of drinking. It also argues that the study of values must be supplemented by study of social organization and social control in order to determine which values and costs become dominant in a society or are brought to bear in drinking situations. In societies in which moralistic concepts of drinking and stigma-management problems of drinkers are absent, a value-cost model may explain the absence of addictive drinking in individuals as well as be useful to account for the collective forms of drinking. Possibly it may have uses in understanding how drinking histories are interrupted or truncated short of addiction in our own society.

14 THE SECULAR USE OF KAVA—
WITH SPECIAL REFERENCE TO TONGA

In the course of recent research on alcohol use in Polynesian Islands my interest in kava drinking was originally limited to establishing lines of cultural continuity between early forms of kava use and patterns of alcohol consumption which developed subsequent to European and American cultural contacts. While in Tonga, however, I was impressed by a widespread secular use of kava, which seems to have largely escaped the attention of anthropologists. This oversight, plus the possible implications of findings for the crosscultural study of alcohol and narcotics use, suggested a need to examine kava drinking in other than the formal ceremonial context which has been the subject of extensive study and description.

A few facts will suffice to provide a background setting for the discussion. Kava, known by a variety of names, is an infusion made by adding water to the macerated root of the pepper tree, the *Piper methysticum*. Originally in Polynesia it was chewed and spat into a bowl where it was mixed with water and served in folded leaf or coconut cups. Kava has been used in most islands of Polynesia except Easter Island and New Zealand, and also consumed in parts of Melanesia and Micro-

Reprinted by permission of the Quarterly Journal of Studies on Alcohol 28 (1967): 328–41.

nesia. The practice died out in Eastern Polynesia, and the Cook Islands, presumably due to missionary influence, and elsewhere in Polynesia it was modified from chewing to pounding the root. Today it continues to be drunk in Samoa, Tonga, Fiji, and in parts of Melanesia, and on Ponape. I will here direct attention to its informal use in Tonga.

Tonga consists of three island groups, mostly of coral formation, located in the Western Pacific, south of Samoa and at one point no more than 80 miles from the eastern boundary of Fiji. Inhabitants of the islands number between 75,000 and 100,000, many of whom, in recent decades, have migrated townwards. The people have been governed under a monarchy since 1845, and in 1900 the islands became a protectorate of the British Empire. Their religion is predominantly Protestant, but language and culture are essentially Polynesian, with a strong conservative emphasis, most apparent in the land system, which, despite reforms, remains quasi-feudal. Alcohol beverages were unknown to Tongans until introduced to them by early explorers, runaway sailors, and traders. Kava, of course, is an ancient and integrated element of the culture.

FAI-KAVA

Tongans distinguish three types of kava drinking: (1) *taumafa kava*, (2) *ilo kava*, and (3) *fai-kava*. The first is the Queen's kava, the second the nobles' kava, and the third, which is no more than a generic term for making kava, is kava for commoners. Generally speaking, fai-kava can be described as a relatively informal gathering or "party" for drinking kava, having some tenuous associations with courtship, but primarily convivial in nature.

Ordinarily a fai-kava is convened at the house of a young unmarried girl which is large enough to accommodate the group. The party is initiated by the action of a young man who in the company of friends takes a supply of kava root to the house and asks the girl to make kava from them. Permission is also sought from the girl's parents and if favorable, the participants, from six to eight in number, enter and seat themselves cross-legged in a circle on the floor. The girl, or *toa*, is at the head of the circle, where the bowl is placed. The male host, who has set up the party, sits at the left of the girl and his close friend may sit at her right.

The boy pounds the kava root and the girl mixes it with water in the bowl according to traditional procedures. Her movements are slow and measured. After it is ready the male host serves the kava in a coconut cup proceeding clockwise or counterclockwise around the circle. No particular precedence is followed unless someone of importance is present.

Serving is anticipated in each instance by clapping of hands of others in the circle. The server waits patiently in front of each drinker until he has finished. Drinkers usually utter a stylized salutation, then down the contents of the cup at one draught. A fresh batch of kava ordinarily is made for each of the servings, which are repeated at intervals of 20 to 30 minutes.

Social interaction at a fai-kava is variously conditioned by the circular positioning of the drinkers, the family setting, and the subjective dispositions of the drinkers. In the early stages of the party, drinkers focus much of their attention on preparation of the kava, particularly on the movements of the toa and all indications are that her presence and actions lend a highly important esthetic element to the proceedings. A good deal of wry face-making accompanies the act of drinking by the individuals, particularly after several rounds.

Conversation at a fai-kava ranges over a wide variety of topics: crops, actions of government officials, religion, rumors of events in the larger world, and local gossip. Verbal interaction, while spirited at times, tends to be desultory, and it may die away to muttered dialogues or even to complete silence. As the evening wears away, some drinkers doze or let their heads hang loosely to the front of their shoulders. Interaction now and then is punctuated by drinkers leaving the house to urinate in the nearby bush.

Singing to the accompaniment of guitars may occur; songs deal with love themes or may be laments for persons who have suffered misfortunes. At one fai-kava the writer witnessed dancing as follows: singly by the toa, the toa with a female partner, and finally the toa with a male partner. The dance movements were slow, stylized, and not even remotely erotic.

Although fai-kavas may be held in the afternoon, or even in the mornings, they most frequently begin in early evening. In Nukualofa, the capital, many such parties commence when the local movies terminate, at eleven o'clock. Parties may continue from seven o'clock until midnight or until the small hours of the morning depending on the amenability of the hosts and the wearing qualities of the toa. In certain instances parties continue for a day and night, or for several days and nights.

Interaction at a fai-kava is seldom if ever disorderly. The only jarring note may come if uninvited guests show up late, and especially if they try to squeeze in to sit close to the girl. Such latecomers may be given a special, large cup of kava or several cups to finish before being accepted in the circle. If they fail they are openly ridiculed. Tensions also may occasionally arise if talk shifts to genealogies, or to "talking of chiefs," a touchy subject in most Polynesian societies, but persons introducing such topics usually are shouted down.

While having the kava prepared and served by a young girl is ideally prescribed, if none is available a man performs the duties.

THE PREVALENCE OF FAI-KAVA

There is little doubt that fai-kava parties are a commonplace feature of contemporary Tongan life. For example, informants seemed agreed that they are more prevalent than homebrew parties, whose number is not inconsequential. In Nukualofa there is a numerous coterie of young men who are continually in search of kava parties day and night. Two kava saloons conspicuously operate near the center of town, where bowls of kava can be purchased for a shilling each. Older men can be seen there most nights and on many afternoons consuming the beverage. Most households have kava plantings nearby. Kava roots are ordinary stock in trade of many local stores, being vended at four shillings per bunch.

More precise information of the prevalence of kava drinking parties in a particular Tongan village is provided by Beaglehole. In this community of 50 households, located on *Vava'u*, during a 16-day period there were 45 kava parties, ranging in frequency from one per day to nine, with an average of three per day. There was only one day out of 16 chosen for tabulation on which no kava was made. At most only one or two of the kava sessions were held to welcome visitors.[1]

DIFFERENTIAL PARTICIPATION

Throughout Polynesia, as well as in Melanesia where it occurs, kava drinking is recognized as a prerogative of older males, although there are areas and occasions which allow female drinking. In the past in Hawaii and in the Cook Islands women could and did hold kava circles of their own, and currently in Tonga this may happen. Otherwise women participate marginally with men, usually to make the kava. Beaglehole in the aforementioned study found that 32 percent of the village women had attended kava parties in the 16-day period, with most of them having participated in one party. On the other hand 81 percent of the men took part in parties, the median number of parties attended being 3.2. This reflects a broad range of participation; some men were but occasional participants, while others were daily participants. One man stood high with a total of 32 parties for 15 days.[2]

[1] Ernest Beaglehole and Pearl Beaglehole, "Pangai, Village in Tonga," *Memoirs of the Polynesian Society* 18 (Wellington, 1941): 112–23.

[2] Ibid.

While I have said that kava has been recognized in Polynesia as a prerogative of older men, this may have been due to the fact that originally it was prepared by chewing, thus more likely drunk by those able to command the labor of others. In Samoa at the present time there has been concern about young men drinking kava, but mainly centering around secret use of the kava ritual (e.g. clapping the hands at each serving), which is a status prerogative of chiefs. Whatever may have been true in the past, both young and older men drink kava in Tonga today, excluding, however, those whom we would regard as children or adolescents.

KAVA IN SOCIAL STRUCTURE

In Eastern and Central Polynesia in early times kava occupied an important place in ceremonies venerating and establishing communication with gods. In Hawaii it was employed in sorcery and in the treatment of disease, as well as being used to induce sleep and counteract fatigue. There are also historical references to drinking parties among chiefs for this area, and after the time of Kamehameha I it was increasingly drunk by commoners in small convivial male groups.[3] However, more elaborate ceremonial uses of kava seem to have been absent from Hawaii and other areas of Eastern Polynesia.

The ritual function of kava drinking as a means of symbolizing and overtly validating status positions in Samoa, of course, is well known, as it is in Tonga. However, in the latter area particularly, there remains a need to account for the widespread use of kava among commoners, which at least in present times, far outweighs the general social importance of formal kava drinking on occasions which designate complexities of the chiefly and royal leadership hierarchy.

As far as I know, Beaglehole has made the only attempt at explaining secular kava forms. Generally he sees them as a kind of Tongan equivalent of the New England town meeting, which provides outlets for social impulses not otherwise possible in a society where older forms of social aggregation have become attenuated or disappeared. Thus kava parties offer opportunities for casual social interaction and the formation of public opinion in a society which due to conflicting groups and interests has no other common socializing agency.

I have no quarrel with the general outlines of Beaglehole's interpretation except that it fails to explain why drinking kava rather than other beverages continues to function as an integrating force in Tongan life. This

[3] Margaret Titcomb, "Kava in Hawaii," *Journal of the Polynesian Society* 57 (1948): 105–71.

is particularly important when it is noted that making and drinking of homebrew for some time has been and still is an alternative medium of male interaction.

There are, of course, a number of things which could be immediately said on this question, touching such things as relative costs of the beverages (kava is cheaper), cultural conservatism, and the prohibitive controls which make homebrew illegal. However, I would first like to dwell upon some of the physiological and psychological effects of kava in relation to its social function and to possible satisfaction of needs or dispositions which may be reactional products of social and cultural claims upon the individual.

The first thing which needs to be said is that intoxication from kava stands in marked contrast to that of alcohol. It does not release aggressive impulses; if anything it inhibits or dissociates them. Furthermore, kava is anaphrodisiac in effect, a point agreed on by all informants, in Tonga and elsewhere.[4] The inhibition of aggressiveness and the extinction of sexual desire are well illustrated by the following statement of a Tongan subject:

> Not feeling like beer when drunk on kava. It makes me tired. It makes me to sleep. Makes my face feel funny, but not make me happy. Homebrew make me happy to speak, and don't mind. The kava make you finished. You don't want anything. Also make you hungry—you go look for food. After eat you go to sleep. Boys never want girls after kava . . .

There are, of course, effects of kava more positively valued than those indicated by the Tongan. Some of these have been described by Tom Harrison, an articulate biologist who became a notable kava drinker during his stay in the New Hebrides.[5]

> The head is affected most pleasantly . . . you don't get drunk on kava. But it speeds up your slowness. You feel friendly, not beer sentimental, never cross. The world gains no new color or rose tint; it fits in its place and is one easily understandable whole. Talk, talk, talk, the world becomes a beauty of voices . . . you cannot hate with kava in you.

Kava taken in limited amounts has a mild tranquilizing effect which sets a mood of amiability. After some initial stimulation, substantial quantities depress bodily functions such as heart rate, respiration, and temperature. Sensory changes occur, most frequently reported by informants as distor-

---

[4] In Fiji a panel of kava drinkers in a village near Nandi were interviewed on this subject. One drinker about 70 years of age claimed kava made him want women. The entire group laughed with great amusement at this.

[5] Tom Harrison, *Savage Civilization* (New York: Knopf, 1937), pp. 275–78.

tion of perception in various forms.[6] Yet with this, the higher cortical processes remain unimpaired. It is quite possible that the sense of time and sense of bodily identification with the self are affected in ways which are not now clear. Dreamy exhaltation is a term which has been applied to kava intoxication, suggesting similarities in effects with marihuana or hashish. Lewin [7] classes it as a soporific and hypnotic.

If the effects I have chosen to assign to kava are valid they immediately speak of a clear superiority over alcohol as a social reagent at least in certain sociocultural contexts. The inhibition of two kinds of impulses or motivations most likely to be socially disruptive, namely sex and aggression, together with a kind of dissociation of the psychic processes, which gives pleasure, intrigue or new meaning to prosaic images, thoughts, and words, may explain the special utility which kava has for Polynesian social interaction. In part this may lie in its use as a counteractive to apathy and boredom associated with routine existence and unpleasant labor in island societies. More importantly kava may well acquire its social function as a way of satisfying paramount Polynesian values which center around psychic rapport without triggering the status rivalries and conflicts which are held to be more or less endemic in Polynesian society.[8] Note, in this connection, that the esthetic values of the kava ritual itself are not impaired by intoxication of the drinkers, and ritual performance is insured by the fact that ordinarily those who prepare and serve the kava, especially the female participants, do not drink.

Kava drinking also provides the opportunity to express in a specialized way emulative and competitive values of Polynesian society. It is obvious from the extent and form of their participation that some Tongans derive kinds of satisfactions from kava parties which differ from those sought by other drinkers. Here I refer to so-called kava addicts, whose interests and manner of inbibing kava have conspicuous cult-like qualities. Such persons are known as *tangata inu kava*, "big kava drinkers." Generally, such persons have gained notoriety for their ability to consume large amounts of kava—30 or 40 cups, and to drink continuously for lengthy periods, as many as three days and nights. They are well versed in kava lore, know of and have drunk from famous kava cups such as *To'nofo* ("to fall to stay") and are a kind of walking registry of current kava parties. They also are

[6] David Cerna, "A Study of the Physiological Action of Kava-Kava," *The Therapeutic Gazette*, 3rd Series, 7 (1891): 7–16; C. Cuzent, "Du Kava on Kava—*Piper Methysticum*," in *Iles de la Société* (Tahiti: Rocheforte, 1860), pp. 82–102; F. Keller and M. W. Khoha, "A Review of the Chemistry and Pharmacology of the Constituents of *Piper methysticum*," *Lloydia* 26 (1963): 1–15.

[7] Louis Lewin, *Phantastica* (London: Kegan, Trench and Trubner, 1931).

[8] Irving Goldman, "Status Rivalry and Cultural Evolution in Polynesia," *American Anthropologist* 57 (1955): 680–97.

acquainted with kava drinkers in many areas, so that in a village away from home they can look up the local tangata inu kava and gain entree to a party.

It is difficult to say how many "kava addicts" there are in Tonga. One informant, however, said he was personally acquainted with over 100. Another counted ten in his village alone. Beaglehole enumerated seven men and one woman in his village of study who were sufficiently heavy drinkers to be regarded as having an obsession for kava.[9] A brief case history of a tangata inu kava who became known to the writer follows:

> This man comes from Nukualofa. He is 55 years of age and is known as Tofo inu kava. He began to drink kava at age 19. Before this for two years he was a general handy boy for a kava drinking group and was finally admitted to the group as a drinker. Older people had advised him to take one cup of kava as a tonic for stomach disorders or influenza, from which he periodically suffered. In the last 30 years since drinking kava he has suffered from neither.
>
> He did not like kava at first but after drinking it for one year he liked it well enough to drink it every day. When he was younger he drank for three or four days at a time. The longest he ever drank was five days and nights, at which time he drank 100 cups. On days following kava bouts he was sleepy and it affected his ability to work on the plantation. He developed scales over his body and his skin cracked. His eyes became sore and inflamed; his lips became chapped and peeled, which he sought to remedy with vaseline. People laughed at his appearance.
>
> While Tofo usually drank with groups, there were times when he became too lazy to find one, so he pounded his own kava and drank alone. At the time he was supported by his parents which explains why he could spend so much of his time drinking kava. He doesn't work much now and he suffers from dizziness.

KAVA PATHOLOGY

It is possible to speak of a limited degree of kava pathology. Prolonged heavy use of the drug is associated with icthyosis—dry scaliness of the skin—and the eyes may become irritated, bloodshot, sometimes prurient. There is evidence that heavy users occasionally suffer from constipation and possibly intestinal obstructions.[10] Loss of weight may occur. However, these signs or conditions quickly disappear when the drink is discontinued.

There are no references in the literature on kava nor indications from

[9] Beaglehole and Beaglehole, "Pangai, Village in Tonga."

[10] Tongan kava lore tells of heavy kava users who have died and later been disinterred. Lumps, or concretions, of kava called *mongea* are said to be sometimes found among the bones. Discerning drinkers claim that kava made from *mongea* is top quality.

user informants that abstention from kava after habitual consumption is followed by withdrawal stress symptoms. Nor do hangovers comparable to those with alcohol occur. Yet it seems clear that a definite craving for the beverage does indeed develop with time, the relative intensity of which was well appraised by Emerson's Hawaiian informant: ". . . awa does not seem to have such a claim on its votary as alcohol; it does not surely kill and it can be abandoned without as fierce a struggle." [11]

That kava drinking can be addictive is supported by the fact of its persistence in the face of social penalties. Preoccupation with the drug may render the drinker less fit or even unfit for work. Marital difficulties may appear, with complaints from the distaff side because of nights or days the drinker spends away from home. Wives also complain of the sexual incapacity or lack of erotic interest of their heavily imbibing husbands, and some cases are known in Tonga where this has been a cause of divorce. In the community, kava addicts are definitely regarded as deviants and gossiped about.

Despite these sequelae, heavy secular use of kava as well as its ritual use to all appearances is an integrated aspect on Tongan society. The addict participates in behavior which is socially accepted for the adult male, and he may find support for his indulgence from older sacred connotations of kava intoxication as a sign of god-like affinity, as well as from the admiration of those who are part of the cult.

The scarcity of studies of Polynesian personality, and the lack of any such data for Tonga make statements about the possible psychic basis of kava addiction difficult. Since repressed sexuality and aggressiveness are not manifest motives for continual kava intoxication it may be meaningful to see it as some form of retreatist or avoidance behavior, related to heavy or onerous claims which Polynesian social organization periodically makes upon the individual. In this connection Mead asserts that cultural demands fall most heavily upon young untitled persons in Samoan society, which, on the surface would be inconsistent with the reported tendency for kava addiction to be most common among older men of higher status. However, she notes, too, that responsibilities resting upon titled Samoans also are heavy and, furthermore, more difficult to evade.[12] This, of course, is a reflection of the more general Polynesian tendency for responsibility (as opposed to requisitions of labor and goods) to go with older age, and the tendency to recognize the years up to 30 as an age of irresponsibility.

In direct reference to Tonga, data show that ideal kinship reciprocity in practice frequently is disordered by death or spatial separation of rela-

[11] Oliver P. Emerson, "The Awa Habit of the Hawaiians," *Hawaiian Almanac and Annual* (Honolulu, 1903), pp. 130–40.

[12] Margaret Mead, "The Role of the Individual in Samoan Culture," *Journal of the Royal Anthropological Institute* 57–58 (1927–28): 481–95.

tives, with the result that burdens for support get unequally distributed. Parents also may be frustrated in efforts to meet responsibility for children both in regard to economic support and educational training.[13] Superficially, at least, the work and allocative system seems to lend itself to interpersonal exploitation, and at the present time there appear to be no well-defined techniques for dealing with the "freeloader."

It seems plausible that Tongan society, as well as other Polynesian societies, produce a share of personalities temperamentally or otherwise ill suited to the strong *gemeinschaft* values of their cultures, which are expressed in food sharing, symbolic aspects of sexual communion, and reinforced by kinship claims and physical intimacy of household arrangements. At the same time there seems to be little cultural support for social withdrawal in Polynesian societies,[14] Tongan not excluded. Indeed, such tendencies are likely to invoke disapproval, particularly if they carry the implications of non-sharing or stinginess.

For those with ambivalent attitudes toward the central values of Tongan culture, kava intoxication may be a well evolved means by which they can preserve the form of psychic identification with others and at the same time maintain identity, individuality, or detachment important for their personal existence. While Tongans apparently believe that kava addiction makes a person less responsible, it also may be true that less responsible persons are the ones who become big drinkers. The heavy user in effect finds a culturally valid explanation for the undesirable consequences of his drinking in causes external to himself. Hence, secondary anxieties from consequences of social penalties are minimal in contrast to those seen, for example, with alcoholism in American society. To this extent there may be less psychic reinforcement of the anxieties associated with kava craving.

CONCLUSION

The current situation in Tonga raises challenging questions in regard to sociocultural change and preferences for intoxicants, centering around concurrent use of kava and alcohol. In recent decades, particularly during and after World War II when the influence of a large contingent of American soldiers was felt, the illegal manufacture and consumption of homebrew coupled with public drunkenness grew into a critical police

[13] Beaglehole and Beaglehole, "Pangai, Village in Tonga."

[14] Samoans recognize a kind of fugue-like state during which individuals for varying periods lapse into sullen disregard for or resistance to orders. This is known as *musu*. However, it was not encountered in Tonga. C. C. Marsack, *Samoan Medley* (London: Robt. Hale Ltd., 1961), pp. 29–30.

problem, ultimately leading to more permissive liquor laws. Along with this, kava drinking has steadily become more prevalent and it is now drunk at a younger age than was true in the past.

There has been little development of culturally patterned preferences for one intoxicant over the other, such as Carstairs [15] found to hold between Brahmin and the Rajput castes of an Indian village in their evaluations of liquor and bhang. Older Tongans can be found who distinctly prefer kava to alcoholic beverages, and church pastors refrain from alcohol on principle, but many or most Tongans—even kava addicts—will drink both. When asked which they prefer, a common response is, "It depends on the circumstances." Thus, if it is available, a young man may prefer to drink homebrew, or if he has a liquor permit and the money, custom beer. On the other hand if his friends are drinking kava or he wants to meet a new girl at a kava party he may forego the chance to drink liquor.

Such facts allow little more in the way of conclusion than that alcohol and kava satisfy different needs felt by individuals at different times. Wider alcohol use may be an expression of unintegrated impulses and desires growing from changes due to missionization, contact with American soldiers, population growth, and drift to urban centers. It may to some extent reflect patterned conformity with white elite culture represented by Commonwealth expatriates, affinity with the privileged nobility, or restlessness and protest of a growing youth population. Increased kava drinking on the other hand suggests a kind of cultural reaction formation in which the attendant intoxication has an altered or expanded function of allowing psychic detachment from the immediate situation and a retreat to older Tongan values.

Such guesses, however informed, are not overly satisfying. Moreover it is doubtful that the adoption and use of particular intoxicants can be reduced to a simple selective process resting upon competing personality needs created by the impact of new and old culture patterns. Much more immediate considerations are ecological and cost factors which affect the availability of materials and energy and investment to manufacture or purchase intoxicants. Of equal importance are differences in the consequences of the two types of intoxication (as opposed to their motives) for social organization and the effects of these on opinion and public policy as they lead to social control.

Older Tongans well appreciate the disruptive potentials in alcohol intoxication both to the authority system and to values placed on female

[15] G. M. Carstairs, "Daru and Bhang Cultural Factors in the Choice of Intoxicant," *Quarterly Journal of Studies on Alcohol* 15 (1954): 29–30; D. L. Gerard, "Intoxication and Addiction, Psychiatric Observations on Alcoholism and Opiate Addiction," *Quarterly Journal of Studies on Alcohol* 16 (1955): 675–99.

virginity. This is illustrated in the occasional efforts of young men who have homebrew or liquor to seek out a receptive girl whose home can be used in the manner of the fai-kava prototype. Generally such overtures get curtly rebuffed by the girl, her parents, or both. The contrast between the fai-kava and the liquor party is sharply drawn in those instances when liquor is added surreptitiously to the kava, for what starts out as ritual drinking soon deteriorates into disorders or fights over a girl. Significantly, an aggressor may expunge his transgressions next day by taking kava to drink at the house of those he has offended.

The reigning Queen of Tonga [now deceased] disapproves of liquor and takes only a little wine occasionally. The ruling Prince Tungi and his brother both renounced alcohol some years ago and the Prince now drinks only kava. Nobles and foreigners must do their drinking in one of four private clubs, three of which are in Nukualofa. Official police policy denies liquor permits to natives under 30 years of age and continues to allocate liquor according to the status of permit holders—a practice dating from the late nineteenth century. The system seems to work well enough at the present. The dominant missionary church forbids alcohol to pastors and discourages its use by young persons. The general attitude of controlling elites is that youth and commoners (unless proven otherwise) are incapable of being trusted with liquor. So long as this attitude prevails it is doubtful that youth will be taught by parents to "behave yourself" when drinking alcohol, as is done for kava. Thus while the tradition of kava drinking has been continuously reinforced in Tongan society, liquor at best has remained a marginal cultural alternative.

In another paper I have held that liquor drinking in Eastern Polynesia, especially in the Society and Cook Islands, has in the course of time become adapted to the expression of older esoteric values of those societies.[16] This has been done by the use of beverages of low alcohol content, which allow a "long slow drunk" without passing out, and a system of small group discipline. The comparative recency with which liquor has been drunk on a large scale in Western Polynesia, Tonga, and Samoa, suggests that sufficient time has not elapsed for a comparable adaptation to occur there. On the other hand it is entirely possible that elements of culture and social organization in Western Polynesia may be basically uncongenial to alcohol use. This doesn't mean that alcohol will not be increasingly used, but that such increasing use will be a measure of the alteration or disappearance of such distinctive elements.

[16] Edwin M. Lemert, "Forms and Pathology of Drinking in Three Polynesian Societies," *American Anthropologist* 66 (1964): 361–74.

15 PARANOIA AND THE DYNAMICS OF EXCLUSION

One of the few generalizations about psychotic behavior which sociologists have been able to make with a modicum of agreement and assurance is that such behavior is a result or manifestation of a disorder in communication between the individual and society. The generalization, of course, is a large one, and, while it can be illustrated easily with case history materials, the need for its conceptual refinement and detailing of the process by which disruption of communication occurs in the dynamics of mental disorder has for some time been apparent. Among the more carefully reasoned attacks upon this problem is Cameron's formulation of the paranoid pseudocommunity.[1]

In essence, the conception of the paranoid pseudocommunity can be stated as follows: [2]

Paranoid persons are those whose inadequate social learning leads them in situations of unusual stress to incompetent social reactions. Out of

Reprinted with permission from Sociometry 25 *(March 1962): 2–25.*

[1] Norman Cameron, "The Paranoid Pseudocommunity," *American Journal of Sociology* 46 (1943): 33–38.

[2] In a subsequent article Cameron modified his original conception, but not of the social aspects of paranoia, which mainly concern us. Norman Cameron, "The Paranoid Pseudocommunity Revisited," *American Journal of Sociology* 65 (1959): 52–58.

the fragments of the social behavior of others the paranoid person symbolically organizes a pseudocommunity whose functions he perceives as focused on him. His reactions to this *supposed community* of response which he sees loaded with threat to himself bring him into open conflict with the actual community and lead to his temporary or permanent isolation from its affairs. The "real" community, which is unable to share in his attitudes and reactions, takes action through forcible restraint or retaliation *after* the paranoid person "bursts into defensive or vengeful activity." [3]

That the community to which the paranoid reacts is "pseudo" or without existential reality is made unequivocal by Cameron when he says:

> As he (the paranoid person) begins attributing to others the attitudes which he has toward himself, he unintentionally organizes these others into a functional community, a group unified in their supposed reactions, attitudes, and plans with respect to him. He in this way organizes individuals, some of whom are actual persons and some only inferred or imagined, into a whole which satisfies for the time being his immediate need for explanation but which brings no assurance with it, and usually serves to increase his tensions. The community he forms not only fails to correspond to any organization shared by others but actually contradicts this consensus. More than this, the actions ascribed by him to its personnel are not actually performed or maintained by them; *they are united in no common undertaking against him.*[4] [Italics ours.]

The general insightfulness of Cameron's analysis cannot be gainsaid and the usefulness of some of his concepts is easily granted. Yet a serious question must be raised, based upon empirical inquiry, as to whether in actuality the insidious qualities of the community to which the paranoid reacts are pseudo or a symbolic fabrication. There is an alternative point of view, which is the burden of this paper, namely that, while the paranoid person reacts differentially to his social environment, it is also true that "others" react differentially to him and this reaction commonly if not typically involves covertly organized action and conspiratorial behavior in a very real sense. A further extension of our thesis is that these differential reactions are reciprocals of one another, being interwoven and concatenated at each and all phases of a process of exclusion which arises in a special kind of relationship. Delusions and associated behavior must be understood in a context of exclusion which attenuates this relationship and disrupts communication.

By thus shifting the clinical spotlight away from the individual to a relationship and a process, we make an explicit break with the conception

[3] Cameron, "The Paranoid Pseudocommunity."
[4] Ibid.

of paranoia as a disease, a state, a condition, or a syndrome of symptoms. Furthermore, we find it unnecessary to postulate trauma of early childhood or arrested psychosexual development to account for the main features of paranoia—although we grant that these and other factors may condition its expression.

This conception of paranoia is neither simple *a priori* theory nor is it a proprietary product of sociology. There is a substantial body of writings and empirical researches in psychiatry and psychology which question the sufficiency of the individual as primary datum for the study of paranoia. Tyhurst, for example, concludes from his survey of this literature that reliance upon intrapsychic mechanisms and the "isolated organism" have been among the chief obstacles to fruitful discoveries about this disorder.[5] Significantly, as Milner points out, the more complete the investigation of the cases the more frequently do unendurable external circumstances make their appearance.[6] More precisely, a number of studies have ended with the conclusions that external circumstances—changes in norms and values, displacement, strange environments, isolation, and linguistic separation—may create a paranoid disposition in the absence of any special character structure.[7] The recognition of paranoid reactions in elderly persons, alcoholics, and the deaf adds to the data generally consistent with our thesis. The finding that displaced persons who withstood a high degree of stress during war and captivity subsequently developed paranoid reactions when they were isolated in a foreign environment commands special attention among data requiring explanation in other than organic or psychodynamic terms.[8]

From what has been said thus far, it should be clear that our formulation and analysis will deal primarily with what Tyhurst[9] calls paranoid patterns of behavior rather than with a clinical entity in the classical Kraepelinian sense. Paranoid reactions, paranoid states, paranoid personality disturbances, as well as the seldom-diagnosed "true paranoia," which are found superimposed or associated with a wide variety of individual behavior or "symptoms," all provide a body of data for study so long as they assume priority over other behavior in meaningful social inter-

---

[5] James S. Tyhurst, "Paranoid Patterns," in *Exploration in Social Psychiatry*, eds. Alexander H. Leighton, John A. Clausen, and Robert N. Wilson (New York: Basic Books, 1957), chap. II.

[6] K. O. Milner, "The Environment as a Factor in the Etiology of Criminal Paranoia," *Journal of Mental Science* 95 (1949): 124–32.

[7] S. Pederson, "Psychological Reactions to Extreme Social Displacement (Refugee Neuroses)," *Psychoanalytic Review* 36 (1946): 344–54.

[8] F. F. Kine, "Aliens' Paranoid Reaction," *Journal of Mental Science* 98 (1951): 589–94; I. Listivan, "Paranoid States: Social and Cultural Aspects," *Medical Journal of Australia* (1956), pp. 776–78.

[9] Tyhurst, "Paranoid Patterns."

action. The elements of behavior upon which paranoid diagnoses are based —delusions, hostility, aggressiveness, suspicion, envy, stubbornness, jealousy, and ideas of reference—are readily comprehended and to some extent empathized by others as social reactions, in contrast to the bizarre, manneristic behavior of schizophrenia or the tempo and affect changes stressed in manic-depressive diagnoses. It is for this reason that paranoia suggests, more than any other forms of mental disorder, the possibility of fruitful sociological analysis.

DATA AND PROCEDURE

The first tentative conclusions which are presented here were drawn from a study of factors influencing decisions to commit mentally disordered persons to hospitals, undertaken with the cooperation of the Los Angeles County Department of Health in 1952. This included interviews by means of schedules with members of 44 families in Los Angeles County who were active petitioners in commitment proceedings and the study of 35 case records of public health officer commitments. In 16 of the former cases and in seven of the latter, paranoid symptoms were conspicuously present. In these cases family members and others had plainly accepted or "normalized" paranoid behavior, in some instances longstanding, until other kinds of behavior or exigencies led to critical judgments that "there was something wrong" with the person in question, and, later, that hospitalization was necessary. Furthermore, these critical judgments seemed to signal changes in the family attitudes and behavior toward the affected persons which could be interpreted as contributing in different ways to the form and intensity of the paranoid symptoms.

In 1958 a more refined and hypothesis-directed study was made of eight cases of persons with prominent paranoid characteristics. Four of these had been admitted to the state hospital at Napa, California, where they were diagnosed as paranoid schizophrenic. Two other cases were located and investigated with the assistance of the district attorney in Martinez, California. One of the persons had previously been committed to a California state hospital, and the other had been held on an insanity petition but was freed after a jury trial. Added to these was one so-called "White House case," which had involved threats to a President of the United States, resulting in the person's commitment to St. Elizabeth's Hospital in Washington, D. C. A final case was that of a professional person with a history of chronic job difficulties, who was designated and regarded by his associates as "brash," "queer," "irritating," "hypercritical," and "thoroughly unlikeable."

In a very rough way the cases made up a continuum ranging from one with very elaborate delusions, through those in which fact and misinterpretation were difficult to separate, down to the last case, which comes closer to what some would call paranoid personality disturbance. A requirement for the selection of the cases was that there be no history or evidence of hallucinations and also that the persons be intellectually unimpaired. Seven of the cases were of males, five of whom were over 40 years of age. Three of the persons had been involved in repeated litigations. One man published a small, independent paper devoted to exposures of psychiatry and mental hospitals. Five of the men had been or were associated with organizations, as follows: a smalltown high school, a government research bureau, an association of agricultural producers, a university, and a contracting business.

The investigations of the cases were as exhaustive as it was possible to make them, reaching relatives, work associates, employers, attorneys, police, physicians, public officials, and any others who played significant roles in the lives of the persons involved. As many as 200 hours each were given to collecting data on some of the cases. Written materials, legal documents, publications, and psychiatric histories were studied in addition to the interview data. Our procedure in the large was to adopt an interactional perspective which sensitized us to sociologically relevant behavior underlying or associated with the more apparent and formal contexts of mental disorder. In particular we were concerned to establish the order in which delusions and social exclusion occur and to determine whether exclusion takes conspiratorial form.

THE RELEVANT BEHAVIOR

In another paper [10] we have shown that psychotic symptoms as described in formal psychiatry are not relevant bases for predictions about changes in social status and social participation of persons in whom they appear. Apathy, hallucinations, hyperactivity, mood swings, tics, tremors, functional paralysis, or tachychardias have no intrinsic social meanings. By the same token, neither do such imputed attributes as "lack of insight," "social incompetence," or "defective role-taking ability" favored by some sociologists as generic starting points for the analysis of mental disorders. Rather, it is behavior which puts strain on social relationships that leads to status changes: informal or formal exclusion from groups, definition as a "crank," or adjudication as insane and commitment to a mental hospital.[11] This is

[10] Edwin M. Lemert, "Legal Commitment and Social Control," *Sociology and Social Research* 30 (1946): 370–78.
[11] Ibid.

true even where the grandiose and highly bizarre delusions of paranoia are present. Definition of the socially stressful aspects of this disorder is a minimum essential, if we are to account for its frequent occurrence in partially compensated or benign form in society, as well as account for its more familiar presence as an official psychiatric problem in a hospital setting.

It is necessary, however, to go beyond these elementary observations to make it preeminently clear that strain is an emergent product of a relationship in which the behaviors of two or more persons are relevant factors, and in which the strain is felt both by ego and *alter* or *alters*. The paranoid relationship includes reciprocating behaviors with attached emotions and meanings which, to be fully understood, must be described cubistically from at least two of its perspectives. On one hand the behavior of the individual must be seen from the perspective of others or that of a group, and conversely the behavior of others must be seen from the perspective of the involved individual.

From the vantage of others the individual in the paranoid relationship shows:

1. a disregard for the values and norms of the primary group, revealed by giving priority to verbally definable values over those which are implicit, a lack of loyalty in return for confidences, and victimizing and intimidating persons in positions of weakness.
2. a disregard for the implicit structure of groups, revealed by presuming to privileges not accorded him, and the threat or actual resort to formal means for achieving his goals.

The second items have a higher degree of relevancy than the first in an analysis of exclusion. Stated more simply, they mean that, to the group, the individual is an ambiguous figure whose behavior is uncertain, whose loyalty can't be counted on. In short, he is a person who can't be trusted because he threatens to expose informal power structures. This, we believe, is the essential reason for the frequently encountered idea that the paranoid person is "dangerous." [12]

If we adopt the perceptual set of ego and see others or groups through his eyes, the following aspects of their behavior become relevant:

1. The spurious quality of the interaction between others and himself or between others interacting in his presence;
2. The overt avoidance of himself by others;
3. The structured exclusion of himself from interaction.

[12] Robert A. Dentler and Kai T. Erikson, "The Functions of Deviance in Groups," *Social Problems* 7 (1959): 102.

The items we have described thus far—playing fast and loose with the primary group values by the individual, and his exclusion from interaction—do not alone generate and maintain paranoia. It is additionally necessary that they emerge in an interdependent relationship which requires trust for its fulfillment. The relationship is a type in which the goals of the individual can be reached only through cooperation from particular others, and in which the ends held by others are realizable if cooperation is forthcoming from ego. This is deduced from the general proposition that cooperation rests upon perceived trust, which in turn is a function of communication.[13] When communication is disrupted by exclusion, there is a lack of mutually perceived trust and the relationship becomes dilapidated or paranoid. We will now consider the process of exclusion by which this kind of relationship develops.

THE GENERIC PROCESS OF EXCLUSION

The paranoid process begins with persistent interpersonal difficulties between the individual and his family, or his work associates and superiors, or neighbors, or other persons in the community. These frequently or even typically arise out of bona fide or recognizable issues centering upon some actual or threatened loss of status for the individual. This is related to such things as the death of relatives, loss of a position, loss of professional certification, failure to be promoted, age and physiological life cycle changes, mutilations, and changes in family and marital relationships. The status changes are distinguished by the fact that they leave no alternative acceptable to the individual, from whence comes their "intolerable" or "unendurable" quality. For example: the man trained to be a teacher who loses his certificate, which means he can never teach; or the man of 50 years of age who is faced with loss of a promotion which is a regular order of upward mobility in an organization, who knows that he can't "start over"; or the wife undergoing hysterectomy, which mutilates her image as a woman.

In cases where no dramatic status loss can be discovered, a series of failures often is present, failures which may have been accepted or adjusted to, but with progressive tension as each new status situation is entered. The unendurability of the current status loss, which may appear unimportant to others, is a function of an intensified commitment, in some cases born of an awareness that there is a quota placed on failures in our society. Under some such circumstances, failures have followed the person, and his

[13] James L. Loomis, "Communications, The Development of Trust, and Cooperative Behavior," *Human Relations* 12 (1959): 305–15.

reputation as a "difficult person" has preceded him. This means that he often has the status of a stranger on trial in each new group he enters, and that the groups or organizations willing to take a chance on him are marginal from the standpoint of their probable tolerance for his actions.

The behavior of the individual—arrogance, insults, presumption of privilege, and exploitation of weaknesses in others—initially has a segmental or checkered pattern in that it is confined to status-committing interactions. Outside of these, the person's behavior may be quite acceptable—courteous, considerate, kind, even indulgent. Likewise, other persons and members of groups vary considerably in their tolerance for the relevant behavior, depending on the extent to which it threatens individual and organizational values, impedes functions, or sets in motion embarrassing sequences of social actions. In the early generic period, tolerance by others for the individual's aggressive behavior generally speaking is broad, and it is very likely to be interpreted as a variation of normal behavior, particularly in the absence of biographical knowledge of the person. At most, people observe that "there is something odd about him," or "he must be upset," or "he is just ornery," or "I don't quite understand him." [14]

At some point in the chain of interactions, a new configuration takes place in perceptions others have of the individual, with shifts in figure-ground relations. The individual, as we have already indicated, is an ambiguous figure, comparable to textbook figures of stairs or outlined cubes which reverse themselves when studied intently. From a normal variant the person becomes "unreliable," "untrustworthy," "dangerous," or someone with whom others "do not wish to be involved." An illustration nicely apropos of this came out in the reaction of the head of a music department in a university when he granted an interview to a man who had worked for years on a theory to compose music mathematically:

> When he asked to be placed on the staff so that he could use the electronic computers of the University I *shifted my ground* . . . when I offered an objection to his theory, he became disturbed, so I changed my reaction to "yes and no."

As is clear from this, once the perceptual reorientation takes place, either as the outcome of continuous interaction or through the receipt of biographical information, interaction changes qualitatively. In our words it becomes *spurious*, distinguished by patronizing, evasion, "humoring," guiding conversation onto selected topics, underreaction, and silence, all calculated either to prevent intense interaction or to protect individual and group values by restricting access to them. When the interaction is between

[14] Elaine Cumming and John Cumming, *Closed Ranks* (Cambridge: Harvard University Press, 1957), chap. VI.

two or more persons in the individual's presence it is cued by a whole repertoire of subtle expressive signs which are meaningful only to them. The net effects of spurious interaction are to:

1. stop the flow of information to ego;
2. create a discrepancy between expressed ideas and affect among those with whom he interacts;
3. make the situation or the group image an ambiguous one for ego, much as he is for others.

Needless to say this kind of spurious interaction is one of the most difficult for an adult in our society to cope with, because it complicates or makes decisions impossible for him and also because it is morally invidious.[15]

The process from inclusion to exclusion is by no means an even one. Both individuals and members of groups change their perceptions and reactions, and vacillation is common, depending upon the interplay of values, anxieties, and guilt on both sides. Members of an excluding group may decide they have been unfair and seek to bring the individual back into their confidence. This overture may be rejected or used by ego as a means of further attack. We have also found that ego may capitulate, sometimes abjectly, to others and seek group reentry, only to be rejected. In some cases compromises are struck and a partial reintegration of ego into informal social relations is achieved. The direction which informal exclusion takes depends upon ego's reactions, the degree of communication between his interactors, the composition and structure of the informal groups, and the perceptions of "key others" at points of interaction which directly affect ego's status.

ORGANIZATIONAL CRISIS AND FORMAL EXCLUSION

Thus far we have discussed exclusion as an informal process. Informal exclusion may take place but leave ego's formal status in an organization intact. So long as this status is preserved and rewards are sufficient to validate it on his terms, an uneasy peace between him and others may prevail. Yet ego's social isolation and his strong commitments make him an unpredictable factor; furthermore the rate of change and internal power

[15] The interaction in some ways is similar to that used with children, particularly the *"enfant terrible."* The function of language in such interaction was studied by Sapir years ago. Edward Sapir, "Abnormal Types of Speech in Nootka," *Geological Survey Memoir* 62, Anthropological Series (Ottawa: Canada Department of Mines, 1915).

struggles, especially in large and complex organizations, means that preconditions of stability may be short lived.

Organizational crises involving a paranoid relationship arise in several ways. The individual may act in ways which arouse intolerable anxieties in others, who demand that "something be done." Again, by going to higher authority or making appeals outside the organization, he may set in motion procedures which leave those in power no other choice than to take action. In some situations ego remains relatively quiescent and does not openly attack the organization. Action against him is set off by growing anxieties or calculated motives of associates—in some cases his immediate superiors. Finally, regular organizational procedures incidental to promotion, retirement, or reassignment may precipitate the crisis.

Assuming a critical situation in which the conflict between the individual and members of the organization leads to action to formally exclude him, several possibilities exist. One is the transfer of ego from one department, branch, or division of the organization to another, a device frequently resorted to in the armed services or in large corporations. This requires that the individual be persuaded to make the change and that some department will accept him. While this may be accomplished in different ways, not infrequently artifice, withholding information, bribery, or thinly disguised threats figure conspicuously among the means by which the transfer is brought about. Needless to say, there is a limit to which transfers can be employed as a solution to the problem, contingent upon the size of the organization and the previous diffusion of knowledge about the transferee.

Solution number two we call encapsulation, which, in brief, is a reorganization and redefinition of ego's status. This has the effect of isolating him from the organization and making him directly responsible to one or two superiors who act as his intermediators. The change is often made palatable to ego by enhancing some of the material rewards of his status. He may be nominally promoted or "kicked upstairs," given a larger office, or a separate secretary, or relieved of onerous duties. Sometimes a special status is created for him.

This type of solution often works because it is a kind of formal recognition by the organization of ego's intense commitment to his status and in part a victory for him over his enemies. It bypasses them and puts him into direct communication with higher authority who may communicate with him in a more direct manner. It also relieves his associates of further need to connive against him. This solution is sometimes used to dispose of troublesome corporation executives, high-ranking military officers, and academic *personae non gratae* in universities.

A third variety of solution to the problem of paranoia in an organization is outright discharge, forced resignation or non-renewal of appointment. Finally, there may be an organized move to have the individual in the paranoid relationship placed on sick leave, or to compel him to take psychiatric treatment. The extreme expression of this pressure (as on the family) or direct action to have the person committed to a mental hospital.

The order of the enumerated solutions to the paranoid problem in a rough way reflects the amount of risk associated with the alternatives, both as to the probabilities of failure and of damaging repercussions to the organization. Generally, organizations seem to show a good deal of resistance to making or carrying out decisions which require expulsion of the individual or forcing hospitalization, regardless of his mental condition. One reason for this is that the person may have power within the organization, based upon his position or monopolized skills and information,[16] and unless there is a strong coalition against him the general conservatism of administrative judgments will run in his favor. Herman Wouk's novel, *The Caine Mutiny*, dramatizes some of the difficulties of cashiering a person from a position of power in an essentially conservative military organization. An extreme of this conservatism is illustrated by one case in which we found a department head retained in his position in an organization even though he was actively hallucinating as well as expressing paranoid delusions.[17] Another factor working on the individual's side is that discharge of a person in a position of power reflects unfavorably upon those who placed him there. In-group solidarity of administrators may be involved, and the methods of the opposition may create sympathy for ego at higher levels.

Even when the person is almost totally excluded and informally isolated within an organization, he may have power outside. This weighs heavily when the external power can be invoked in some way, or when it automatically leads to raising questions as to the internal workings of the organization. This touches upon the more salient reason for reluctance to eject an uncooperative and retaliatory person, even when he is relatively unimportant to the organization. We refer to a kind of negative power derived from the vulnerability of organizations to unfavorable publicity and exposure of their private lives that are likely if the crisis proceeds to formal hearings, case review, or litigation. This is an imminent possibility where paranoia exists. If hospital commitment is attempted, there is a possibility that a jury trial will be demanded, which will force leaders of the organization to defend their actions. If the crisis turns into a legal contest of this sort, it is not easy to prove insanity, and there may be damage suits. Even

---

[16] For a systematic analysis of the organizational difficulties in removing an "unpromotable" person from a position see B. Levenson, "Bureaucratic Succession," in *Complex Organizations*, ed. Amitai Etzioni (New York: Holt, Rinehart & Winston, 1961), pp. 362–95.

[17] One of the cases in the first study.

if the facts heavily support the petitioners, such contests can only throw unfavorable light upon the organization.

THE CONSPIRATORIAL NATURE OF EXCLUSION

A conclusion from the foregoing is that organizational vulnerability as well as anticipations of retaliations from the paranoid person lay a functional basis for conspiracy among those seeking to contain or oust him. Probabilities are strong that a coalition will appear within the organization, integrated by a common commitment to oppose the paranoid person. This, the exclusionist group, demands loyalty, solidarity, and secrecy from its members; it acts in accord with a common scheme and in varying degrees utilizes techniques of manipulation and misrepresentation.

Conspiracy in rudimentary form can be detected in informal exclusion apart from an organizational crisis. This was illustrated in an office research team in which staff members huddled around a water cooler to discuss the unwanted associate. They also used office telephones to arrange coffee breaks without him and employed symbolic cues in his presence, such as humming the Dragnet theme song when he approached the group. An office rule against extraneous conversation was introduced with the collusion of supervisors, ostensibly for everyone, actually to restrict the behavior of the isolated worker. In another case an interview schedule designed by a researcher was changed at a conference arranged without him. When he sought an explanation at a subsequent conference, his associates pretended to have no knowledge of the changes.

Conspiratorial behavior comes into sharpest focus during organizational crises in which the exclusionists who initiate action become an embattled group. There is a concerted effort to gain consensus for this view, to solidify the group and to halt close interaction with those unwilling to join the coalition completely. Efforts are also made to neutralize those who remain uncommitted but who can't be kept ignorant of the plans afoot. Thus an external appearance of unanimity is given even if it doesn't exist.

Much of the behavior of the group at this time is strategic in nature, with determined calculations as to "what we will do if he does this or that." In one of our cases, a member on a board of trustees spoke of the "game being played" with the person in controversy with them. Planned action may be carried to the length of agreeing upon the exact words to be used when confronted or challenged by the paranoid individual. Above all there is continuous, precise communication among exclusionists, exemplified in one case by mutual exchanging of copies of all letters sent and received from ego.

Concern about secrecy in such groups is revealed by such things as carefully closing doors and lowering of voices when ego is brought under discussion. Meeting places and times may be varied from normal procedures; documents may be filed in unusual places and certain telephones may not be used during a paranoid crisis.

The visibility of the individual's behavior is greatly magnified during this period; often he is the main topic of conversation among the exclusionists, while rumors of the difficulties spread to other groups, which in some cases may be drawn into the controversy. At a certain juncture steps are taken to keep the members of the in-group continually informed of the individual's movements and, if possible, of his plans. In effect, if not in form, this amounts to spying. Members of one embattled group, for example, hired an outside person unknown to their accuser to take notes on a speech he delivered to enlist a community organization on his side. In another case, a person having an office opening onto that of a department head was persuaded to act as an informant for the nucleus of persons working to depose the head from his position of authority. This group also seriously debated placing an all-night watch in front of their perceived malefactor's house.

Concomitant with the magnified visibility of the paranoid individual, come distortions of his image, most pronounced in the inner coterie of exclusionists. His size, physical strength, cunning, and anecdotes of his outrages are exaggerated, with a central thematic emphasis on the fact that he is dangerous. Some individuals give cause for such beliefs in that previously they have engaged in violence or threats, others do not. One encounters characteristic contradictions in interviews on this point, such as: "No, he has never struck anyone around here—just fought with the policemen at the State Capitol," or "No, I am not afraid of him, but one of these days he will explode."

It can be said parenthetically that the alleged dangerousness of paranoid persons storied in fiction and drama has never been systematically demonstrated. As a matter of fact, the only substantial data on this, from a study of delayed admissions, largely paranoid, to a mental hospital in Norway, disclosed that "neither the paranoiacs nor paranoids have been dangerous, and most not particularly troublesome." [18] Our interpretation of this, as suggested earlier, is that the imputed dangerousness of the paranoid individual does not come from physical fear but from the organizational threat he presents and the need to justify collective action against him.[19]

However, this is not entirely tactical behavior—as is demonstrated by

[18] O. Odegard, "A Clinical Study of Delayed Admissions to a Mental Hospital," *Mental Hygiene* 42 (1958): 66–77.

[19] Supra.

anxieties and tensions which mount among those in a coalition during the more critical phases of their interaction. Participants may develop fears quite analogous to those of classic conspirators. One leader in such a group spoke of the period of the paranoid crisis as a "week of terror," during which he was wracked with insomnia and "had to take his stomach pills." Projection was revealed by a trustee who, during a school crisis occasioned by discharge of an aggressive teacher, stated that he "watched his shadows," and "wondered if all would be well when he returned home at night." Such tensional states, working along with a kind of closure of communication within the group, are both a cause and an effect of amplified group interaction which distorts or symbolically rearranges the image of the person against whom they act.

Once the battle is won by exclusionists, their version of the individual as dangerous becomes a crystallized rationale for official action. At this point misrepresentation becomes part of a more deliberate manipulation of ego. Gross misstatements, most frequently called "pretexts," become justifiable ways of getting his cooperation, for example, to get him to submit to psychiatric examination or detention preliminary to hospital commitment. This aspect of the process has been effectively detailed by Goffman, with his concept of a "betrayal funnel" through which a patient enters a hospital.[20] We need not elaborate on this, other than to confirm its occurrence in the exclusion process, complicated in our cases by legal strictures and the ubiquitous risk of litigation.

THE GROWTH OF DELUSION

The general idea that the paranoid person symbolically fabricates the conspiracy against him is in our estimation incorrect or incomplete. Nor can we agree that he lacks insight, as is so frequently claimed. To the contrary, many paranoid persons properly realize that they are being isolated and excluded by concerted interaction, or that they are being manipulated. However, they are at a loss to estimate accurately or realistically the dimensions and form of the coalition arrayed against them.

As channels of communication are closed to the paranoid person, he has no means of getting feedback or consequences of his behavior, which is essential for correcting his interpretations of the social relationships and organization which he must rely on to define his status and give him identity. He can only read overt behavior without the informal context. Although he may properly infer that people are organized against him, he

[20] Erving Goffman, "The Moral Career of the Mental Patient," *Psychiatry* 22 (1959): 127 ff.

can only use confrontation or formal inquisitorial procedures to try to prove this. The paranoid person must provoke strong feelings in order to receive any kind of meaningful communication from others—hence his accusations, his bluntness, his insults. Ordinarily this is non-deliberate; nevertheless, in one complex case we found the person consciously provoking discussions to get readings from others on his behavior. This man said of himself: "Some people would describe me as very perceptive, others would describe me as very imperceptive."

The need for communication and the identity which goes with it does a good deal to explain the preference of paranoid persons for formal, legalistic, written communications, and the care with which many of them preserve records of their contracts with others. In some ways the resort to litigation is best interpreted as the effort of the individual to compel selected others to interact directly with him as equals, to engineer a situation in which evasion is impossible. The fact that the person is seldom satisfied with the outcome of his letters, his petitions, complaints, and writs testifies to their function as devices for establishing contact and interaction with others, as well as "setting the record straight." The wide professional tolerance of lawyers for aggressive behavior in court and the nature of Anglo-Saxon legal institutions, which grew out of a revolt against conspiratorial or star-chamber justice, mean that the individual will be heard. Furthermore his charges must be answered; otherwise he wins by default. Sometimes he wins small victories, even if he loses the big ones. He may earn grudging respect as an adversary, and sometimes shares a kind of legal camaraderie with others in the courts. He gains an identity through notoriety.

REINFORCEMENT OF DELUSION

The accepted psychiatric view is that prognosis for paranoia is poor, that recoveries from "true" paranoia are rare, with the implication that the individual's delusions more or less express an unalterable pathological condition. Granting that the individual's needs and dispositions and his self-imposed isolation are significant factors in perpetuating his delusional reactions, nevertheless there is an important social context of delusions through which they are reinforced or strengthened. This context is readily identifiable in the fixed ideas and institutionalized procedures of protective, custodial, and treatment organizations in our society. They stand out in sharpest relief where paranoid persons have come into contact with law enforcement agencies or have been hospitalized. The cumulative and interlocking impacts of such agencies work strongly to nurture and sustain the massive sense of injustice and need for identity which underlie the delusions and aggressive behavior of the paranoid individual.

Police in most communities have a well-defined concept of cranks, as they call them, although the exact criteria by which persons are so judged are not clear. Their patience is short with such persons: in some cases they investigate their original complaints and if they conclude that the person in question is a crank they tend to ignore him thereafter. His letters may be thrown away unanswered, or phone calls answered with patronizing reassurance or vague promises to take steps which never materialize.

Like the police, offices of district attorneys are frequently forced to deal with persons they refer to as cranks or soreheads. Some offices delegate a special deputy to handle these cases, quaintly referred to in one office as the "insane deputy." Some deputies say they can spot letters of cranks immediately, which means that they are unanswered or discarded. However, family or neighborhood quarrels offer almost insoluble difficulties in this respect, because often it is impossible to determine which of two parties is delusional. In one office some complaints are called "50–50," which is jargon meaning that it is impossible to say whether they are mentally stable. If one person seems to be persistently causing trouble, deputies may threaten to have him investigated, which, however, is seldom if ever done.

Both police and district attorney staffs operate continuously in situations in which their actions can have damaging legal or political repercussions. They tend to be tightly in-grouped and their initial reaction to outsiders or strangers is one of suspicion or distrust until they are proved harmless or friendly. Many of their office procedures and general manner reflect this—such as carefully recording in a log book names, time, and reason for calling of those who seek official interviews. In some instances a complainant is actually investigated before any business will be transacted with him.

When the paranoid person goes beyond local police and courts to seek redress through appeals to state or national authorities, he may meet with polite evasion, perfunctory treatment of his case, or formalized distrust. Letters to administrative people may beget replies up to a certain point, but thereafter they are ignored. If letters to a highly-placed authority carry threats, they may lead to an investigation by security agencies, motivated by the knowledge that assassinations are not unknown in American life. Sometimes redress is sought in legislatures, where private bills may be introduced, bills which by their nature can only be empty gestures.

In general, the contacts which the delusional person makes with formal organizations frequently disclose the same elements of shallow response, evasion, or distrust which played a part in the generic process of

262 SOME FORMS OF DEVIANCE

exclusion. They become part of a selective or selected pattern of inter-action which creates a social environment of uncertainty and ambiguity for the individual. They do little to correct and much to confirm his suspicion, distrust, and delusional interpretations. Moreover, even the en-vironment of treatment agencies may contribute to the furtherance of paranoid delusion, as Stanton and Schwartz have shown in their comments on communication within the mental hospital. They speak pointedly of the "pathology of communication" brought about by staff practices of ignoring explicit meanings in statements or actions of patients and reacting to in-ferred or imputed meanings, thereby creating a type of environment in which "the paranoid feels quite at home." [21]

Some paranoid or paranoid-like persons become well known locally or even throughout larger areas to some organizations. Persons and groups in the community are found to assume a characteristic stance toward such people—a stance of expectancy and preparedness. In one such case, police continually checked the whereabouts of the man and, when the governor came to speak on the courthouse steps, two officers were assigned the special task of watching the man as he stood in the crowd. Later, whenever he went to the state capitol, a number of state police were delegated to accompany him when he attended committee hearings or sought inter-views with state officials.[22] The notoriety this man acquired because of his reputed great strength in tossing officers around like tenpins was an obvious source of pleasure to him, despite the implications of distrust con-veyed by their presence.

It is arguable that occupying the role of the mistrusted person be-comes a way of life for these paranoids, providing them with an identity not otherwise possible. Their volatile contentions with public officials, their issuance of writings, publications, litigations in *persona propria*, their over-riding tendency to contest issues which other people dismiss as unim-portant or as "too much bother" become a central theme for their lives, without which they would probably deteriorate.

If paranoia becomes a way of life for some people, it is also true that the difficult person with grandiose and persecutory ideas may fulfill certain marginal functions in organizations and communities. One is his scapegoat function, being made the subject of humorous by-play or conjectural gossip as people "wonder what he will be up to next." In his scapegoat role, the person may help integrate primary groups within larger organizations by directing aggressions and blame toward him and thus strengthening feel-ings of homogeneity and consensus of group members.

[21] Alfred H. Stanton and Morris S. Schwartz, *The Mental Hospital* (New York: Basic Books, 1954), pp. 200–210.

[22] This technique in even more systematic form is sometimes used in protecting the President of the United States in "White House cases."

There are also instances in which the broad, grapeshot charges and accusations of the paranoid person function to articulate dissatisfactions of those who fear openly to criticize the leadership of the community, organization, or state, or of the informal power structures within these. Sometimes the paranoid person is the only one who openly espouses values of inarticulate and politically unrepresented segments of the population.[23] The "plots" which attract the paranoid person's attention—dope rings, international communism, monopolistic "interests," popery, Jewry, or "psychopoliticians"—often reflect the vague and ill-formed fears and concerns of peripheral groups, which tend to validate his self-chosen role as a "protector." At times in organizational power plays and community conflicts his role may even be put to canny use by more representative groups as a means of embarrassing their opposition.

THE LARGER SOCIOCULTURAL CONTEXT

Our comments draw to a close on the same polemic note with which they were begun, namely, that members of communities and organizations do unite in common effort against the paranoid person prior to or apart from any vindictive behavior on his part. The paranoid community is real rather than pseudo in that it is composed of reciprocal relationships and processes whose net results are informal and formal exclusion and attenuated communication.

The dynamics of exclusion of the paranoid person are made understandable in larger perspective by recognizing that decision-making in American social organization is carried out in small, informal groups through casual and often subtle male interaction. Entry into such groups is ordinarily treated as a privilege rather than a right, and this privilege tends to be jealously guarded. Crucial decisions, including those to eject persons or to reorganize their status in larger formal organizations, are made secretly. The legal concept of "privileged communication" in part is a formal recognition of the necessity for making secret decisions within organizations.

Added to this is the emphasis placed upon conformity in our organization-oriented society and the growing tendency of organization elites to rely upon direct power for their purposes. This is commonly exercised to isolate and neutralize groups and individuals who oppose their policies both inside and outside of the organization. Formal structures may be manipulated or deliberately reorganized so that resistant groups and individuals are

[23] Judd Marmor, "Science, Health and Group Opposition," mimeographed paper, 1958, UCLA School of Social Work.

denied or removed from access to power or the available means to promote their deviant goals and values. One of the most readily effective ways of doing this is to interrupt, delay, or stop the flow of information.

It is the necessity to rationalize and justify such procedures on a democratic basis which leads to concealment of certain actions, misrepresentation of their underlying meaning, and even the resort to unethical or illegal means. The difficulty of securing sociological knowledge about these techniques, which we might call the "controls behind the controls," and the denials by those who use them that they exist are logical consequences of the perceived threat such knowledge and admissions become to informal power structures. The epiphenomena of power thus become a kind of shadowy world of our culture, inviting conjecture and condemnation.

CONCLUDING COMMENT

We have been concerned with a process of social exclusion and with the way in which it contributes to the development of paranoid patterns of behavior. While the data emphasize the organizational forms of exclusion, we nevertheless believe that these are expressions of a generic process whose correlates will emerge from the study of paranoia in the family and other groups. The differential responses of the individual to the exigencies of organized exclusion are significant in the development of paranoid reactions only insofar as they partially determine the "intolerable" or "unendurable" quality of the status changes confronting him. Idiosyncratic life history factors of the sort stressed in more conventional psychiatric analyses may be involved, but equally important in our estimation are those which inhere in the status changes themselves, age being one of the more salient of these. In either case, once situational intolerability appears, the stage is set for the interactional process we have described.

Our cases, it will be noted, were all people who remained undeteriorated, in contact with others, and carrying on militant activities oriented toward recognizable social values and instituitions. Generalized suspiciousness in public places and unprovoked aggression against strangers were absent from their experiences. These facts, plus the relative absence of "true paranoia" among mental-hospital populations, lead us to conclude that the "pseudo-community" associated with random aggression (in Cameron's sense) is a sequel rather than an integral part of paranoid patterns. They are likely products of deterioration and fragmentation of personality appearing, when and if they do, in the paranoid person after long or intense periods of stress and complete social isolation.

Name

Name Index

Subject Index

271